Juvenile Sex Offenders

What the Public Needs to Know

CAMILLE GIBSON AND
DONNA M. VANDIVER

PRAEGER

Westport, Connecticut
London

Library of Congress Cataloging-in-Publication Data

Gibson, Camille, 1971–
  Juvenile sex offenders : what the public needs to know / Camille Gibson and
Donna M. Vandiver.
    p.   cm.
  Includes bibliographical references and index.
  ISBN-13: 978–0–313–34853–2 (alk. paper)
  1. Teenage sex offenders—United States.   2. Child sex offenders—United
States.   3. Sex crimes—United States.   I. Vandiver, Donna M., 1972–   II. Title.
  HV9067.S48G53   2008
  364.15′308350973—dc22   2008015610

British Library Cataloguing in Publication Data is available.

Library of Congress Catalog Card Number: 2008015610
ISBN-13: 978–0–313–34853–2

First published in 2008

Praeger Publishers, 88 Post Road West, Westport, CT 06881
An imprint of Greenwood Publishing Group, Inc.
www.praeger.com

Printed in the United States of America

The paper used in this book complies with the
Permanent Paper Standard issued by the National
Information Standards Organization (Z39.48–1984).

10 9 8 7 6 5 4 3 2 1

Contents

Preface

The impetus for this book came from a concern about prevailing misconceptions about the nature of juvenile sex offenders and of juvenile sex offending. Many of these inaccurate notions have resulted in laws that do more harm than good. Some of our laws force a deviant identity on those tagged as "sex offenders," making their rehabilitation particularly difficult. In so doing, we jeopardize ourselves needlessly, for sex offenders are highly amenable to treatment, especially juvenile sex offenders. Much of our response to sex offenders in recent years has been reactionary and poorly considered. It has been a knee-jerk response to a relatively few but very shocking high-profile cases involving violent predatory adult sex offenders. Although well intentioned, the effects of these efforts were not thoroughly thought through. Having had the chance to note our missteps in laws and practice it is time to make corrections and promptly. To this end, this book is an effort to educate the public. The literature abounds with information on adult sex offenders but works specifically about juvenile sex offenders are far more limited and usually written for an academic audience. In plain talk we offer the facts and food for thought. Change is needed not only legislatively, but also in our homes and any place where juveniles may be.

The facts on juvenile sex offenders include that they do offend sexually. Often, we assume that by virtue of youth's assumed innocence that they could not. So, more vigilance and care is needed when choosing those young babysitters, including one's kin. The fact is that much of the juvenile activities tagged as "sex offending" are no more than fairly innocent developmental exploratory sexual activity. The fact is that most juvenile sex offenders do not recidivate sexually. The fact is that adult sex offenders tend to not just pop up as adult offenders. Often they begin their sex offending as juveniles. Amongst these juveniles are some with a paraphilia, including sexual compulsions, that is difficult to control without professional intervention. The fact is that the information on many sex offender registries is not up to date or always accurate and most of us do not check these registries anyway. Public sex offender registries then, offer a false sense of safety. This plus other laws have created a new stigmatized class—sex offenders. The fact is that the sex offender is more likely to be someone we know than a stranger cruising by. The fact is that a seven-year-old will rape a two-year-old for a reason. We should think about what that reason might be. The fact is that we should pay attention to issues involving juveniles—both victims and those we call "the offenders." The fact is that help is available. There are sex offender treatment providers (SOTP) available in many communities. You can contact groups like the Association for the Treatment of Sexual Abusers (ATSA) for information.

In Chapter 1 juvenile sex offending is defined and described. Myths about sex offenders are addressed, including normal versus abnormal juvenile interest in the topic of sex. The circumstances of most juvenile sex offending are described including the likelihood of an arrest. The chapter ends with information on how one might proceed when addressing inappropriate juvenile sexual contact. Chapter 2 describes what we know about why juveniles offend sexually with examples of cases. The explanations available have included elements of biology, evolutionary need, behavioral conditioning, learned violence, social-psychological peer situations, poor early parental attachment, and various environmental variables. Chapter 3 presents examples of the variety of those who might be labeled "juvenile sex offenders." The chapter begins with a few of the most concerning cases but goes on to present examples of most juvenile sex offenders where rehabilitation is very likely if facilitated. The chapter presents an argument for change. Chapter 4 addresses the variety of juvenile sex offenders in detail and how these typologies were developed. Proper assessment is important in determining the best individualized response. Chapter 5 describes less common cases of sex offenders such as females, individuals with a developmental disability, and very young offenders. Chapter 6 (by Philip Ikomi) addresses the issue of juvenile sex offender recidivism. It includes a review of assessment instruments and treatment approaches. Chapter 7 is an indictment on our legal response to juvenile sex offenders with ideas about how circumstances might improve. Finally, Chapter 8 urges readers to separate the facts regarding juvenile sex offenders from fiction. Once the public knows and accepts the true circumstances of juvenile sex offenders, we can do better as individuals and collectively to protect the more vulnerable among us.

1

When? How? And by Whom? The Circumstances of Juvenile Sex Offending

Since 1990 there has been a flurry of activity in response to some high-profile cases of adults who kidnapped, sexually molested and, in some instances, murdered children. The result has been the enactment of punitive policies for dealing with adult sex offenders. Much of these responses have been emotionally reactionary and not informed by research. They have had a spillover effect on juvenile sex offenders. Consequently, there has been government-sanctioned harm to the physiology, psyche, and families of some juveniles—including at least one case where the juvenile sex offender was murdered by vigilantes and other cases of suspected suicides. This book is a call for reflection toward rethinking what we have done in haste and how we might fix the damage to rescue more victims of juvenile sexual deviance and the juvenile offenders themselves from greater harm.

Juvenile sexual activity is deviant, but how much of it should be illegal? That is difficult to say given that juvenile sexual activity is inherently covert. Also shrouding the phenomenon from study is the fact that it tends to occur between relatives and friends; in some cases the child victims are so young or too disabled to articulate their abuse; and there is a powerful stigma associated with disclosing sexual victimization, especially for males. When such behavior is uncovered, it is usually by family members of the victim and, or the offender. If there is a relationship between the parties involved, the common tendency is to attempt to address the circumstances privately, further adding to the intellectual and scientific enigma of such activities. So, what we know comes largely from official numbers, juvenile self-reports, and retrospective accounts from adult sex offenders.

What is very clear is that adult sex offenders and juvenile sex offenders tend to be very different in how and why they sexually offend and in their amenability to treatment. We assume adults know what they are doing. However, in some cases that we call "juvenile sex crimes" there is no apparent harm (example, children playing doctor, or two teens agreeing to heavy petting). In a few cases, the motivation of the juvenile sex offender is to harm and there is serious harm for the victim. In other cases, the juvenile may claim he or she meant no "real" harm (for example, when a juvenile reluctantly participates in a sex "train" or coerced group sex with one victim because the juvenile does not want to be perceived as less than manly by his peers). In such cases, regardless of the offender's intentions, serious harm to the victim is evident and the circumstance of both victim and offender will necessitate intervention. Consider the following example:

> *Several 8-year-old girls have complained that a 10-year-old boy keeps touching them and grabbing them between the legs. This has happened in the corridor and in the playground. The girls say the way he touches them makes then feel uncomfortable. The boy initially denies he has touched them but then says it was just for fun. There are no further incidents after he has been spoken to. Other things known about the boy are that he is not particularly popular and is clumsy in his attempts to make friends.[1]*

What response seems best?

Because juveniles today will be the adults of tomorrow, we should *pay attention*—a theme that will be repeated throughout this book.

Back in 1950 Paul Tappan noted some common misperceptions of sex offenders. Recently, Karen Terry[2] reminded us of these and the fact that the misperceptions persist: They include:

- That sex offenders are oversexed. If true, castration could be a cure. However, the truth here is that sex offenders are usually undersexed, but motivated by a need to exercise power and control over someone. Sex, then is merely the weapon of choice.

- That most sex offenders are out to kill. One poll referenced by Human Rights Watch revealed that most of us are more concerned about sex offenders than about terrorists.[3] Actually, most sex offending is relatively minor like fondling, and being a "peeping Tom." Juvenile sexual homicide is rare. For example, in 1999 there were nine such cases.[4]

- That most sex offenders continue their sex offending. The truth is, most studies report sexual offense recidivism rates from 8 to 14 percent for juvenile males.[5] These numbers are far less than the recidivism rates reported for nonsexual offending, which may be as high as 58 percent.[6]

- That the behavior of sex offenders escalates in seriousness. Actually, most sex offenders stick with one sexual behavior with which they are comfortable.

- That future sex offending may be predicted. Mental health experts do not claim to predict recidivism but they offer an assessment of how dangerous or risky a person is. This is far less definite.

- That passing a bunch of laws will protect us from sex offenders. This may help us to feel safe but if the laws are ill-conceived they could actually increase our jeopardy. Those who get tagged as sex offenders are a mixed group—we need different approaches for different types of sex offenders. Presently, some of our laws in regard to sex offenders are so demanding of resources that they go largely unenforced. What good are unenforced laws?

WHAT IS JUVENILE SEX OFFENDING?

Juvenile sex offending refers to sexual behavior that involves another person or persons and is exploitive, manipulative, aggressive, threatening, or without true consent. True consent exists when persons have full knowledge and complete freedom to engage or not.[7] Who is considered a *juvenile* sex offender depends on the age range for responsibility in that jurisdiction. For example, the age range for juvenile offenders in Arkansas is ten to seventeen years old. Thus, juveniles below age ten who engage in sex acts would not be considered *offenders*. Given their youth they are *doli incapax* or incapable of mentally conceiving the intent or guilty mind (*mens rea*) necessary for an offense. Instead of *offenders* they would be called "juveniles with a sexual behavior problem." Notably, more than half of our states (for example, Montana and Wyoming) have no minimum age limit, so prepubescent children could legally be labeled "juvenile sex offenders." Adolescents over the age limit (for example, in Arkansas, it would be those over age seventeen) would be adult sex offenders.

The victim of a juvenile sex offender could be of any age but it appears that most often they are children or peers. Those juveniles who focus on child victims tend to have different motivations for their offending than those who tend to victimize peers or adults.[8]

Those who prefer children are likely to display traits of some paraphilia or faulty thinking about the circumstances. They are more likely to seize opportunities to offend, utilize seduction rather than force, and have a male victim at some point. For those juveniles who offend against peers and/or adults, the sexual offending is one of a pattern of general criminal offending. Thus, the sexual offense may occur in the process of another offense, in a publicly accessible place, and involve the use of force or a weapon.

The reasons that juveniles engage in sexual activity differs. Some juvenile sex offenses are a part of childhood exploration (e.g., playing "doctor and nurse"); others might be the result of some miseducation (for example, a juvenile observes the behavior, assumes it is appropriate and imitates it); others might reflect predatory opportunistic cruelty, and for others, the behaviors are a manifestation of a mental disorder. These may be diagnosed with the primary instrument of psychiatrists and psychologists, a book called the *Diagnostic and Statistical Manual IV-Text Revision* (or the DSM-IV-TR). These disorders are usually only formally diagnosed in persons who are at least sixteen years of age. The condition must also be present, recurrent, for at least six months and interrupting normal daily activities. Examples include voyeurism, frotterism, exhibitionism, fetishism, autoerotic asphyxiation, unsolicited scatologia, necrophilia, zoophilia, and pedophilia. Pedophilia is the most concerning of these disorders because of the vulnerability of likely victims, often young child victims. A person with pedophilia has a compulsion to engage in sexual activity with minors.

Forcible rape is often predatory and opportunistic. It is largely not about sex, but about power and control, a maladaptive way of dealing with esteem issues and a sense of powerlessness, perhaps an overresponse to feeling very vulnerable to harm in childhood. Learning to cope with such feelings in more appropriate ways often does not happen without professional therapeutic intervention. When the sex offending is the manifestation of a mental disorder, the disorder is called a paraphilia.

Significantly, many of the predictors of juvenile sex offending are the same for juvenile offending. These predictors include: severe physical and emotional abuse, prior offenses, nonrelated victims, stranger victims, male victims, nonsexual convictions, including nonsexual assaults and low IQ scores.[9] Predictors of juvenile sex re-offending include: blaming the victim, deviant arousal, cognitive distortions, the use of threat or force, and the presence of a psychopathology.[10] A recent study of 6,000 persons in Racine, Wisconsin, revealed that for male juvenile sex offenders the best predictor of a juvenile continuing his offending into adulthood was the frequency of the juvenile sex offending.[11] Markedly, most juveniles stop their delinquency, including sex offending, by the time they turn eighteen years old. Noted psychologist Terrie Moffitt has won significant accolades for her work on delinquency. Moffitt concluded that delinquency is normal given that most juveniles do it.

She went on to claim that there are two types of juvenile offenders: a few juveniles are life course persistent offenders (they keep on offending into adulthood) but most are adolescent limited offenders (they stop offending when they become adults). Many juvenile sex offenders fall into the latter category. Thus, a key thing to remember here is that nine times out of ten that juvenile who is taken into custody for a sex offense will not be picked up again for another sex offense—so, why the harsh legal response?[12]

WHO IS A JUVENILE?

Each state's legislature determines who is considered a "juvenile" for legal purposes by setting age limits. All states have an upper age limit, but some have no minimum age limit, meaning that it is legally possible in some states to prosecute even very young children—like three- or seven-year-olds. This however, remains rare.

Age of Juvenile Jurisdiction—Lower and Upper Age Limit		
Alabama		17
Alaska		17
Arizona	8	17
Arkansas	10	17
California		17
Colorado	10	17
Connecticut		15
Delaware		17
District of Columbia		17
Florida		17
Georgia		16
Hawaii		17
Idaho		17
Illinois		17
Indiana		17
Iowa		17
Kansas	10	17
Kentucky		17
Louisiana	10	16
Maine		17
Maryland	7	17

Massachusetts	7	16
Michigan		16
Minnesota	10	17
Mississippi	10	17
Missouri		16
Montana		17
Nebraska		17
Nevada		17
New Hampshire		16
New Jersey		17
New Mexico		17
New York	7	15
North Carolina	6	15
North Dakota		17
Ohio		17
Oklahoma		17
Oregon		17
Pennsylvania	10	17
Rhode Island		17
South Carolina		16
South Dakota	10	17
Tennessee		17
Texas	10	16
Utah		17
Vermont	10	17
Virginia		17
Washington		17
West Virginia		17
Wisconsin	10	16
Wyoming		17

Overall, based on information known to law enforcement in twelve states, it appears that juveniles are roughly responsible for 17 percent of all forcible rapists; 23 percent of rapes with an object; 27 percent of all forcible fondlings, and 36 percent of all forcible sodomies. Juveniles were also responsible for 4 percent of all adult sexual victims but 40 percent of sexual victimizations of children under age six. When the victim was under six, 27 percent of the offenders were twelve to seventeen and 13 percent of the offenders were seven to eleven. Adults, however, were responsible for 67 percent of juvenile victims. The modal age of juvenile sex offenders was fourteen.[13]

Other studies estimate that juveniles are responsible for about half of all child victimizations[14] and approximately 20 percent of all sexual assaults.[15] While the number of all sex offending incidents went up in the 1980s, reports of *child* sexual victimizations went down substantially during the 1990s.[16] We are not sure why. It is important to note that such changes might not mean that the number of actual incidents is going up or down; rather, it indicates whether or not people are reporting these incidents more or less.

How Does It Happen?

Some advocate the "vampire" perspective in that those who are victimized perpetuate the victimization and on and on it goes. Yet, most victims do not repeat their victimization. Plus, there is the huge problem of gender with this explanation—most sex offenders are male, most of the victims of sex offending are females. If the vampire idea were correct, there would be a lot more female sex offenders out there than male offenders—but there is not.[17] Others claim that sex offending is a learnt response via exposure to such acts by others, including via pornography. Significantly, about 20 to 55 percent of juvenile sex offenders report having been sexually abused. These offenders are more likely to report physical abuse than sexual abuse.[18]

Some risk factors mentioned over the years with conflicting research findings include family isolation suggesting that in rural areas where families are isolated sexual abuse might be more common than among urban residents; parental absence, or unavailability where less parental monitoring means a greater likelihood of seeking connections with "others." These could all be facilitated by a mother's mental or physical illness and a distant relationship between mother and child.[19]

Often offenders will claim that drugs and alcohol made them do it. There is no evidence to support that position. Drugs, including alcohol, may make an already motivated person more likely to act and a potential victim more susceptible to harm.

For juvenile offenders much of their sexual abuse and their choice of victim whether male or female, adult or child, is largely about which potential victim is available as opposed to sexual preference for a particular age group or gender. Thus, it is not uncommon for a sex offender to be in a relationship with an age peer, while also sexually abusing others. Notably, adult sex offenders seem more inclined to manipulate and seduce to exploit their victim. Juveniles tend to be less sophisticated. When the attack is between strangers the use of force and penetration seems more likely.[20] It is generally accepted among researchers in the area and clinicians that juvenile sexual recidivism is unlikely. However, some speculate that the recidivism might simply be undetected given the covertness of juvenile sex offending.[21] What we know about possible causes of juvenile sex offending is addressed in detail in the next chapter.

WHO ARE THE OFFENDERS?

Our answer to this question is a very limited one given that we can speak only of those juvenile sex offenders who have come to the attention of legal authorities. These are often the same juveniles discussed in clinical studies. This is likely a small portion of all juvenile sex offenders. So, who are the juveniles who get caught? They tend to be the ones who have offended outside of their family (for when it happens in the family we tend to be hush-hush about it); those who use violence or who were particularly bizarre.[22]

Of course, adult sex offenders tend to not just appear as adults. Sixty to 80 percent of adult sex offenders report beginning their sexual offending as juveniles, but even this number might be an underestimate because sex offenders tend to underreport their sexual deviance.[23] But note, this 60 to 80 percent could be 10 percent or less of all juvenile sex offenders. The public concern is those predatory and chronic sex offenders and these are who we need to focus on identifying, treating, and controlling.

In terms of who gets tagged as a "juvenile sex offender," there are three general types of circumstances:

1. Juveniles engaged in "consensual" sexual activity. Some estimates are that a third of United States' juveniles have had sexual intercourse.[24] But, here's the catch and something very important that everyone including juveniles need to know: *A juvenile cannot consent to sex in the eyes of the law.* It doesn't matter that the twelve-year-old acted seductively or that the fourteen-year-old lied and said that he was twenty-one. In the eyes of the law, and many child development professionals, a minor is incapable of "consent." Consent suggests that the person has a reasonable grasp of the risks and benefits involved with an action and then voluntarily, from an informed position, makes a choice to engage or not. Many juveniles do not know all of the ramifications of sexual contact, nor is their brain fully developed until about age twenty-five. Yes, the age of majority (that age that we think people are old enough to consent to sex) seems like an arbitrary number. It is eighteen years in many states. *What this means*

is that any sexual contact with a minor is a sex crime. When any form of intercourse is involved, it might be called "statutory rape" and in many jurisdictions claiming "ignorance" or a "mistake" is no excuse. In some states, if both persons are underage, both could be called "sex offenders."

2. First time sex offenders who use force or coercion. This is the largest group of juvenile sex offenders to come to the attention of authorities. Often there is a substantial age gap between victim and offender. The rearrest rate for this group, however, is low.[25]

3. The repeat abusive juvenile sex offender. This group constitutes 4 to 8 percent of all juvenile sex offenders taken into custody, perhaps 1,000 such juveniles per year.[26] Notably, among adult sex offenders those who are violent predators are a relatively small number. We might assume that predatory juvenile sex offenders are similarly a relatively small percent of the total number. The behaviors, nonetheless, cause significant harm, so these persons should certainly be identified and addressed.

In the United States, juvenile sex offenders are primarily white males from two parent homes without a record of prior sexual offending who have experienced a period of significant parental loss.[27] One federal study of twelve states revealed that of all sexual assaults known to police 96 percent of the offenders were male, with female offenders mostly involved with victims under six years of age; 23 percent of sex offenders were seven to seventeen years at the time of the offense; of these 3.6 percent were seven to eleven years; 19.5 percent were twelve to seventeen years; 16 percent of juvenile sexual assault offenders were under twelve and their most common sexual offense was forcible fondling (representing 19 percent of all juvenile forcible fondlings).[28] Learning disabilities and poor school performance are not uncommon among juvenile sex offenders known to authorities. Academic difficulties existed for 30 to 60 percent of juvenile sex offenders[29] or shall we say, for those not savvy enough to avoid getting caught.

The younger the victim the more likely the offender was to be a family member; for those victims under six, abused in a residence, the offender was most likely to be a family member, twenty-five to thirty-four years old, or an acquaintance, twelve to seventeen years old. For those victims six to eleven years old, the offender was slightly more likely to be an acquaintance than a family member but, for victims twelve to seventeen, victimized in a residence, the offender was usually a family member. When a child victim of sexual assault was victimized away from a residence the likelihood of the offender being a family member declined. When the victim was twelve to seventeen, and victimized away from home the likely offender was a juvenile. In all cases of sexual assault only about 14 percent of offenders were strangers to the victim. For male victims under twelve, 40 percent of the offenders were family; for females under twelve, 47 percent were family.[30]

Some juvenile sex offenders largely victimize younger juveniles, others target peers and adults, while a third group, the "mixed type," will victimize younger juveniles, peer, and adults if possible. The mixed type group may present the greater risk of recidivism followed by those with a preference for sexual contact with young children. In the latter group, a preoccupation with sex and deviant sexual arousal patterns are more common.[31] When the deviant arousal is coupled with cognitive distortions this is usually indicative of a maladaptive sexual conditioning and/or a paraphilia. Examples of cognitive distortions include: "She must have wanted to—she never said 'no'"; "I did no more than what happened to me"; "I paid for her Coke so she owes me"; "Women are all the same and I know what they want."[32] In such cases the juvenile offenders' reaction when confronted about the inappropriate behavior tends to include denial, minimization, and victim blaming.[33]

GENDER, AGE, AND RACE

Of course, the offenders may be male or female, of any ethnicity, race, class, nationality, or sexual orientation. Juvenile females are responsible for 1 percent of forcible rapes and 7 percent of juveniles arrested for a sex offense—prostitution excluded.[34] Usually, juvenile female sex offenders evidence having experienced more types of abuse than their male counterparts and their offending occurs most often in a childcare setting.[35]

On age, while the juvenile sex offender could be very young, the most common age of onset for prepuberty sex offenders is between six and nine years of age.[36] Their victims are usually comparably young (simply because victims of sex offenses in general tend to be younger than their perpetrators and in these cases the offenders are also young). Victims of child sex offenders are often acquaintances or relatives. The older the juvenile sex offender, the greater the severity of the harm that is likely (in particular, penetration and the use of force).[37] These child sex offenders tend to have poor relationships with peers and academic difficulties.[38] Nevertheless, the International Association for the Treatment of Sexual Offenders[39] does not recommend considering juveniles under twelve as sex offenders, but rather as children in need of supervision or other assistance.

Are these young offenders sexual abuse victims? Results vary widely among studies from 4 to 62 percent saying "no."[40] Why the range? Often, convenience samples (whoever is available) constitute the sex offenders who are studied, as opposed to random samples, which would be more objective.

Advisedly, we should be careful about responding to adolescents by tagging them as "sex offenders." Adolescence is a time of normal development that includes a sexual awakening; thus, sexual exploration of various sorts is not uncommon for teens. Incidents involving female offenders and very young offenders are discussed in detail in Chapter 5.

Regarding race, one study involving a comparison of Caucasian and African American juvenile sex offenders revealed more severe physical abuse and emotional abuse for the Caucasian sex offenders than for the African American sex offender.[41] It also revealed that Caucasians were more likely to self-report incest and to commit penetrative acts than the African Americans in the study.

THE DYNAMICS OF THE SEXUAL ASSAULT INCIDENT

The dynamics of the sexual abuse incident can vary per offender motivation. Is the behavior the result of some sexual miseducation? Is it between age peers or younger or older juveniles, but clearly without an intent to harm? There is a lot written about this. From a criminal justice perspective there are three setups that are common.[42] The first involves juveniles with what might be called pedophiliac tendencies. These juveniles feel some compulsion to engage in sexual activity. They have sexual fantasies about being with others that are so intense that they interfere with their normal activity. The sexual activity is shrouded in secrecy and does not occur suddenly. For those with a pedophilia paraphilia sexual activity often occurs after some seduction of a minor involving friendship and gifts. Then there are the more opportunistic aggressive sex offenders who acting alone or with peers take advantage of a vulnerable person. Finally, there are the criminalistic offenders for whom sex offending is merely one type of offending among other law-violating behaviors.

The cycle generally begins when:

1. An event triggers negative self-perception and feelings, which often includes some sense of helplessness.
2. The juvenile then expects negative things to happen.
3. He/she engages in behavior to avoid a problem or some emotional discomfort.

4. The juveniles then attempt to compensate with sexualized efforts at power/control (a maladaptive way of responding to people or circumstances).

5. In the of sexual arousal—often through masturbation.

6. When a sex-related incident occurs.

7. The Fear of being discovered.

8. Efforts to reframe the event ("he/she wanted it," "I was drunk," "it's no big deal").

9. Experiences and worldview influence how event is viewed.

With a trigger, such as family trouble, anger, or boredom, these events can begin again.[43] The inappropriate sexual conduct may be a maladaptive response to a stressor. There might be a situation involving a misinterpretation of the words or actions of others.

In a review of the research Righthand and Welch[44] report the following as common characteristics of the juvenile sex offense:

- more often the victim is female
- the victim is usually much younger than the offender
- the victim is usually a relative or acquaintance
- the offense occurs when someone other than a parent is responsible for supervision
- the victim is intimidated, or threatened in some way
- the older the victim, the greater the force employed for victim compliance.

Additionally, sibling incest seems common, but underreported. Sibling sex offenders appear more troubled when compared to those who offend against nonrelatives.[45] While adults are more likely to be the sole victims of a sexual assault (96 percent of such victimizations), with juveniles multiple victims are more likely (19 percent of such victimizations). This is especially true for juvenile victims under twelve years (25 percent), and for older juveniles (13 percent). Among the youngest victims, multiple victims were more common between ages six to eleven years (28 percent) compared to under age six (21 percent). Usually multiple victims of a sex offense tend to be close in age.[46] According to another researcher[47] females have been more likely to experience multiple sexual offenses than male victims. This difference is less significant for juvenile victims of sexual assault (5 percent for females; 3 percent for males).

WARNING SIGNS

Signs of sexual victimization in children include chronic lying, in boys a strong reaction to being touched around the face or neck, sexual promiscuity, seductiveness, overeating, fear of being alone with a particular adult, bedwetting, sudden poor school performance, sexual—sometimes frighteningly so—thoughts and dreams, depression, rage or temper tantrums, bruises or pain around the mouth or genitalia, substance abuse, special friendship with an older person, particular bashfulness about undressing before others, mistrust of adults, personality changes, self-mutilation, suicidal behavior, soreness, a sexually transmitted disease and in prepubescent juveniles—pregnancy.

YOUR ANSWERS TO QUESTIONS ON JUVENILE SEX OFFENDING

Much of the data that follow are from a 2000 Bureau of Justice Statistics government study by Howard Synder called *Sexual Assault of Young Children as Reported to Law Enforcement: Victim, Incident, and Offender Characteristics.*[48] While not nationally generalizeable (because the data reflect the situation in only twelve states) it appears to come as close as it gets at this point. Note, the information reflects those cases of sexual assault known to law enforcement—not the very many incidents that we do not know about.

AT WHAT AGE ARE JUVENILES MOST AT RISK OF A SEXUAL VICTIMIZATION?

The victims of juvenile sex offenders, at least the ones we know about, are much younger than their offenders.[49] From Bureau of Justice Statistics data from twelve states—the modal age of juvenile victims of a sex offense that came to the attention of law enforcement was fourteen. Of all victims under twelve years old, four-year-olds were at most risk. Most sexual assault victims (67 percent) were under eighteen years; more than half of these were under twelve. One in seven victims who come to law enforcement attention was under six. Juveniles most at risk of forcible rape were those ten to fourteen years old, peaking at age fourteen. As one got older, past fourteen years, the risk of being raped decreased. The risk of forcible sodomy peaked at age four. It dropped thereafter and then increased from about age eleven to age thirteen. Risk of being assaulted with an object peaked at ages three and four followed by ages eight to fourteen years (again—these are based on cases the police know about); forcible fondling was most common when victims were thirteen, followed by age four.[50] Recent Idaho data indicate that 61 percent of juvenile sex offender victims (from summer 2005 to June 2006) were less than age eleven.[51] The modal age of male victimization known to law enforcement is four, for females it is fourteen.[52]

WHICH SEX OFFENSES HAPPEN TO JUVENILES?

Forcible fondling was the most common sex offense overall (45 percent of all sex assaults), followed by forcible rape (42 percent); forcible sodomy (8 percent); then, sexual assault with an object (4 percent). Regarding the sexual assault of juveniles 46 percent were victims of forcible rape; 84 percent were victims of forcible fondling; 79 percent were victims of forcible sodomy; and 75 percent were victims of sexual assault with an object.[53] When the victim was older than the offender sexual penetration was less likely.[54] Child abuse victimizations in general appear to vary minimally across social class and ethnic and racial categories and regions of the country.[55]

WHERE DO VICTIMIZATIONS OCCUR?

Seventy percent of all sexual assaults happened in a residence—whether the victim's, another victim's, or the offender's. Indeed, 64 percent of all forcible rapes; 74 percent of forcible sodomy; 76 percent of sexual assault with an object, and 74 percent of forcible fondling occur in a residence. This was especially so in cases of female sexual victimizations (77 percent female: 69 percent male victimizations occur in a residence); for juveniles, 77 percent of sexual victimizations occur in a residence compared to 55 percent of adult sexual victimizations. Children in children's homes are acutely vulnerable because of a lack of care in assessing, placing, and monitoring troubled children.[56] Following residences juvenile sexual victimizations occurred at schools, in hotels/motels, along roadways, and in fields/woods. Alternatives to residences in adult sexual victimizations included commercial/office buildings, hotels/motels, roadways, parking lots, and fields/woods.[57] Often juvenile victims were conned into accompanying the offender to the location where they were eventually victimized. It is assumed that juveniles are easier to deceive in this regard than a potential adult victim.[58] Also, once in a less familiar location escape becomes more difficult and thus, penetration appears more likely.[59]

WHAT WEAPONS ARE COMMONLY USED?

In 14 percent of all sexual assaults, no weapons were reported, but most often when weapons are mentioned they were "hands, feet or fists"; 2 percent of the incidents involve a firearm; and, 6 percent involve a knife or club. The infrequency of weapons is indicative of a physical strength differential between victim and offender.[60] While female victimizations might occur with physical restraint, male victimizations usually involve a weapon.[61] Adult female victims seemed more likely to be threatened by violence and injured than young female victims.[62] Violence is also more likely with a group of offenders as opposed to a single juvenile sex offender.[63] The more difficult the victim the greater the likelihood of violence, which would seem more likely if someone is facing victimization by several persons. Massed in a group each offender might feel less responsible for inflicting violence than when such actions are more direct. Some reports are that juvenile sex offenders tend to use more force than adult sex offenders.[64]

WHEN DO SEXUAL VICTIMIZATIONS OCCUR?

When the victims are adults, the victimizations were most common from midnight to 2 A.M. The number of victimizations of adults began to peak at 8 P.M., cresting around 2 A.M. For victims under six, the victimizations peaked modally around 3 P.M.[65] Juvenile sex offending seemed most likely, off school grounds and between 3:00 and 6:00 P.M.[66]

WHO ARE THE VICTIMS OF SEXUAL ASSAULT BY JUVENILE SEX OFFENDERS?

We tend to believe that our children are safe and that "these things" happen to other children, poor children, and minority children.[67] The fact is, juvenile sex offenders are of any demographic—race, gender, class, and nationality. Juvenile sex offenders are less discriminating in their choice of victims than their adult counterparts in that they usually victimize those who are simply available and vulnerable. These are mostly females, of any age, but usually early teens.[68] Eighty-six percent of all sexual assault victims (known to police) were females. The number of female victims of sexual assault peaks at 95 percent for nineteen-year-olds and 90 percent for thirteen-year-olds. Females were 99 percent of forcible rape victims; 87 percent of those assaulted with an object; 82

percent of forcible fondling. Female juvenile victims (83 percent) were more likely to be victimized alone than were males (71 percent).[69] Some research indicate that while females who are victims of child sexual abuse may not become abusers themselves as adults, they are more likely to be the mothers of children who are sexually abused than women who were not sexually abused.[70] Thus, parents may be contributors to the risk of harm based on whom they expose to their children.

Male victims (known to police) were more likely to be victims at younger rather than older ages.[71] Males were 31 percent of all victims under age six, 27 percent of victims under age twelve, and 18 percent of all victims under eighteen years. Most victims of forcible sodomy (54 percent) were males. This does not mean older males are not victimized, but rather that there is no parent or guardian to insist on the victimization being reported. Given the stigma of male victimization one might suspect the numbers are much higher—but not reported. Eighteen percent of juvenile sexual assault victims known to police were males. Male juvenile victims of sexual assault with an object were 15 percent of all juvenile victims, 20 percent of forcible fondling victims, and, 59 percent of forcible sodomy victims. The numbers were higher for boys under twelve years—with an object, 19 percent; forcible fondling, 26 percent; and forcible sodomy, 64 percent.[72]

WHAT IS THE LIKELIHOOD OF AN ARREST?

Sex offenses are our most underreported crimes. However, arrests appear more likely when there is a juvenile victimization (29 percent of the cases) than an adult victimization (22 percent of cases).[73] The exception here is when the victim is a very young child (about 19 percent of cases involve a victim under six—which is not surprising because young children are not likely to reveal their victimization articulately). The likelihood of an arrest increased when the sexual assault involved more than one victim at the same incident; when there was more than one offender; and, when the victim was a female. The likelihood of an arrest decreased when the offender was a stranger, when the incident occurred away from a residence, and when the victim was physically injured. In 2003 there were approximately 22,540 juvenile arrests for sex offending (excluding prostitution).[74]

Children will often not reveal being sexually victimized, sometimes not until adulthood. They may feel so bonded with the abuser that they do not want to cause him or her any harm especially if the person is a family member. There is often a reluctance to be considered the one responsible for sending a sibling, cousin, uncle, or other kin "to jail." If the young victim was threatened with harm or the harm of someone close to him or her, the victim may also remain silent. Guilt, shame, embarrassment, or hoping the situation will resolve itself also keeps some victims quiet. At times confusion feeds the silence because the abuser has otherwise been so generous and friendly, the young victim wonders—whether the sexual abuse is really wrong; whether anyone would believe it; and, whether the sexual contact is normal. If the victim is disabled or a very young child he or she may not be able to articulate the victimization.[75] In some cases class differences (juvenile offender from a wealthy family; victim from a low-income family) are a disincentive to report the victimization because justice so often comes with a price tag.

SEXUAL DEVIANCE OR NORMAL BEHAVIOR?

Exactly what constitutes sexual abuse is debatable, particularly when juveniles are involved. There are several situations that most would agree are sexual abuse or are not sexual abuse. For example, if two eight-year-olds, one male and one female, engage in a game of doctor where one pulls up the other's shirt and pokes their stomach as they pretend to give a shot—most would perceive this as normal child's play and part of a normal peer relations. If a grown woman, however, walked into a colleague's office pretending to be a nurse and giving her colleague a shot—and still proceeded after the colleague objected—most would agree this constitutes sexual harassment, but not sexual abuse. Most would agree the following situations constitute some form of sexual abuse/assault: (1) person A holds down person B against his/her own will and touches their genitals or penetrates him/her; (2) person A threatens person B against his/her own will and person B submits to having sex with person A; or (3) person A has a knife or gun and uses it against person B to force him or her to have sex/touch their genitals. Most would agree person B in all circumstances did not consent to person A touching him or her in a sexual way or having sex with him or her. Additionally, most would agree there are certain groups of people in vulnerable situations who lack the ability to consent. For example, those who are mentally disabled or physically disabled do not have the capacity to consent to someone who is in a primary care-giving role. Thus, any staff or employee who works in an institution or residential facility where these individuals live, cannot touch their clients in a sexual way or have sex with them, even when these clients seemingly accept these invitations. Also, children cannot consent to having sex with an adult. They lack the capacity to fully understand what they are agreeing to do.

When juveniles or young children are involved, the lines may become blurred. For example, while it is inappropriate and illegal for adults to sexually harass adults, what about juveniles? What if a young boy looks up a little girl's skirt? Most would probably consider this a "no-no," but not be ready to take action if the boys and girls were in elementary school, but may not be so quick to dismiss the incident if the boys and girls are in junior high school. The same would be true if a boy or girl ran up to another boy or girl and slapped them in their buttocks and ran away. OK, if they are in elementary school, but not if they are in high school. It is questionable and perhaps the context of the situation needs to be considered if it occurred in junior high school. These examples just show that it isn't so clear-cut to determine appropriateness of sexual behavior when it occurs as one develops into an adult.

With so much focus on sex offenders and inappropriate sexual behavior in the news and in the media, the question comes to our minds: Have we gone too far and do we even know the difference between what is and what is not inappropriate sexual behavior? In the following incident, an eight-year-old was removed from school for his sexual behavior.

> *Lorain school official this week executed an "emergency removal" of an 8-year-old boy who they say sexually harassed a girl in class. The boy's mother, Tammy . . . said yesterday her son was playing in gym on Tuesday when a girl student said he and two other boys may have grabbed her buttocks. He was then questioned in an informal hearing by school officials and he admitted he had been passing love notes to the same girl. The second-grader then asked to sign a notice of emergency removal form for sexual harassment without a parent present, . . . [his mother] said. The boy printed his first name on the portion of the form asking for his signature. School documents . . . did not give specifics on the incident but showed that the second-grader was removed from school on Tuesday for "sexual harassment during gym." It also states the student "admits to writing notes saying 'I love you' and giving them to a student." "It's an embarrassment to me and it's an embarrassment to him because he doesn't understand what's going on," [His mother] said.[76]*

The new article also stated the school officials insisted they were only providing discipline to the child because his behavior was inappropriate and he was not being disciplined at home. His mother said it was difficult to discipline him because she felt he was being reprimanded for passing a love note and the child did not understand what he did was wrong. The parents were considering taking legal action against the school and removing their children from the school system.

In the preceding example, it may be debatable whether the second-grader committed a bona fide sexual offense or whether it constitutes sexual harassment. The problem is that research shows many who have committed serious sexual offenses (i.e., rape and child molestation) as adults began by merely committing sexual deviancy (i.e., sexual harassment or fetishes) when they were really young.[77] On the flip side of this, however, experts also know some sexual exploration during childhood and during adolescence is part of normal development. And even those who draw outside the lines, so to speak, with regard to their sexual behavior during childhood adolescence, do not necessarily grow up to become rapists or child molesters.[78] Thus, we are left in a quandary: do we admonish all sexual behavior during childhood or adolescence and label it as deviance or do we turn our heads when children and juveniles engage in sexually inappropriate behavior? The answer is somewhere in between and we, as a society, have to decide where the line should be drawn. That is exactly where we are. Some are drawing the line more conservatively by considering the second-grader's behavior as deviant and in need of punishment. Others, however, may be drawing the line liberally, by possibly defining some excessively sexually deviant behavior as normal development. Again, with so much focus in the media on sex offenders, we have become sensitive to the issue of sexual deviancy and we are currently redefining how such behavior should be handled when the (alleged) offender is not an adult yet and not fully aware of the consequences of such behavior.

Additionally, a surprising fact about juveniles who sexually abuse is that they rarely use overt aggression or violence.[79] This only makes it more difficult to define as a sexual abuse incident. Typically, no more force is used than what is necessary to complete the abuse. Juveniles have been known to use bribes and promises to gain compliance.[80] In an examination of approximately 500 juvenile sex offenders, 35 percent reported the behavior was mutual.[81] Almost one-fourth (24 percent) promised the child something, such as money, a toy, or candy. Only 10 percent threatened the child and the remaining 9 percent used some sort of physical force ranging from mild to severe (one caused the death of a child). Thus, when juveniles engage in sexual behavior and one is accused of molestation, it may be difficult to prove it was sexual abuse when the offender encouraged or enticed the victim without the use of physical force. The simple fact is that the more evidence (e.g., bruises and other injury) there is, the more likely people will believe a genuine offense occurred.

NORMAL BEHAVIOR EXAMINED

Anyone working with minors (especially parent and teacher) needs to know what is relatively normal versus abnormal juvenile sex-related behavior. Supervising adults should manage risk in the home and in the school environment.

Sexual exploration is usually cause for less concern if it is between age peers than between juveniles with a large age gap.

Stop it Now,[82] an American and European child abuse prevention group, offers the following guidelines on common versus uncommon juvenile sex interests:

Up to age 5:

Common includes: talk of pregnancy and childbirth, discussing differences about body parts and bathroom functions, attempting to look at nude persons and touching their private parts in public and, or, in private.

Uncommon: Specific sex actions and talk of such behaviors.

Ages 6 to 12:

Common: questions about menstruation, pregnancy and sexual activity, same age kissing, touching, role-play games, exhibitionism, and, or, touching their private parts secretively.

Uncommon: specific sex acts, public masturbation.

Ages 13 to 16:

Common: questions about relationships, private masturbation, same age kissing, fondling, or petting. Among a third of persons in this age group there is intercourse.

Uncommon: public masturbation, sexual interest in younger children.

Understanding what appears sexually normal is important to avoid the needless stigmatization and criminalization of juveniles. Markedly, some regional studies indicate that over 40 percent of persons have had some childhood sexual contact with peers. The numbers are similar for those who report masturbation before puberty.[83] There is also evidence that some young children (who masturbate) are capable of orgasmic feelings before puberty, but most do not engage in activities to make such discoveries.[84] John Bancroft[85] emphasizes the significance of understanding "the normal" in interpreting data that indicate that children in foster care tend to be considered more sexually aggressive than their peers. Bancroft suggests that this finding might be the result of a lack of close monitoring in foster care and a lack of privacy in such homes. When the sexual exploratory play, et cetera, occurs in such settings with the loss of privacy, it is more likely to be discovered and labeled as *deviant* with negative consequences for the juvenile. The implications are similar for low-income persons who live in small residences and children with certain disabilities who are likely to be monitored a bit more closely than others.[86]

Think back to your experiences with puberty—a crazy time—a physiological evolution, a time that peaked the curiosity of some individuals more than others to go exploring. From childhood into adolescent, the juvenile experiences usually include some sexual arousal (often prepuberty), sexual attraction to another (which might occur sooner in boys [about age eleven] than in girls [about age thirteen]), and sexual fantasies (which tend to begin prepuberty in most boys and postpuberty in most girls) according to admittedly limited data on the subject.[87] Another study by Reynolds and colleagues in 2003 reported that first crushes were common by ages eight or nine, a first boyfriend or girlfriend by age thirteen, and a first date by age fifteen.[88] Details on the initiation of sexual activity in juveniles are scarce given a general prudence about sex talk. Nevertheless, there have been suggestions that among juveniles oral sex has become a substitute for intercourse (like Bill Clinton, they might not view oral sex as "sex"), but some evidence suggests that many juveniles who have oral sex have already had intercourse or utilize it as a precursor to intercourse.[89]

It is worth remembering that we are talking about juveniles here, little sponges—not adults. So when their behavior goes awry— often the source is external to them. Maybe they saw something on television, perhaps they are imitating their parents, peers, or somebody else in their life. Of course, we could say that all of us see or experience some degree of negativity—but, no, we don't all act on it. What's the difference? Odds are there was some intervention to keep most of us on the straight and narrow.

WHAT ARE THE SIGNS THAT MY CHILD COULD BECOME A JUVENILE SEX OFFENDER?

Indicators of a child at risk of sexual offending include: Minimizing the impact of inappropriate behavior on others; ignoring or missing social cues of others' sexual boundaries, a preference for socializing with younger children rather than peers, insisting on physical contact with a child who does not want such contact, responding sexually to gestures of mere friendliness; reluctance to be alone with a particular child; offering inappropriate substances or materials like alcohol/pornography to younger children. More serious signs include forced sexual contact, sexual exploration with a younger child, secretive touching as opposed to age-peer exploration, and continuing sexually inappropriate behavior after being instructed to stop.[90]

PEER INFLUENCE

Looks that way, but the research on peer influence on sex offending is very limited. Generally, as children grow older the regard of parents tends to diminish in comparison to what peers think. Many children who sexually offend have trouble getting along with peers from a young age. Some scholars believe that this problem relating to peers is what might develop into a preference for intimacy with much younger children, associated with cognitive distortions and sexual fantasies.

So, something happens! You catch a child or adolescent doing something. Stay calm. Depending on how you react, you could turn something simple or innocent into a lifetime stigma. There is a need to understand what happened and to eliminate sexual activity of juveniles that might be fairly normal (innocent, exploratory—"playing doctor," or "show me yours and I'll show you mine," etc.).

DISTINGUISHING MORE SERIOUS SITUATIONS

Among prepubescent children signs of trouble include: if the behavior is frequent, interferes with normal activity, involves force, is a part of the manifestation of an emotional problem, if children involved are at very different developmental levels or ages, and the behaviour occurs in secret, even after adult intervention.[91]

When is more care needed versus more control? Often what's necessary is both care and control. There is certainly need for early intervention in dysfunctional families for it is often those in need of care who eventually become those in need of control. Judges need not be sex offender experts but they certainly need to be knowledgeable enough to do the right thing when dealing with children in need of services (those who are not delinquent, but who have no parents or guardians seeing to their well-being).

Example of a *cause for much concern* case:

Sam, aged 16 years, had presented with problematic behavior since early childhood, for which he has received on-going monitoring and [professional] input . . . At the age of 7 he reported sexual abuse by a stranger and at 9 he [was found to be in need of child protection services given] physical abuse from his mother, who consistently found him difficult to manage . . . Over the last 18 months Sam has committed a series of sexual offenses which appear to have increased in frequency and severity over time. He is charged with indecent assault and . . . assault having attacked a 15 year old girl in a local park. Despite clear evidence, Sam is unable to take responsibility for his actions.[92]

Example of a *cause for low concern* case:

Sally aged 11 years was sexually abused by her mother's partner. Her mother did not believe Sally's disclosure and disowned her because she was causing "trouble." Sally went

Table 1.1 Guideline for Discerning the Level of Concern Warranted When Juveniles Behave Sexually

Cause for Much Concern	Low Concern Points Prior Instances of
Sexual activity, especially related convictions	It is the first such incident
Diagnosis of conduct disorder, or a history of interpersonal aggression	Nonpenetrative assault
Poor social skills/deficits in intimacy skills	No history of significant trauma or abuse
Self-reported sexual interest in children	Remorse, empathy for the victim
Victim-blaming	Behavior seems peer-influenced and, or, experimental
High levels of trauma e.g., witnessing domestic violence, physical, psychological, sexual abuse, neglect	No significant history of nonsexual assault
High levels of family dysfunction (abusiveness, harshness)	Healthy peer relations
Detailed planning of the incident	No school problems
Early dropout from treatment	No history or behavioral or emotional problems
Marked compulsive, impulsive behaviors	

Note: The high concern points are based on strong research data and the low concern points are based on clinical assessments.

Source: Adapted from a table of indicators for concern by Tony Morrison and Julie Henniker.[93]

to live with her maternal aunt. Soon after she was found playing a "mummy and daddy" game in which she got her 8-year-old cousin Peter to touch her genetalia on top of her clothes.[94]

SEXUALLY VICTIMIZED JUVENILES

Significantly, the abuser might also be the victim of sexual abuse. Sexually victimized minors may come to associate sex with negative feelings—anger, fear, and powerlessness. Boys may wonder if they are gay; girls may wonder if they have become sexually impaired.[95] Finkelhor and Browne[96] described four possible impacts of the sexual victimization of minors:

1) *Traumatic sexualization*: where sexual feelings and attitudes are developmentally inappropriate, for example, the child comes to believe that sexually inappropriate behaviors might bring rewards—gifts, attention, et cetera. So sex becomes a tool for manipulation. The range of traumatization tends to vary, given the child's level of awareness of the circumstances and the circumstances themselves. For example whether the child is, say, a fairly passive instrument in the abuser's masturbation to the use of violence to garner sexual access. The trauma comes from the sexual misconceptions and confusions that can follow as the child matures.

Behavioral manifestations include:
- Sexual preoccupation
- Precocious sexual activity
- Aggressive sexual behaviors
- Promiscuity
- Prostitution
- Sexual dysfunction
- Phobic reactions to sexual intimacy.

2) *Betrayal*: the realization that someone the child needs to be positive toward him or her has caused hurt instead. They had been manipulated, lied to, not protected, or blamed.

Behavioral manifestations include:
- Clinging
- Allow own children to be victimized
- Discomfort with intimacy
- Aggression.

3) *Powerlessness*: where the victim's will is disregarded or invaded. This usually occurs repeatedly and the victim's efforts to stop it—fail. Thus, the victim feels powerless in his or her circumstances.

Behavioral manifestations include:
- Nightmares
- Phobias
- Eating and sleeping disorders
- Depression

- Running away
- School/employment problems
- Bullying
- Delinquency
- Becoming an abuser.

4) *Stigmatization*: when the child's self-image comes to include guilt, shame, and messages that he or she somehow caused was complicit with his or her own victimization. The messages may come from the abuser or even relatives and others.

Behavioral manifestations include:

- Delinquency
- Substance abuse
- Isolation
- Self-mutilation.

DO JUVENILE SEX OFFENDERS RE-OFFEND SEXUALLY?

NO. Chapter 6 offers details on the juvenile sex offender recidivism research. Yet, it bears repeating here that *most juvenile sex offenders do not continue their sex offending.* The rate of adolescent sex offense recidivism is approximately 5 to 14 percent.[97] Most juvenile delinquents whether sexual or nonsexual offenders desist their offending after the age of majority. They age out of the behavior. This is presently attributed to the newly accepted fact that it is more or less normal for juveniles to exercise poor judgment given that their brain is generally not fully developed until about age twenty-five.

Examples of recent studies on juvenile sex offender recidivism include: (1) a Texas Youth Commission study of seventy-two violent juvenile sex offenders who were followed for three years after release. Only three of them re-offended sexually[98]; (2) a study that reported on the findings of thirteen recidivism studies that looked at juvenile sex offense recidivism where most followed at least seventy-five offenders for over a year,[99] rearrest for a sexual offense was in the range of 1.8 to 12.2 percent across the studies; (3) using follow-up data for three or four years, less than one out of ten of those juveniles taken into custody for a first-time sex offense recidivate with a sex offense[100]; (4) a study of 300 male juvenile sex offenders who were followed for three to six years found that only thirteen re-offended sexually.[101] Significant predictors were the age of the offender, the age of the victim, and the sex of the victim; (5) a study of 156 male adolescent sex offenders 6.4 percent re-offended sexually[102]; and (6) when the offender is five to twelve years old, one study of 135 children indicated (much in line with other works) that they are unlikely to continue the behavior into adulthood.[103]

WHAT IF THE PERSON RE-OFFENDED SEXUALLY BUT WAS NOT CAUGHT AND CERTAINLY DOES NOT TELL?

Well, odds are these low recidivism rates are correct because most juveniles are just not that sophisticated. Juvenile sex offenders need to be properly assessed—who are the ones with pedophiliac tendencies? The compulsion, fantasy, or aggression? Treat them! Also, pay attention to female juvenile sex offenders—they "fly under the radar" and too often, by our neglectful trust we help them to do this.

NOTES

1. Carol Carson, "Looking after Young Sexual Abusers: Child Protection, Risk Management and Risk Reduction," in *Children and Young People Who Sexually Abuse Others: Current Development and Practice Responses*, ed. Marcus Erooga and Helen Masson (London: Routledge, 2006), 55.

2. Karen J. Terry, *Sexual Offenses and Offenders: Theory, Practice, and Policy* (Belmont, CA: Wadsworth, 2006), 30–31.

3. The Gallup Poll, "Sex Offenders," video report, June 9, 2005, as cited in Human Rights Watch, http://www.hrw.org/reports/2007/us0907/1.htm#_Toc176672548.

4. Wade C. Myers, *Juvenile Sexual Homicide* (London: Academic Press, 2002).

5. Donna M. Vandiver, "A Prospective Analysis of Juvenile Male Sex Offenders: Characteristics and Recidivism Rates as Adults," *Journal of Interpersonal Violence* 21(5) (2006): 676.

6. National Center of Sexual Behavior of Youth, "Frequently Asked Questions about Children with Sexual Behavior Problems," http://www.ncsby.org/pages/registry.htm.

7. David Finkelhor, *Sexually Victimized Children* (New York: Free Press, 1979), 50.

8. John A. Hunter, Robert Hazelwood, and David Sleslinger, "Juvenile Perpetrated Sex Crimes: Patterns of Offending and Predictors of Violence," *The FBI Law Enforcement Bulletin* 69(3) (2000): 2.

9. Joan Williams, Auburn University, http://graduate.auburn.edu/auetd/search.aspx, *Juvenile Sex Offenders: Predictors of Recidivism*, 91.

10. Ibid.

11. Franklin E. Zimring, Alex R. Piquero, and Wesley G. Jennings, "Sexual Delinquency in Racine: Does Early Sex Offending Predict Later Sex Offending in Youth and Young Adulthood," *Criminology and Public Policy* 6(3) (2007): 507.

12. Franklin Zimring, *An American Travesty: Legal Responses to Adolescent Sexual Offending* (Chicago: University of Chicago Press, 2004), 66.

13. Howard N. Snyder, "Sexual Assault of Young Children as Reported to Law Enforcement: Victim, Incident and Offender Characteristics" (Washington, DC: Bureau of Justice Statistics: National Center for Juvenile Justice. NCJ 182990, 2000), 8.

14. Howard Barbaree and William Marshall, *The Juvenile Sex Offender*, ed. Howard Barbaree and William Marshall (New York: Guilford Press, 2006), 4.

15. Ibid., 2.

16. Ibid., 4.

17. David Finkelhor, "Prevention: A Review of Programs and Research," in *A Sourcebook on Child Sexual Abuse*, ed. David Finkelhor et al. (Newbury Park, CA: Sage, 1986), 127.

18. National Center of Sexual Behavior of Youth, "Frequently Asked Questions about Children with Sexual Behavior Problems," http://ncsby.org/pages/FAQ.htm1.

19. Finkelhor, "Prevention: A Review of Programs and Research," 71–76.

20. Jessica Woodhams, Raphael Gilley, and Tim Grant, "Understanding the Factors That Affect the Severity of Juvenile Stranger Sex Offenses: The Effect of Victim Characteristics and Number of Suspects," *Journal of Interpersonal Violence* 22(2) (2007): 218.

21. Michael Caldwell, "What We Do Not Know about Juvenile Sexual Reoffense Risk," *Child Maltreatment* 7(4) (2002): 294.

22. Ibid.

23. National Task Force on Juvenile Sexual Offending, *Juvenile and Family Court Journal* (1993), 55.

24. Caldwell, "What We Do Not Know about Juvenile Sexual Reoffense Risk," 293.

25. Zimring, *An American Travesty: Legal Responses to Adolescent Sexual Offending*, 67.

26. Ibid.

27. Gail Ryan, "Sexually Abusive Youth: Defining the Population," in *Juvenile Sexual Offending: Causes, Consequences and Corrections*, ed. Gail Ryan and Sandy Lane (San Francisco, CA: Jossey-Bass, 1997).

28. Ibid., 6.

29. John A. Hunter, "Understanding Juvenile Sex Offenders: Research Findings and Guidelines for Effective Management and Treatment," in *Juvenile Justice Fact Sheet* (Charlottesville, VA: Institute of Law, Psychiatry, and Public Policy, 2000), n.p.

30. Snyder, "Sexual Assault of Young Children as Reported to Law Enforcement: Victim, Incident and Offender Characteristics," 10–11.

31. Gregory A. Parks and David E. Bard, "Risk Factors for Adolescent Sex Offender Recidivism: Evaluation of Predictive Factors and Comparison of Three Groups Based upon Victim Type," *Sexual Abuse: A Journal of Research and Treatment* 18(4) (2006): 334.

32. Marcus Erooga and Helen Masson, "Children and Young People with Sexually Harmful or Abusive Behaviors: Underpinning Knowledge, Principles, Approaches and Service Provision," in *Children and Young People Who Sexually Abuse Others: Current Development and Practice Responses*, ed. Marcus Erooga and Helen Masson (London: Routledge, 2006), 15.

33. Helen Masson and Marcus Erooga, in *Children and Young People Who Sexually Abuse Others: Current Development and Practice Responses*, ed. Marcus Erooga and Helen Masson (London: Routledge, 2006), 14.

34. National Center of Sexual Behavior of Youth, "Frequently Asked Questions about Children with Sexual Behavior Problems."

35. Sue Righthand and Carlann Welch, "Juveniles Who Have Sexually Offended: A Review of the Professional Literature," (Washington, DC: Office of Juvenile Justice and Delinquency Prevention, 2001), 16–17.

36. Sharon Araji, *Sexually Aggressive Children: Coming to Understand Them* (Thousand Oaks, CA: Sage Publications, 1997), 72–79.

37. Howard Barbaree, Stephen Hudson, and Michael Seto, 1993, as cited in Elizabeth. J. Letourneau, Sonja. K. Schoenwald, and Ashli. J. Sheidow, "Children and Adolescents with Sexual Behavior Problems," *Child Maltreatment* 9(1) (2004): 50.

38. Araji, *Sexually Aggressive Children: Coming to Understand Them*.

39. Association for the Treatment of Sexual Abusers, "The Effective Legal Management of Juvenile Sex Offenders," ATSA, http://www.atsa.com/ppjuvenile.html (March 11, 2000).

40. National Center of Sexual Behavior of Youth, "Frequently Asked Questions about Children with Sexual Behavior Problems."

41. David L. Burton and William Meezan, "A Preliminary Examination of Racial Differences in Trauma and Sexual Aggression among Adolescent Sexual Abusers," *Smith College Studies in Social Work* 77(1) (2007): 113.

42. David Canter, Derek Hughes, and Stuart Kirby, "Paedophilia: Pathology, Criminality, or Both? The Development of a Multivariate Model of Offense Behaviour in Child Sexual Abuse," *Journal of Forensic Psychiatry* 9 (1998): 538.

43. Sandy Lane, "The Sexual Abuse Cycle," in *Juvenile Sexual Offending*, ed. Sandy Lane and Gail Ryan (San Francisco, CA: Jossey-Bass Inc., 1997), 80.

44. Righthand and Welch, "Juveniles Who Have Sexually Offended: A Review of the Professional Literature," 4.

45. Ibid., xiv.

46. Snyder, "Sexual Assault of Young Children as Reported to Law Enforcement: Victim, Incident and Offender Characteristics," 4–5.

47. Ibid., 5.

48. Ibid.

49. Righthand and Welch, "Juveniles Who Have Sexually Offended: A Review of the Professional Literature," 4.

50. Snyder, "Sexual Assault of Young Children as Reported to Law Enforcement: Victim, Incident and Offender Characteristics," 2.

51. Parker Howell, "Sex Abuse Cases Hit Record Number. Better Awareness, Enforcement Cited," *Knight Ridder Tribune Business News*, February 4, 2007, 1.

52. Snyder, "Sexual Assault of Young Children as Reported to Law Enforcement: Victim, Incident and Offender Characteristics," 4.

53. Ibid.

54. Woodhams, Gillett, and Grant, "Understanding the Factors That Affect the Severity of Juvenile Stranger Sex Offenses: The Effect of Victim Characteristics and Number of Suspects," *Journal of Interpersonal Violence* 22(2) (2007): 232.

55. Doyle Peters, Gail Elizabeth Wyatt, and David Finkelhor, "Ch 1: Prevalence," in *A Sourcebook on Child Sexual Abuse*, ed. David Finkelhor et al. (Newbury Park, CA: Sage, 1986), 28–30.

56. Kevin Epps, "Looking after Young Sexual Abusers: Child Protection, Risk Management and Risk Reduction," in *Children and Young People Who Sexually Abuse Others: Current Development and Practice Responses*, ed. Marcus Erooga and Helen Masson (London: Routledge, 2006), 96.

57. Snyder, "Sexual Assault of Young Children as Reported to Law Enforcement: Victim, Incident and Offender Characteristics," 6.

58. Woodhams, Gillett, and Grant, "Understanding the Factors That Affect the Severity of Juvenile Stranger Sex Offenses: The Effect of Victim Characteristics and Number of Suspects," *Journal of Interpersonal Violence* 22(2) (2007): 220.

59. Ibid., 232.

60. Snyder, "Sexual Assault of Young Children as Reported to Law Enforcement: Victim, Incident and Offender Characteristics," 6.

61. Pino and Meier, 1999, as cited in Woodhams, Gillett, and Grant, "Understanding the Factors That Affect the Severity of Juvenile Stranger Sex Offenses: The Effect of Victim Characteristics and Number of Suspects," *Journal of Interpersonal Violence* 22(2) (2007): 220.

62. Muram, Hostetler, Jones, and Speck, 1995, as cited in Woodhams, Gillett, and Grant, "Understanding the Factors That Affect the Severity of Juvenile Stranger Sex Offenses: The Effect of Victim Characteristics and Number of Suspects," 220.

63. Ibid., 221.

64. Ibid., 219.

65. Snyder, "Sexual Assault of Young Children as Reported to Law Enforcement: Victim, Incident and Offender Characteristics," 7.

66. Michele McNeil, "Concerned about Juvenile Sex Offenders, States Move to Tighten Their Regulations," *Education Week* (2007): 18.

67. Finkelhor, "Prevention: A Review of Programs and Research," 230.

68. Woodhams, Gilley, and Grant, "Understanding the Factors That Affect the Severity of Juvenile Stranger Sex Offenses: The Effect of Victim Characteristics and Number of Suspects," 219.

69. Snyder, "Sexual Assault of Young Children as Reported to Law Enforcement: Victim, Incident and Offender Characteristics," 4–5.

70. David Finkelhor, "Abusers: Special Topics," in *A Sourcebook on Child Sexual Abuse*, ed. David Finkelhor et al. (Newbury Park, CA: Sage, 1986), 127.

71. Snyder, "Sexual Assault of Young Children as Reported to Law Enforcement: Victim, Incident and Offender Characteristics," 5, Awad and Saunders, 1991, as cited in Woodhams, Gilley, and Grant, "Understanding the Factors That Affect the Severity of Juvenile Stranger Sex Offenses: The Effect of Victim Characteristics and Number of Suspects," 219.

72. Snyder, "Sexual Assault of Young Children as Reported to Law Enforcement: Victim, Incident and Offender Characteristics," 4.

73. Ibid., 11–12.

74. Howard N. Snyder, "Sexual Assault of Young Children as Reported to Law Enforcement: Victim, Incident and Offender Characteristics," Washington, DC: U.S. Department of Justice, Bureau of Justice Statistics, NCJ 182990 (2000): 125.

75. Stop It Now, *Do Children Sexually Abuse Other Children? Preventing Sexual Abuse among Children and Youth* (Brandon, VT: The Safer Society Press, 2007), 9.

76. Beth Stallings, "Boy, 8 Accused of Sexual Harassment," *Morning Journal*, April 2006.

77. Gene G. Abel, Candice A. Osborn, and Deborah A. Twigg, "Sexual Assault through the Life Span: Adult Offenders with Juvenile Histories," in *The Juvenile Sex Offender*, ed. Howard E. Barbaree, William S. Marshall, and Stephen M. Hudson (New York: The Guilford Press, 1993).

78. Judith V. Becker, Jerry Cunningham-Rathner, and Meg S. Kaplan, "Adolescent Sexual Offenders: Demographics, Criminal and Sexual Histories, and Recommendations for Reducing Future Offenses," *Journal of Interpersonal Violence* 1(4) (1987).

79. Gail Ryan et al., "Trends in a National Sample of Sexually Abusive Youths," *Journal of the American Academy of Child and Adolescent Psychiatry* 35(1) (1996).

80. Jeffrey Metzner and Gail Ryan, "Sexual Abuse Perpetration," in *Conduct Disorder in Children and Adolescents*, ed. Pirooz Sholevar (Washington, DC: American Psychiatric Publishing, 1995).

81. Stacey O. Zolondek et al., "The Self-Reported Behaviors of Juvenile Sex Offenders," in *Sexual Deviance*, ed. Christopher Hensley and Richard Tewksbury (Boulder, CO: Lynne Rienner Publishers, Inc, 2003).

82. Stop It Now, *Do Children Sexually Abuse Other Children? Preventing Sexual Abuse among Children and Youth* (Brandon, VT: The Safer Society Press, 2007), 5.

83. John Bancroft, "Normal Sexual Development," in *The Juvenile Sex Offender*, ed. Howard Barbaree and William Marshall (New York: Guilford Press, 2006), 29–30.

84. Ibid., 34.

85. Ibid., 33.

86. Gilby, Wolf, and Goldberg, 1989 as cited in Righthand and Welch, "Juveniles Who Have Sexually Offended: A Review of the Professional Literature," 23.

87. Bancroft, "Normal Sexual Development," 35–36.

88. Ibid., 37.

89. Ibid., 38.

90. Stop It Now, *Do Children Sexually Abuse Other Children? Preventing Sexual Abuse among Children and Youth*, 6.

91. National Center of Sexual Behavior of Youth, "Frequently Asked Questions about Children with Sexual Behavior Problems." 2.

92. Tony Morrison and Julie Henniker, "Building a Comprehensive Inter-Agency Assessment and Intervention System for Young People Who Sexually Harm: The Aim Project," in *Children and Young People Who Sexually Abuse Others: Current Development and Practice Responses*, ed. Marcus Erooga and Helen Masson (London: Routledge, 2006), 41.

93. Ibid., 49.

94. Ibid.

95. David Finkelhor and Angela Browne, "Initial and Long Term Effects: A Conceptual Framework," in *A Sourcebook on Child Sexual Abuse*, ed. David Finkelhor et al. (Newbury Park: CA: Sage, 1986), 189.

96. Ibid., 181–87.

97. National Center of Sexual Behavior of Youth, "Frequently Asked Questions about Children with Sexual Behavior Problems."

98. D. Poole, D. Leidecke, and M. Marbibi, "Risk Assessment and Recidivism in Juvenile Sex Offenders: A Validation Study of the Static-99" (Austin, TX: Texas Youth Commission, 2000).

99. Caldwell, "What We Do Not Know About Juvenile Sexual Reoffense Risk," 293.

100. Zimring, *An American Travesty: Legal Responses to Adolescent Sexual Offending*, 128.

101. Vandiver, "A Prospective Analysis of Juvenile Male Sex Offenders: Characteristics and Recidivism Rates as Adults," 683.

102. Parks and Bard, "Risk Factors for Adolescent Sex Offender Recidivism: Evaluation of Predictive Factors and Comparison of Three Groups Based Upon Victim Type," 327.

103. Melissa Carpentier, Jane F. Silovsky, and Mark Chaffin, "Randomized Trial of Treatment for Children with Sexual Behavior Problems: Ten-Year Follow-Up," *Journal of Consulting and Clinical Psychology* 74(3) (2006): 482.

REFERENCES

Abel, Gene G., Candice A. Osborn, and Deborah A. Twigg. "Sexual Assault through the Life Span: Adult Offenders with Juvenile Histories." In *The Juvenile Sex Offender*, edited by Howard E. Barbaree, William S. Marshall, and Stephen M. Hudson, 104–116. New York: The Guilford Press, 1993.

Araji, Sharon. *Sexually Aggressive Children: Coming to Understand Them.* Thousand Oaks, CA: Sage Publications, 1997.

Association for the Treatment of Sexual Abusers. "The Effective Legal Management of Juvenile Sex Offenders." ATSA, http://www.atsa.com/ppjuvenile.html (accessed November 24, 2007).

Bancroft, John. "Normal Sexual Development." In *The Juvenile Sex Offender*, edited by Howard Barbaree and William Marshall. New York: Guilford Press, 2006.

Barbaree, Howard, and William Marshall. *The Juvenile Sex Offender*, edited by Howard Barbaree and William Marshall. New York: Guilford Press, 2006.

Becker, Judith V., Jerry Cunningham-Rathner, and Meg S. Kaplan. "Adolescent Sexual Offenders: Demographics, Criminal and Sexual Histories, and Recommendations for Reducing Future Offenses." *Journal of Interpersonal Violence* 1(4) (1987): 431–445.

Burton, David L., and William Meezan. "A Preliminary Examination of Racial Differences in Trauma and Sexual Aggression among Adolescent Sexual Abusers." *Smith College Studies in Social Work* 77(1) (2007): 101–121.

Caldwell, Michael. "What We Do Not Know about Juvenile Sexual Reoffense Risk." *Child Maltreatment* 7(4) (2002): 291–302.

Canter, David, Derek Hughes, and Stuart Kirby. "Paedophilia: Pathaology, Criminality, or Both? The Development of a Multivariate Model of Offense Behaviour in Child Sexual Abuse." *Journal of Forensic Psychiatry* 9 (1998): 532–555.

Carpentier, Melissa, Jane F. Silovsky, and Mark Chaffin. "Randomized Trial of Treatment for Children with Sexual Behavior Problems: Ten-Year Follow-Up." *Journal of Consulting and Clinical Psychology* 74(3) (2006): 482–488.

Carson, Carol. "Looking after Young Sexual Abusers: Child Protection, Risk Management and Risk Reduction." In *Children and Young People Who Sexually Abuse Others: Current Development and Practice Responses*, edited by Marcus Erooga and Helen Masson. London: Routledge, 2006.

Epps, Kevin. "Looking after Young Sexual Abusers: Child Protection, Risk Management and Risk Reduction." In *Children and Young People Who Sexually Abuse Others: Current Development and Practice Responses*, edited by Marcus Erooga and Helen Masson. London: Routledge, 2006.

Erooga, Marcus, and Helen Masson. "Children and Young People with Sexually Harmful or Abusive Behaviors: Underpinning Knowledge, Principles, Approaches and Service Provision." In *Children and Young People Who Sexually Abuse Others: Current Development and Practice Responses*, edited by Marcus Erooga and Helen Masson, 3–17. London: Routledge, 2006.

Finkelhor, David. "Abusers: Special Topics." In *A Sourcebook on Child Sexual Abuse*, edited by David Finkelhor, Sharon Araji, Larry Baron, Angela Browne, Stefanie Doyle Peters, and Gail Elizabeth Wyatt, 119–142. Newbury Park, CA: Sage, 1986.

———. "Prevention: A Review of Programs and Research." In *A Sourcebook on Child Sexual Abuse*, edited by David Finkelhor, Sharon Araji, Larry Baron, Angela Browne, Stefanie Doyle Peters, and Gail Elizabeth Wyatt, 224–254. Newbury Park, CA: Sage, 1986.

Finkelhor, David, and Angela Browne. "Initial and Long Term Effects: A Conceptual Framework." In *A Sourcebook on Child Sexual Abuse*, edited by David Finkelhor, Sharon Araji, Larry Baron, Angela Browne, Stefanie Doyle Peters, and Gail Elizabeth Wyatt. Newbury Park: CA: Sage, 1986.

Howell, Parker. "Sex Abuse Cases Hit Record Number. Better Awareness, Enforcement Cited." *Knight Ridder Tribune Business News*, February 4, 2007, 1.

Hunter, John A. "Understanding Juvenile Sex Offenders: Research Findings and Guidelines for Effective Management and Treatment." In *Juvenile Justice Fact Sheet*. Charlottesville, VA: Institute of Law, Psychiatry, and Public Policy, 2000.

Hunter, John A., Robert Hazelwood, and David Sleslinger. "Juvenile Perpetrated Sex Crimes: Patterns of Offending and Predictors of Violence." *The FBI Law Enforcement Bulletin* 69(3) (2000): 1–7.

Lane, Sandy. "The Sexual Abuse Cycle." In *Juvenile Sexual Offending*, edited by Sandy Lane and Gail Ryan. San Francisco, CA: Jossey-Bass Inc., 1997.

Letourneau, Elizabeth. J., Sonja. K. Schoenwald, and Ashli. J. Sheidow. "Children and Adolescents with Sexual Behavior Problems." *Child Maltreatment* 9(1) (2004): 49–61.

Masson, Helen, and Marcus Erooga. In *Children and Young People Who Sexually Abuse Others: Current Development and Practice Responses*, edited by Marcus Erooga and Helen Masson, 3–17, 2006.

McNeil, Michele. "Concerned about Juvenile Sex Offenders, States Move to Tighten Their Regulations." *Education Week* (2007): 1–18.

Metzner, Jeffrey, and Gail Ryan. "Sexual Abuse Perpetration." In *Conduct Disorder in Children and Adolescents*, edited by Pirooz Sholevar. Washington, DC: America Psychiatric Publisher, 1995.

Morrison, Tony, and Julie Henniker. "Building a Comprehensive Inter-Agency Assessment and Intervention System for Young People Who Sexually Harm: The Aim Project." In *Children and Young People Who Sexually Abuse Others: Current Development and Practice Responses*, edited by Marcus Erooga and Helen Masson, 31–50. London: Routledge, 2006.

Myers, Wade C. *Juvenile Sexual Homicide*. London: Academic Press, 2002.

National Center of Sexual Behavior of Youth. "Frequently Asked Questions about Children with Sexual Behavior Problems," http://www.ncsby.org/pages/registry.htm (accessed November 1, 2007).

Parks, Gregory A., and David E. Bard. "Risk Factors for Adolescent Sex Offender Recidivism: Evaluation of Predictive Factors and Comparison of Three Groups Based Upon Victim Type." *Sexual Abuse: A Journal of Research and Treatment* 18(4) (2006): 319–342.

Peters, Doyle, Gail Elizabeth Wyatt, and David Finkelhor. "Ch 1: Prevalence." In *A Sourcebook on Child Sexual Abuse*, edited by David Finkelhor, Sharon Araji, Larry Baron, Angela Browne, Stefanie Doyle Peters, and Gail Elizabeth Wyatt, 15–59. Newbury Park: CA: Sage, 1986.

Poole, D., D. Leidecke, and M. Marbibi. "Risk Assessment and Recidivism in Juvenile Sex Offenders: A Validation Study of the Static-99." Austin: Texas Youth Commission, 2000.

Righthand, Sue, and Carlann Welch. "Juveniles Who Have Sexually Offended: A Review of the Professional Literature," 1–59. Washington, DC: Office of Juvenile Justice and Delinquency Prevention, 2001.

Ryan, Gail. "Sexually Abusive Youth: Defining the Population." In *Juvenile Sexual Offending: Causes, Consequences and Corrections*, edited by Gail Ryan and Sandy Lane, 3–9. San Francisco, CA: Jossey-Bass, 1997.

Ryan, Gail, Thomas J. Miyoshi, Jeffrey L. Metzner, Richard D. Krugman, and George E. Fryer. "Trends in a National Sample of Sexually Abusive Youths." *Journal of the American Academy of Child and Adolescent Psychiatry* 35(1) (1996): 17–25.

Snyder, Howard N. "Sexual Assault of Young Children as Reported to Law Enforcement: Victim, Incident and Offender Characteristics." Washington, DC: Bureau of Justice Statistics: National Center for Juvenile Justice. NCJ 182990, 2000.

———. "Sexual Assault of Young Children as Reported to Law Enforcement: Victim, Incident and Offender Characteristics." Washington, DC: U.S. Department of Justice, Bureau of Justice Statistics, NCJ 182990 (2000).

Stallings, Beth. "Boy, 8 Accused of Sexual Harassment." *Morning Journal*, March 25, 2006, 1.

Stop It Now. *Do Children Sexually Abuse Other Children? Preventing Sexual Abuse among Children and Youth*. Brandon, VT: The Safer Society Press, 2007.

Terry, Karen J. *Sexual Offenses and Offenders: Theory, Practice, and Policy*. Belmont, CA: Wadsworth, 2006.

Vandiver, Donna M. "A Prospective Analysis of Juvenile Male Sex Offenders: Characteristics and Recidivism Rates as Adults." *Journal of Interpersonal Violence* 21(5) (2006): 673–688.

Williams, Joan. *Juvenile Sex Offenders: Predictors of Recidivism*, Auburn University, 2007, http://graduate.auburn.edu/auetd/search.aspx (accessed November 15, 2007).

Woodhams, Jessica, Raphael Gillett, and Tim Grant. "Understanding the Factors That Affect the Severity of Juvenile Stranger Sex Offenses: The Effect of Victim Characteristics and Number of Suspects." *Journal of Interpersonal Violence* 22(2) (2007): 218–237.

Zimring, Franklin. *An American Travesty: Legal Responses to Adolescent Sexual Offending*. Chicago: University of Chicago Press, 2004.

Zimring, Franklin E., Alex R. Piquero, and Wesley G. Jennings. "Sexual Delinquency in Racine: Does Early Sex Offending Predict Later Sex Offending in Youth and Young Adulthood." *Criminology and Public Policy* 6(3) (2007): 507–534.

Zolondek, Stacey O., Gene G. Abel, William F. Northey, and Alan D. Jordan. "The Self-Reported Behaviors of Juvenile Sex Offenders." In *Sexual Deviance*, edited by Christopher Hensley and Richard Tewksbury. Boulder, CO: Lynne Rienner Publishers, Inc, 2003.

2

Explanations: What We Know and Don't Know

As sex offender and juvenile justice experts, one of the most frequently questions we are asked, is why—why do some juveniles sexually offend? This is perhaps why we have dedicated years to studying and examining this population of offenders—we also want to know the answer to this question. Unfortunately, after examining all of the research that has been conducted and conducting our own research we still cannot fully answer this question. The current state of research has informed us of the following: (1) there are certain factors that put youth at an increased risk for committing sexual offenses; (2) just because someone is exposed to these risk factors does not mean they will become a sex offender; (3) many adults who sexually offend began their offending when they were juveniles or even younger; (4) some children/juveniles who do engage in sexual offenses or sexual deviance, however, do not necessarily become sex offenders. What this tells us is that the cause and effect relationship between risk factors and becoming a sex offender is by no means a simple one. Thus, we cannot say if "X" is present, sexual abuse is always the result. It is not a one-to-one relationship. What we can say, if "X" is present, sexual abuse is more likely to occur. In the following case study, there are several suspicious risk factors that exist. The following excerpt is Billy's Story:

> When I was young, my dad kept moving from place to place. He left us when I was six years old . . . my mom [told] us that he wouldn't be back . . . I used to run over to my grandpa's house a lot . . . Later on, my grandpa tried to take us kids from my mom because my stepfather was so mean, but the court said nope . . . My stepfather was an idiot and a drinker. If you didn't do something the way it should be done, you got throwed around the

room. He would hold your hand up and burn your fingers with a cigarette lighter . . . He mostly did it to mom and me . . . My mother never stuck up for me with my stepfather. I guess she loved him . . . [My stepfather] told me to clean the dishes one night, and instead of walking around the table to pick up a glass, I just reached across the table for it. He said to put it down and walk around there. I took the glass and slammed it down on the table, and it went all over. So we had a fight. I was twelve or thirteen and I was having none of him. He went to hit me, but I was a little too quick and took off . . . That's how I got the broken nose, the busted eye. My mom didn't do nothing about it . . . I was gone for three days . . . my uncle . . . made me go back home . . . I had been about five years old when I first had sex. It was with my cousin underneath the old horse barn. She showed me what to do. She was only about five—about the same age as me—but she still knew about sex. Years later, I found out my uncle had molested all my cousins. After my cousin and I did it, there was a neighbor girl. We were like seven or eight years old and did everything, except I could never figure out how to get my penis into her so I always used my fingers . . . After that, I just kept messing around with all my cousins and the neighbor girls. I figured if they ain't yelling, then it must be all right. I've taken all these courses while I've been in prison and they keep telling me that those girls didn't want it, but none of the girls hollered like it was bothering them . . . [Later, after I got married] my cousins started bringing my niece over, and for some reason, that is when I crossed the line. I don't know if it was because I was getting back at everybody or what . . . I'd play with Cindy, make her stand upside down or give me blow jobs . . . The thing with my niece went on for like two years . . . After I left my first wife, I didn't have no more contact with Cindy . . . [After getting married to Elaine, who] had two kids, a little boy and girl named Annie. The first time Annie came into the bathroom when I was in there . . . she was looking at me so hard . . . I thought well, maybe she likes me, so I started trying to get her to have sex with me.[1]

Billy later sodomized Annie after he got drunk and became angry with her. The question is inevitable: why would someone commit such a horrible offense? Billy, though he lacked insight, began sexually offending when he was very young and continued such behavior, which eventually led to his incarceration.

There are several possible causes of his behavior. Perhaps, it was because he was abused. Though, he doesn't admit sexual abuse, he did experience physical abuse at the hands of his stepfather. Maybe Billy sexually molested because he needed to feel bonded to someone; as his father was absent and his relationship with his stepfather was not a loving or caring one. Perhaps Billy's normal developmental cycle was stunted due to his dysfunctional family. Billy's living environment was unstable, moving around a lot when he was younger. His grandfather was not allowed to raise him. Billy was exposed to sex at an excessively young age and although he wasn't sexually abused, there appeared to be a ripple effect of his cousins being sexually abused. That is, his young cousin learned about sexual abuse and passed it on to Billy. There was also a cognitive belief that if the girl did not yell, she was saying yes to sex.

In this chapter, we review the most well-known explanations of juveniles who sexually offend. Also, the empirical support for each explanation is provided.

Where it is possible, case examples of real juvenile sex offenders are presented to further explore explanations of sexual abuse.

FROM SEXUAL DEVIANCY TO SEXUAL OFFENDING: A SINGLE CONTINUUM?

It is important to note many of the explanations of sexual offending are much broader than just simply explaining the sexual offense; rather, they include explanations of sexual deviancy in addition to sexual abuse. Sexual deviance is defined in the *Diagnostic and Statistical Manual*, Fourth edition, Revised (*DSM-IV-R*), which is a bible of sorts for psychiatric/psychological disorders. It includes paraphilias and fetishes. Paraphilias are defined as "recurrent, intense sexual urges, fantasies, or behaviors that involve unusual objects, activities, or situations and cause clinical significant distress or impairment in social, occupational, or other important functioning."[2] Fetishes involve sexual arousal to nonliving objects. Common fetishes include, but are not limited to, bras, stockings, shoes, boots, etc. Having a fetish usually involves masturbating while holding, rubbing, or smelling the object or asking their sex partner to wear the object. It is noted in the DSM-IV that paraphilias typically begin by adolescence. Fetishes may involve an object that has some significance to the individual during their childhood. Fetishes tend to be lasting and persistent.

It is important to note many fetishes do not constitute criminal behavior; only those that involve other people without their consent are criminal. For example, receiving sexual gratification from watching others undress when they are not aware of it (i.e., voyeurism) or exposing one's self to another un-suspecting person (i.e., exhibitionism) are criminal, yet receiving sexual grati-fication from women's high-heeled shoes is not criminal. Additionally, while there is no conclusive research that shows that if someone has a paraphilia or fetish, he or she will later become a pedophile or rapist; however, many adult pedophiles and rapists have paraphilias and/or fetishes.[3] Additionally, it has been shown that when one paraphilia is present, there are usually multiple paraphilias present.[4] Perhaps sexual abuse is simply a slippery slope: those with slight sexual deviance transition from slightly odd behavior to outright sexual abuse. Additional research is needed to test this possible relationship.

Current research of approximately 500 juvenile sex offenders, however, in-dicates more than 30 percent reported using pornography and more than 25 percent reported fetishes, including, voyeurism, zoophilia (sexual at-traction to animals), masochism (sexual arousal from being beaten, bound, humiliated), sadism (sexual arousal from beating, bounding, humiliating others), pedophilia, and phone sex.[5] More specifically, juvenile sex offenders are more likely than adults to report obscene phone calls, child molestation, and phone sex. Adults, however, were more likely to engage in zoophilia. Juveniles and adults did not differ with regard to their prevalence of exhibitionism, voyeurism, masochism, sadism, pornography use, transsexualism, and transvestitism. Thus, paraphilias appear to be common among juvenile sex offenders, but more research is needed to assess whether such behaviors represent a gateway to sexual abuse.

In the following news article, exposure to pornography at a young age is just one of several theories posed to explain juvenile sex offending.

> Over a 10-month period, prosecutors allege, a Lombard teenager embarked on a criminal sexual assault rampage that left five adult women traumatized and prompted questions about how and why a youth of 15 would develop sexually violent behavior. The answers vary dramatically. Some experts say that most sexual offenders are victims of sexual abuse. Others say they are likely exposed to pornography at an early age ... The case is extremely rare in the world of juvenile criminal sexual assault, according to police, prosecutors and psychologists. The victims of child sexual predators typically are the same age as or younger than the offenders. In many cases, teenagers who commit sexual assault will target someone they know: a date, for example, or a relative. Police and prosecutors allege that the Lombard youth began assaulting women when he was 14 and that he targeted his victims at random, sometimes stalking them. The victims, who were attacked outside their homes and, in two cases, in the home, ranged in age from 23 to 62, police said. "The current thought is that (sexual assault) is a learned behavior, that somewhere along the line, (offenders) were sexually abused, witnessed sexual abuse, or were exposed to pornography or films that depict sexual violence against women," [said Robert E. Freeeman-Longo a licensed counselor who treats sexual offenders]. Some sexual offenders may be on a power trip; some may have sexual fantasies and severe anxiety that prompts them to act on the desires compulsively. For others, such attacks are an expression of unleashed rage.[6]

In this news excerpt, early exposure to sexual deviance (i.e., pornography) is only one of several theories posed.

COGNITIVE THEORY: MY THOUGHTS MADE ME DO IT

Thinking errors have long been attributed to criminal behavior and, more recently, attributed to sexual offending. Oftentimes, offenders develop rationalizations or support misperceptions in order to justify their behavior. For example, an offender may believe he/she is not harming anyone when he/she files a false insurance claim. He or she may rationalize that the insurance company has a lot of money and has paid the company several hundred or thousands of dollars and deserves to get his or her money back (i.e., Why should I feel guilty when they are the real crooks?). This type of thinking allows one to reconcile their behavior with their thoughts. Researchers coined this criminological theory and called it techniques of neutralization—denial of responsibility ("it wasn't my fault"), denial of injury ("you enjoyed it"), denial of victim ("you deserve it"), admonishing the admonishers ("you are just as bad"), appeal to a higher loyalties ("I did it to teach you a lesson").[7]

Similar rationalizations were also identified for adolescent sex offenders. These included: (1) denying the behavior, (2) minimizing the extent of the behavior, (3) denying the seriousness of the behavior, (4) denying responsibility, and (5) fully admitting with responsibility and guilt. With the exception of the last, all are ways to avoid personal involvement in the sexual abuse. These are psychological views the offender adopts to lessen the severity of what they did.[8]

Cognitive distortions have also been examined in sexual coercion and rape, more specifically in date-rape incidents. Cognitive distortions include holding sex-role stereotypes, negative attitudes toward women, and acceptance of violence toward women.[9] Thinking errors, particularly unfavorable attitudes toward women, have been used to show a correlation with rape-favorable attitudes. For example, it has been found some use rape myths to justify violent behavior toward their victims.[10]

Rape myths include believing in the following: all women want to be raped; no woman can be raped against her will; if a woman is raped, she asked for it, and a woman might as well relax and enjoy it if she is being raped.[11] Having such beliefs has shown to correlate with rape rates. For example, in one study it was hypothesized that countries with higher rapes would have more favorable attitudes toward rape myths than countries with lower rapes.[12] This hypothesis was tested by comparing attitudes of U.S. students to Scottish students. The results showed support for the hypothesis: Americans held more favorable attitudes toward rape myths.

It has also been found that rape myths are prevalent among U.S. college students. A student-led research project at a midwestern university assessed approximately 200 U.S. college students' attitudes toward rape myths also found support for this.[13] The results showed 23 percent of the students felt if a woman is raped while she is drugged, she is at least somewhat responsible for letting things get out of control. Also, 4 percent agreed that although most women wouldn't admit it, they generally find being physically forced into sex a real "turn-on." These findings show moderate support for rape myths among young Americans.

Although the initial indication is that there is some relationship between rape myths and committing rape, attempts to find cognitive thinking errors that discriminate juvenile sex offenders from juvenile nonsexual offenders have not been successful.[14] Additional research is needed in this area. Also, it may be that some factor or combination of factors leads to sexual abuse. Cognitive elements may simply be an effect of something that has occurred in the youth's life and the result is cognitive misperceptions, which leads the youth to commit sexual abuse. Thus, the cognitive element may be a mediating factor—caused by something and later leads to abuse.

BIOLOGICAL THEORY: MY OVERACTIVE TESTOSTERONE MADE ME DO IT

Biological explanations have the potential to revolutionize the way we identify and treat sexual offenders. For example, if there was some biological component, whether it is a gene, a brain deformity, or an excessive level of testosterone—we can treat it. We can even perform tests to detect it before the person offends. The biological makeup of a person can be altered through surgery or pharmacological treatment. Most of the current-day biological theories involve chemicals or other aspects in our environments that change the way we feel, and therefore, the way we behave. Everyone has likely experienced this. After waking up after a good night's rest and a good breakfast, I feel better and I am more social and friendly throughout the day. If, however, I didn't sleep well, I haven't exercised, and have been eating too much fast food, I feel groggy, irritable, and more likely to engage in hostile conversations.

Biological explanations of aberrant behavior are often thought of as Draconian or simply out of date. One of the first empirical assessments of why people engage in criminal behavior can be dated back to Cesare Lombroso, an Italian scholar, doctor, and philosopher. He proposed criminals were evolutionary throwbacks—*atavists*. Thus, criminals could be identified by their primitive appearances, which included such features as a low-sloping forehead, large jaw, flattened or upturned nose, handle-shaped ears, shifty eyes, baldness, and fleshy lips. His research, though not highly supported through scientific assessments, spawned an entire school of thought when attempting to explain criminal behavior—biological theories.

Although Lombroso's explanation has not received empirical support, subsequent research efforts have identified environmental factors that cause biological reactions that may precipitate criminal behavior. For example, research has shown increased sugar and carbohydrates,[15] some food dyes and artificial colors,[16] and lead ingestion,[17] serve as catalysts for aggressive and violent behavior.

More specific to sex offenders, high levels of testosterone, have been cited as possibly the primary culprit to explain their behavior. These explanations, however, have usually been geared toward explaining adult rape and not necessarily juveniles who commit sexual abuse. If the problem for some juveniles is that they have high levels of testosterone, providing treatment when they are still developing creates an ethical dilemma.[18] Treating high levels of testosterone is often referred to as chemical castration because it dramatically decreases testosterone levels. Antitestosterone drugs, such as Depo-Provera, are often used. The effects of taking this drug, originally approved as birth control for women, can negatively affect growth and maturation when administered to a juvenile. There may be situations where this would be used to treat juveniles; for example, if it was an extreme case of compulsive, extremely violent behavior in conjunction with the sexual behavior and if, perhaps, the juvenile is older. Additionally, the National Task Force on Juvenile Sexual Offending has noted that such treatment should not be used unless the youth is extremely sexually abusive and under close supervision of a medical doctor.[19]

EVOLUTIONARY THEORY: MY NEED TO REPRODUCE MADE ME DO IT

One of the most controversial explanations of rape is evolutionary theory. Evolutionary theorists attempt to explain only rape, not child molestation, or other sexual aberrances. Recently, a biologist and an anthropologist, Randy Thornhill and Craig T. Palmer, teamed up to write and publish *A Natural History of Rape: Biological Bases of Sexual Coercion*.[20] The book was sure to cause uproar; our initial reaction to the book's release was that this was sure to ruffle some feathers and we wondered if the book would turn out to be revolutionary or rather just turn the clocks back in terms of how rape was currently perceived in our society. Before we jump ahead to forming a reaction, however, let's discuss what exactly an evolutionary theory of rape entails and specifically, how this relates to juvenile sex offenders.

Relying on some of the most basic biological components, Thornhill and Palmer provide detail of the evolution process.[21] It has been well documented that many species have adapted features through the process of evolution. Through the process of evolution, many species maintain traits that increase reproductive success and eliminate traits that do not contribute to successful reproduction (i.e., continued life for that species).[22] Thornhill and Palmer note that somewhere along the evolution history of humans, rape became a trait that, for men, ensured their continued existence for generations to come. Several studies and explanations are provided to support this notion. For example, it is noted that rape victims are overwhelming in their childbearing age. Also, penile-vaginal rape (as compared to other types of rape that do not result in possible conception) is more likely to occur when the victim is of reproductive age.

The authors note that rape among different species appears to occur in conjunction with the responsibility to raising their offspring.[23] For example, human females bear the responsibility for carrying the fetus for nine months and often take primary care roles in raising their offspring. Men, therefore, will compete for women due to their ability to care for their offspring. In a few species (some insects, birds, frogs, and fish), females do not bear the brunt of parental responsibility. For example, the male pipefish, supplies the nutrients and oxygen for several weeks to the fertilized egg. Female pipefish act more sexually competitive than males, quite the opposite of humans. The authors cite these findings as evidence to support the evolution perspective of rape.

Rape becomes a way for men to one-up, so to speak, the selectiveness that females have toward potential sex partners. It becomes a way for them to circumvent the choosiness exhibited by most females. Thornhill and Palmer note that women have developed a psychological adaptation to protect their own genes. They provide support for this by referring to evidence showing women who suffer rape during their childbearing years suffer more psychological trauma from the event compared to those who are in their childhood or postpuberty. This, the authors suggest, shows women protect themselves, are more selective, and so on during their childbearing years.

Some of their recommendations based on their evolutionary evidence, is that rape should be punished severely. They also suggest exploring chemical castration, which entails injections of medication that lower a males' level of testosterone. With regard to females, they suggest women, particularly of childbearing age, take into account biological and evolutionary causes of rape when they decide what they are going to wear, how they appear, and consider whether to participate in certain types of social activities.

Many researchers and experts in sex offenders/sex offenses admonish perceiving sex crimes as being "sexual"; rather, they are violent and assaultive offenses.[24] Thornhill and Palmer, however, see sex crimes as just that—sexual in nature and cannot be explained by denying the biological nature of sex. They contend the social scientists have it wrong through their examination of rape without examining the sexual nature of the behavior.[25]

While this theory was not proposed as a juvenile sex offender explanation, the theory can definitely apply to explaining why juveniles rape after they reach puberty. This theory, however, does not fully apply to all of the sexual behavior juveniles described in much of the literature. For example, it has been well documented among juvenile sex offenders that force is rarely used;

manipulation and verbal coercion are more likely.[26] Also, many of the victims of juvenile sex offenders are young, usually not in the childbearing stage of their life.[27] What would evolutionary theorists say about this? Perhaps they could pose an explanation. Nevertheless, rape—having vaginal-penile sex against the victim's will and with either use of force or threat of force—is not common among juveniles.

BEHAVIORAL THEORY: I WAS CONDITIONED TO DO IT

It has been long known by experts that pairing masturbation with deviant fantasies leads to abnormal/unusual sexual development.[28] Pairing a neutral stimuli (i.e., shoes) with one that produces satisfaction (i.e., masturbation) can lead to respondent conditioning. That is, the neutral stimuli (i.e., shoes) will later produce the same feeling of satisfaction and pleasure that the paired stimuli (masturbation) will produce. This process was identified by Pavlov when he would simply ring a bell each time he fed his dog.[29] The dog would salivate when he knew he was about to be fed. Later, when Pavlov rang the bell, the dog would salivate even if no food was present. The dog associated the ringing of the bell with being fed. So later the neutral stimuli, bell ringing, produced the same response as if he was being fed. Thus, when applying this to sexual responses, neutral stimuli can produce the same arousal as the masturbatory stimuli. Thus, sexual arousal to abnormal and unhealthy stimuli can result.

It has also been found that pairing a behavior normally associated with positive feelings, such as sexual arousal, with something negative or aversive (such as a negative experience) can lead a young person to believe that normal, healthy, sexual interactions are out of the question for them.[30] This is especially critical if it was one of their first sexual exposures. An additional problem during fantasy is that the individual may inadvertently focus on particular cues (that are not normally associated with sexual arousal). Thus, these cues become the focus and cues normally causing sexual arousal become nonexistent. That means, over time it is possible that the adolescent becomes immune to stimuli that normally produces arousal, such as touching, viewing, and interacting with an age-appropriate mate. Sexual arousal results from inappropriate sexual cues, which includes (but is not limited to) children on nonconsenting partners.

The role that fantasy plays in abnormal sexual interactions has been well researched, particularly in the adult sex offender literature.[31] Fantasy can in fact become a motive in rape cases. Many adult rapists spend a substantial amount of time fantasizing about a rape before they actually rape a victim.

Early research indicates people can easily develop a sexual attraction to an innocuous stimulus rather quickly when it is paired with a sexual photograph. For example, in one study a researcher showed a picture of a partially nude/scantily dressed woman followed by a picture of a pair of boots several times. After showing the set of pictures several times, only the picture of the boot was shown; the result was that the men became sexually aroused only when shown the boots.[32]

Two well-known researchers concluded that the evidence to support a theory of adolescent sexual offending based strictly on a classical conditioning model is rather weak.[33] They note that conditioning does in fact play a role, particularly in those who molest nonrelatives. The role of conditioning, however, appears to be one of many factors explaining sexual deviancy.

CYCLE OF VIOLENCE THEORY: MY PAST ABUSE MADE ME DO IT

Some have speculated prior physical and sexual abuse may make someone more susceptible to becoming a sexual offender. The following case study provides such an example:

Carl, a thirteen-year-old boy referred to Orchard Place with a long-standing history of unmanageability in the home and school, was twelve when he sexually molested Sara, the five-year-old daughter of his mother's fiancée. Carl's natural parents never married and he had no contact with his father. His mother, an alcoholic, was frequently intoxicated and unavailable to Carl both physically and emotionally. When Carl was eight his mother married and sought treatment for alcoholism. Carl was adopted but the marriage ended in divorce when he was ten. The adoptive father remained peripherally involved with Carl and his mother reported Carl was withdrawn following the divorce. His grades and school behavior deteriorated and he refused to obey his mother. Upon admission to Orchard Place, Carl presented as angry and refused to discuss the sexual assault on Sara. Two months after admission he reported being sexually abused at age five, several times each week, for approximately one year by a fifteen-year-old male babysitter . . . During the initial interview with the co-therapists Carl would not discuss the details of his sexual assault on Sara, but he acknowledged that the abuse occurred . . . Encouragement by group members . . . enabled Carl to discuss feelings of social isolation and anger. This resulted in Carl's ability to understand that his anger about being a victim of sexual abuse was associated with his sexual abuse of Sara . . . Carl displayed homophobia in each of the first thirteen group sessions. He reported feeling anxious about others perceptions of him due to being sexually abused by a male. [Later,] he began to identify feelings of powerlessness and anger while sexually molesting Sara. This enabled Carl to understand that his own perpetrator's motivation was similar, and the issue was not the sex of one's victim or abuser, but the misuse of power. This insight reduced Carl's homophobic anxiety and also assisted him in the understanding the victim/perpetrator cycle.[34]

In this case, it seems the most rational explanation: Carl was molested when he was a child and as a result, later molested a child. Some experts speculate maybe it was a learned behavior—that is how someone treated them and that is how they treat others. Others may speculate they want to identify with their aggressor, so they molest someone to feel what their aggressor felt—possibly in hopes of understanding their aggressor's motivation. Some may say they feel angry about what happened to them and feel others should have to pay for this so they take their anger out on someone through the sexual abuse. Regardless of how or why the cycle of violence actually occurs, the research that currently exists does not support the notion that being sexually abused causes one to later commit sexual offenses.[35]

> "Child sexual abuse was like getting bitten by a rattlesnake: Some kids recovered completely, and some didn't, but it wasn't good for anybody."
> —Anna Salter, 2004, p. 63.

Research has reported a high incidence of experiences of sexual abuse among sexual offenders.[36] So, how can sexual abuse not be an explanation for later sexual abuse? When sexual abuse is examined by itself, it does not predict whether one will later commit sexual abuse.[37] This leads one to the explanation that sexual abuse in conjunction with other factors (ones we do not know what they are) may predispose someone toward sexually abusing. Additionally, it is important to note that many sex offenders were not sexually abused themselves.[38] Thus, sexual abusers are not always abused when they were young. But it certainly may serve as an intervening variable of sexual abuse when combined with other risk factors.

SOCIAL-PSYCHOLOGICAL ASSESSMENT: MY PEERS INFLUENCED ME DO IT

One of the noted characteristics of juveniles who commit sexual offenses is that some commit the abuse in the context of a group. Abusing someone in the context of a group allows the individual to diffuse responsibility for the behavior; it is thought that different dynamics occur when one acts in a group, rather than on their own. Deindividuation is a term that has been used to describe this phenomenon.[39]

> "Deindividuation is the process of losing one's sense of individuality or separateness from others and becoming submerged in a group.'"
> —Goldstein, 2002, p. 30.[40]

It has also been found that when juveniles sexually abuse in the context of a group, violence is more likely to occur. In one study, 21 percent of juveniles who acted in a group used violence compared to only 8 percent of lone-offenders who used violence.[41] When persons act in a group, there is an increased perception of legitimacy regarding the behavior. The term "group-think" has also been used to describe this process, which involves a group of people who seek some sort of cohesion and collective agreement.[42] When one person becomes aggressive, the others do not question it. This phenomenon has been well documented in social scientific experiments—people will often take on the characteristics of a group when they are isolated within that group.

A well-known example of this was the prison simulation study conducted at Stanford University.[43] Normal, healthy, male college students who participated in the study were assigned to either prison guard or prisoner roles. Unusually, and unexpectedly, each group quickly submerged into their roles—to the point where the study was cut short due to the aggressive behavior of the "guards" and the unwillingness of the "prisoners" to stand up to the guards. One of the inmates felt he was "losing his mind" and wanted to be released. While this situation does not resemble a sexual abuse situation, psychology experts are familiar with the fact that people behave very differently when immersed into a group.

Such violent behavior is defined as instrumental or expressive. Instrumental violence occurs as a result to achieve a goal, where expressive violence occurs after anger has been aroused.[44] It appears that the violence used in juvenile sexual abuse incidents involving multiple offenders, could be either instrumental or expressive.[45] In many of these offenses, the use of violence was in direct relationship to victim resistance. For a subgroup of juvenile offenders, those who victimized peers or adults where level of victim resistance was low, violence was still used. Perhaps for this small group of offenders, the violence was expressive, rather than instrumental.[46]

In an assessment of juvenile sex offenders who acted alone compared to those who sexually assaulted someone in a group, it was found overall, those who act in a group were more likely to use violence. The results, however, did not support the hypothesis that use of violence was for instrumental purposes.[47] Again, additional research is needed to examine this relationship.

ATTACHMENT THEORY: MY NEED TO BOND WITH OTHERS MADE ME DO IT

Whether someone forms an intimate bond with others, particularly their primary caregivers, may provide a basis for the rest of their life in how they interact and form relationships, especially sexual relationships. It has been suggested, for example, relationships children form when they are young specifically affect self-image. The failure to bond with others has been examined with younger children experiencing sexual problems and more recently with adolescent sex offenders.[48]

It is assumed that some of the first relationships one forms are with one's parents and other family members. One researcher, for example, described the family of sexually abusive youth and in many of the family dynamics, attachment of child to parent was highly affected. For example, an exploitative family is one where the children are used to meet the parents' own needs. Their needs are obtained through a system of bartering with their parents. Such children will learn to manipulate and often fail to develop their own sense of self-worth. This is just one of several types of family dynamics that can lead to sexual abuse.[49]

Many juveniles who commit sexual offenses have gone through several negative emotional experiences, including episodes of abuse, unstable family, and general neglect; these experiences serve as the basis for the juveniles feeling justifiable in committing sexual offenses.[50] In the following case example, a juvenile's history is described and there is an apparent lack of bonding that occurred.

Chuck was arrested at age fourteen for the molestation of several cousins and his sister. Upon interrogation, he revealed that he had been sodomized by an older cousin when he was about six years old, although later, in view of his cousin's anger and denial, he became ambivalent as to whether this had really occurred or was "just a dream."

Chuck was the second of six children, born at a time when his mother's first marriage was both abusive and breaking up. His older brother and younger siblings appeared to have satisfactory relationships with their mother, but Chuck's mother stated she had "always felt different" about him and "never felt as close to him" as to the other children. Chuck had felt this difference, and he and his mother seemed to experience a distorted intimacy only around shared feelings of fear and guilt. His mother reported that Chuck had "always been a problem" and "never been trustworthy," acting up and being in trouble perpetually from age six. Lying, stealing, intimidating his siblings, and incidents that caused his mother to feel like a failure were common occurrences, although he was well liked by peers and had good social skills. The first-grade teacher had reported unusual sexual components in his artwork at age six. Chuck had been discovered trying to sodomize a younger sibling at that time and had gone to counseling for a brief period.

Chuck had felt set apart and different much of his life. His mother's preoccupation with a bad marriage at the time of his birth may have impaired her availability to him and precluded empathic care. Although he had no conscious memory of his natural father, there seemed to be some covert implication that he was like his father: untrustworthy, criminal, and a source of fear for his mother. He had never felt allowed to inquire about that father, and he felt some obscure sense of loss that he described as "an empty place" relative to his perceived abandonment or rejection by his father. In addition to his reported experience to sodomy at age six, he remembered learning about sex by eavesdropping when an older brother and his friends discussed sexual matters in the home.

Chuck showed little genuine affect and was quite unaware of the feelings of self or others. He had difficulty maintaining eye contact with adults and reported feeling very helpless and small, especially with is mother. Although his sexual abuse of boys was quite aggressive, his perception of the long-term molesting relationship he had with one female cousin was that it was a loving and intimate experience, and she agreed. In every molestation, however—and also in subsequent peer relationships—his victims were related to a fierce protector whom he feared: his mother, a very scary uncle, a crazy, gun-toting boyfriend, and so forth. It is possible that the experience of fear in his exploitative sexual relationship made him feel more alive and somehow connected him to that "missing part," which was the father figure whom his mother had feared.[51]

In the above case study, it is evident Chuck experienced several hardships and according to the attachment perspective, the lack of bonding between him and his parents during his developmental stage served as a precursor for his offending. Also, his genuine lack of emotion and insight also show he justified the behavior and, in a weird twisted way, actually saw it as normal. He actually defined some of his molestations as genuine expressions of caring and loving. The care and love he lacked appear to serve as a basis for his inability to express his care and love in appropriate ways.

Juveniles can develop one of four attachment styles. First, they can form a *secure* attachment, which means the juvenile develops positive self-concept and positive view of others. They are able to make age-appropriate friends without difficulty. Those who have a poor self-concept and do not think well of others will develop a *fearful* style of attachment. That is, they are not likely to talk to others about problems and often put blame on themselves for any problems encountered. Someone who has a positive self-concept, high level of confidence, yet they have a negative concept of others will develop a *dismissing* style of attachment. They typically do not seek out support, even when needed. A child who develops a *preoccupied* style is the most likely to abuse a child. They suffer from low self-esteem and low confidence. They are positive toward others, seeking their advice to deal with their own issues.[52]

For juveniles who suffer a lack of attachment or "broken bond," intensive treatment is suggested. Such juveniles should be provided with close, consistent supervision. Consistent discipline and a clear understanding of rules should be in place. The juvenile needs to have a model of good behavior to follow and should be provided with reassurance and positive feedback. Daily contact and communication between the treatment provider and juvenile are essential. Individual therapy should occur two to three times a week in addition to two to four group therapy sessions a week. Clearly, the juvenile who suffers from an attachment disorder needs intensive treatment.[53]

Research for this explanation is moderate, meaning there is some support for its explanation. For example, adults who have sexually abused children often have poor social skills and low self-confidence; they typically do not form age-appropriate relationships.[54] Other researchers have been able to show that sex offenders often misperceive social cues and have social skills deficits, which often leads to an inability to form intimate relationships.[55]

DEVELOPMENTAL THEORY: A HOST OF FACTORS MADE ME DO IT

Following someone's history throughout the course of his or her development can be very telling—watching every mishap, every experience, and every reaction, is likely to reveal there is no single factor that explains why they committed such a serious offense. Someone for example, may explain their deviance by saying, "It was because I was abused," but as we have seen some who offend were not abused. Someone may say, "I was exposed to this behavior by my friends" or perhaps "I felt it was OK for me to engage in this behavior." None of these explanations has given us the answer to what we want to know, which is: Why do some juveniles sexually abuse? While developmental theories may not hold the complete answer, they combine many factors previously identified as precursors to sexual behavior. This perspective pulls back each layer of one's development and looks at the constellation of factors, rather than isolating individual factors.

Back in the 1930s, two sociologists, Eleanor and Sheldon Glueck, began to examine not only sex offenders, but also a group of delinquents and compare it to a group of nondelinquents. They tracked the groups for decades to examine how their offending patterns emerged. What derived from their research was the beginning of examining deviance over the course of one's life. One of the key concepts associated with developmental theory is "early starters." It was found that those who began their deviant career at a young age (before or during early puberty), the more likely they would persist their deviance throughout their life.[56] Also, the earlier they begin, the more likely they will commit serious offenses. It is found that those who begin deviance later in life are more likely to age out; that is, they will desist in the mid-to late twenties. Offenders' criminal careers are often distinguished into two categories: (1) those who commit offenses only during their adolescentce (adolescent-limited delinquents), and (2) those who commit crime in their adolescence and during their adulthood (life-course persistent delinquents).[57]

"Equally important is an exploration of the trajectory of delinquency. Sexual offending behavior cannot be viewed acts as the beginning of the delinquent path but rather behavior that is often the consequence of a history of nonsexual delinquent acts."

—Nancy G. Calley, 2007, 131[58]

This perspective, therefore, proposes that perhaps there is not a single risk factor, but rather when a group of factors exists, delinquent behavior may be the result. For example, researchers have found when a juvenile with biologically based problems, such as learning disabilities and poor impulse control, has a dysfunctional family, fertile ground is established for sexual problems, including sexually abusing someone.[59] It is assumed juveniles are going through a critical developmental stage where they are learning to develop appropriate peer relationships. A combination of the learning disability, poor impulse control, and dysfunctional family short-circuit, so to speak, the process of normal peer relationship development. From this, anger, depression, and a hostile attitude lead to exploiting others through their apathetic attitude. This grouping of characteristics, however, does not fully stand up to testing; by applying these factors, it does not predict juvenile sex offenders from juvenile nonsexual offenders.[60]

In an assessment of a developmental perspective, two researchers compared adolescent sex offenders with a history of other sexual offenses to those without such a history. Part of the thinking behind such examination is that offenders have different trajectories, or developmental tracts. It was presumed adolescent sex offenders with a history of nonsexual offenses (i.e., general crime) have a different developmental trajectory than adolescent sex offenders with no history of committed nonsexual offenses. They, in fact, did find evidence of differences between the two groups. It was shown those without a history of general offenses had fewer current behavior problems, along with more prosocial attitudes/beliefs; they were also less likely than those with a history of general offenses to commit future crimes. Thus, what this shows is that prior developmental experiences can be useful in predicting future risk; adolescent sex offenders with a history of both sexual and nonsexual offenses are more likely to recidivate compared to adolescent sex offenders with a history of only sexual offenses.[61]

ENVIRONMENTAL INFLUENCES: CAN ALCOHOL AND DRUGS CAUSE SOMEONE TO SEXUALLY ABUSE?

Although many have explored the relationship between alcohol/drugs and violence, including sexual abuse, the overwhelming majority of experts agree that one does not cause the other. It has been well documented that many who commit violent crimes were under the influence of alcohol or drugs,[62] it cannot be said that someone who is normally not aggressive will become aggressive and violent.[63] Rather, it is shown many who are antisocial will engage is substance abuse. Thus, alcohol and drugs do not cause or lead someone who normally does not commit sexual offenses to actually commit a sexual offense.

WHY DON'T WE KNOW MORE ABOUT THE CAUSE OF JUVENILE SEXUAL OFFENDERS?

A report (by Mark Weinrott) written for the Center for Study and Prevention of Child Abuse, specifically addressed the lack of research that has been conducted on juvenile sex offenders.[64] The author noted many policies were being developed with regard to this population of offenders, yet no empirical research supported many of the assumptions made in the policies. While additional research has been conducted since his report, the state of the research on juvenile sex offenders is underdeveloped. Borrowing a phrase from Cheri Miller, a psychologist treating sex offenders in Illinois, she states research on sex offenders is beyond its infancy, but still in its toddler-hood phase, meaning we know more than we did a few decades ago, but still have a long way to go. Personally, we are hopeful in the gains we will make in the near future. We are sure in just a few decades we will look back at what we are using today to assess and treat (juvenile and adult) sex offenders and gasp at our archaic measures. We are hopeful we have more knowledge to gain that will be helpful to victims and offenders in the future.

Several factors were identified that had impeded research on juvenile sex offenders. First, Weinrott noted many graduate students (in various fields) are taught very little about sexual abuse; sexual behaviors such as sexual aggression and paraphilias are not officially recognized as social problems. We agree with Weinrott; even in criminal justice rarely are specialized courses offered on sexual offenders. Additionally, it has been our experience that many psychology, social work, and sociology programs also lack sexual deviance courses. A few years ago I was looking for a book to use for a sex offender course I was teaching and came across a book titled, *Predators: Pedophiles, Rapists, and Other Sex Offenders*. It was by far one of the most informative books I have read about adult sex offenders. I was surprised, but not shocked, when I read the following excerpt written by the author, Anna Salter, about her knowledge of sex offenders:

I am known as an expert on sex offenders... Surely I could claim to be the expert in the room. I had a Ph.D. in psychology from Harvard and have lectures on sex offenders in more than forty states and in ten countries. I have given keynote addresses at national conferences on the topic in four of those countries. In 1997 I won the Significant Achievement Award of the Association of the Treatment of Sexual Abusers, given to one person in the world every year. I have made educational films on the topic and have written two academic books, one of which has gone into fifteen printings and has been called the Bible of sex offender treatment. I even write mysteries about sex offenders based on my experience in the field. But my credentials pale next to [name of a sex offender victim].[65]

When the victim asked Dr. Salter about the origin of such behavior, what makes someone engage in such behavior, Dr. Salter states that she really doesn't know. She is referring to the fact that after examining all of the research and theories that do exist about this behavior, they are not enough. She is, in fact, referring to the current state of research regarding adult sex offenders. We imagine that if we asked her about juveniles who sexually offend, the answer would be the same.

Also, it was noted that many of the key researchers in the field of adult sex offenders paid little attention to juveniles who sexually offended.[66] Again, since the publication of Weinrott's report, additional research has been conducted on juvenile sex offenders. Yet, the amount of research still pales in comparison to the adult sex offender literature. Some of the reasons for this may just be the nature of the problem; while the number of juveniles who sexually offend is substantial, they are still far outnumbered by adults.

Another noted reason for the lack of support is that one of the essential organizations in their field, National Adolescent Perpetrator Network (NAPN) had not made an effort to promote research in this field. This particular association, in fact, is not necessarily geared to researchers; it is more focused on practitioners. Weinrott compares the group to the Association for the Treatment of Sexual Abusers, which not only provides support for clinicians, but also supports researchers.

Weinrott also notes that sex offenders do not have a support base compared to women's right's groups or child advocates. In other words, no one is really "for" sex offenders; however, the lack of research in this area not only affects the offenders, but also the victims and society. Weinrott describes this as "a combination of political malaise and outright opposition."[67] Most groups, for instance, who advocate for women and children will often advocate for lengthier sentences, public registries, and community notification.

Also impeding research is that there is little research on juvenile sexual offending because most offenses lack violence. Most sexual offenses committed by juveniles involve manipulation and coercion. Other than the sexual abuse itself, rarely is the victim otherwise physically harmed. Due to the lack of violence, per se, researchers tend to focus on crimes causing more physical harm than juvenile sexual offenses.

WHAT DO WE KNOW ABOUT CAUSES OF JUVENILE SEXUAL OFFENDING?

It is clear that for some of the case examples there were many warning signs or exposures to risk factors that could possibly explain why that juvenile committed a sex offense. For example, at the beginning of the chapter, Billy, was in an unstable living environment, lacked a loving relationship with his stepfather, was exposed to physical abuse, was exposed to sex at age five, and developed a belief that if the girl was not yelling in objection, she must want sex. However, we know there are other children and juveniles who have been exposed to risk factors and do not commit sexual offenses. Maybe those who do not become sex offenders have other factors present that serve as an insulating factor. Additional research in this area is certainly warranted.

For all of the possible explanations explored in this chapter, deviancy turning into sexual abuse, cognitive, biological, evolutionary, conditioning, exposure to sexual abuse, group violence, attachment, and developmental explanations, the current research that exists does not fully support or dismiss any of the these theories. It is clear more research is needed. While some of the theories have some empirical support (i.e., attachment theory, conditioning, group violence), additional research is still needed. For example, some support is shown for the attachment theory; many juveniles who sexually offend do show some sort of broken bond with others; they never formed an attachment to either one or both of their parents. Research, however, has not fully tested whether nonsexual offenders have broken bonds. In other words, a broken bond may not distinguish between sex offenders and nonsexual offenders.

Again, we are hopeful that we are simply at the beginning of the search for answers. We believe more research will be conducted in the future to address some of the discrepancies or gaps that currently exist. For now, we know juveniles who sexually offend are commonly exposed to several risks: physical abuse, sexual abuse, unstable living environment, poor self-esteem, inability to form age-appropriate relationships,[68] early sexual deviance,[69] learning disabilities, developmental problems, and poor impulse control.[70] And these indeed just scratch the surface.

NOTES

1. Pamela Schultz, *Not Monsters: Analyzing the Stories of Child Molesters* (Oxford: Rowman & Littlefield Publishers, Inc., 2005), 82–88.

2. American Psychiatric Association, *Diagnostic and Statistical Manual of Mental Disorders, Fourth Edition* (Washington DC: American Psychiatric Association, 1994), 493.

3. Gene G. Abel, Candice A. Osborn, and Deborah A. Twigg, "Sexual Assault through the Life Span: Adult Offenders with Juvenile Histories," in *The Juvenile Sex Offender*, ed. Howard E. Barbaree, William S. Marshall, and Stephen M. Hudson (New York: The Guilford Press, 1993), 104–116.

4. Ibid.

5. Stacey O. Zolondek et al., "The Self-Reported Behaviors of Juvenile Sex Offenders," in *Sexual Deviance*, ed. Christopher Hensley and Richard Tewksbury (Boulder, CO: Lynne Rienner Publishers, Inc, 2003), 119–130.

6. Janan Hanna, "Teen Rape Suspect Could Face Adult Trial," *Chicago Tribune*, January 14, 1998, 1.

7. Gresham Sykes and David Matza, "Techniques of Neutralization: A Theory of Delinquency," *American Sociological Review* 22(6) (1957): 664–670.

8. See generally Anna Salter, *Treating Child Sex Offenders and Victims: A Practical Guide* (Newbury Park, CA: Sage, 1988).

9. Martha R. Burt and Rochelle Semmel Albin, "Rape Myths, Rape Definitions, and Probability of Conviction," *Journal of Applied Social Psychology* 11(3) (1981): 214.

10. Zoe Peterson and Charlene Muehlenhard, "Was It Rape? The Function of Women's Rape Myth Acceptance and Definitions of Sex in Labeling Their Own Experiences," *Sex Roles* 51(3–4) (2004): 130.

11. Susan Brownmiller, *Against Our Will: Men, Women, and Rape* (New York: Ballantine Books, 1975), 311.

12. Grant Muir, Kimberly Lonsway, and Diana Payne, "Rape Myth Acceptance among Scottish and American Students," *The Journal of Social Psychology* 136(2) (1996): 262.

13. Cori Johnson, "Student Acceptance of Rape Myths," in *Academy of Criminal Justice Services* (Cincinnati, OH, 2008), n.p.

14. John A. Hunter et al., "The Reliability and Discriminative Utility of the Adolescent Cognition Scale for Juvenile Sexual Offenses," *Annals of Sex Research* 4(3–4) (1991): 285.

15. Stephen Schoenthaler and Walter Doraz, "Types of Offenses Which Can Be Reduced in an Institutional Setting Using Nutritional Intervention," *International Journal of Biosocial Research* 4(2) (1983): 74–75.

16. Clyde Hawley and Robert Buckley, "Food Dyes and Hyperkinetic Children," *Academy Therapy* 10(1) (1974): 1485.

17. Deborah Denno, "Considering Lead Poisoning as a Criminal Defense," *Fordham Urban Law Journal* 20(3) (1993): 378.

18. Gail Ryan, "Theories of Etiology," in *Juvenile Sexual Offending*, ed. Gail Ryan and Sandy Lane (San Francisco, CA: Jossey-Bass, 1997), 19–58.

19. National Task Force on Juvenile Sexual Offending (1993) as cited in: Gail Ryan, "Theories of Etiology," in *Juvenile Sexual Offending*, ed. Gail Ryan and Sandy Lane (San Francisco, CA: Jossey-Bass, 1997), 19–58.

20. Randy Thornhill and Craig T. Palmer, *A Natural History of Rape: Biological Bases of Sexual Coercion* (Cambridge, MA: The MIT Press, 2000).

21. Ibid.

22. See generally: George Williams, *Adaptation and Natural Selection* (Princeton: Princeton University Press, 1966).

23. Robert Trivers, "Parental Investment and Sexual Selection," in *Sexual Selection and the Descent of Man, 1881–1971*, ed. B. Campbell (Chicago: Aldine, 1972), 136–207.

24. Nicholas A. Groth and Jean H. Birnbaum, *Men Who Rape: The Psychology of the Offender* (New York: Plenum Press, 1979): 2

25. Thornhill and Palmer, *A Natural History of Rape: Biological Bases of Sexual Coercion*, Preface.

26. Mark Weinrott, "Juvenile Sexual Aggression: A Critical Review," (Portland, OR: Center for the Study and Prevention of Violence, 1996), 25.

27. Sue Righthand and Carlann Welch, "Juveniles Who Have Sexually Offended: A Review of the Professional Literature" (Washington, DC: Office of Juvenile Justice and Delinquency Prevention, 2001), 3–4.

28. R. McGuire, J. Carlisle, and B. Young, "Sexual Deviations as Conditioned Behaviour: A Hypothesis," *Behaviour Research and Therapy* 2 (1965): 185.

29. See generally: Ivan Pavlov, *Conditioned Reflexes* (Oxford: Clarendon Press, 1927).

30. McGuire, Carlisle, and Young, "Sexual Deviations as Conditioned Behaviour: A Hypothesis," 186.

31. Karen Terry, *Sexual Offenses and Offenders: Theory, Practice, and Policy* (Belmont, CA: Wadsworth, 2006), 65–66.

32. S. Rachmen, "Sexual Fetishisms: An Experimental Analogue," *Psychological Record* 16(3) (1966): 293–295.

33. William L. Marshall and A. Eccless, "Issues in Clinical Practice with Sex Offenders," *Journal of Interpersonal Violence* 6(1) (1991): 73–74.

34. Rebecca Scavo and Bruce D. Buchanan, "Group Therapy for Male Adolescent Sex Offenders: A Model for Residential Treatment," *Residential Treatment for Children and Youth* 7(2) (1989): 71–72.

35. Anna C. Salter, *Predators: Pedophiles, Rapists, and Other Sex Offenders* (New York: Basic Books, 2003), 72–75.

36. See generally: Carla Edwards and Rebecca Hendrix, "Traumagenic Dynamics in Adult Women Survivors of Childhood Sexual Abuse vs. Adolescent Male Sex Offenders with Similar Histories," *Journal of Offender Rehabilitation* 33(2) (2001); James R. Worling, "Personality-Based Typology of Adolescent Male Sexual Offenders: Differences in Recidivism Rates, Victim-Selection Characteristics, and Personal Victimization Histories," *Sexual Abuse: A Journal of Research and Treatment* 13(3) (2001); George Zgourides, Martin Monto, and Richard Harris, "Correlates of Adolescent Male Sexual Offense: Prior Adult Sexual Contact, Sexual Attitudes, and Use of Sexually Explicit Materials," *International Journal of Offender Therapy and Comparative Criminology* 41(3) (1997).

37. Raymond A. Knight and Robert A. Prentky, "Exploring Characteristics for Classifying Juvenile Sex Offenders," in *The Juvenile Sex Offender*, ed. Howard E. Barbaree,

William L. Marshall, and Stephen M. Hudson (New York: Guilford Press, 1993), 45–83.

38. Salter, *Predators: Pedophiles, Rapists, and Other Sex Offenders*, 72–75.

39. See generally: Arnold Goldstein, *The Psychology of Group Aggression* (Chichester, UK: John Wiley & Sons, 2002).

40. Ibid., 30.

41. Jessica Woodhams, "Characteristics of Juvenile Sex Offending against Strangers: Findings from a Non-Clinical Study," *Aggression Behavior* 30(3) (2004): 246–247.

42. See generally: Goldstein, *The Psychology of Group Aggression*.

43. See generally: Craig Haney, Burtis Banks, and Philip Zimbardo, "Interpersonal Dynamics in a Simulated Prison," *International Journal of Criminology and Penology* 1(1) (1973).

44. Stephen W. Smallbone and Lynley Milne, "Associations between Trait Anger and Aggression Used in the Commission of Sexual Offenses," *International Journal of Offender Therapy and Comparative Criminology* 44(5) (2000): 607.

45. See generally: John A. Hunter, Robert Hazelwood, and David Sleslinger, "Juvenile Perpetrated Sex Crimes: Patterns of Offending and Predictors of Violence," *The FBI Law Enforcement Bulletin* 69(3) (2000); Woodhams, "Characteristics of Juvenile Sex Offending against Strangers: Findings from a Non-Clinical Study."

46. Smallbone and Milne, "Associations between Trait Anger and Aggression Used in the Commission of Sexual Offenses," 607.

47. Woodhams, "Characteristics of Juvenile Sex Offending against Strangers: Findings from a Non-Clinical Study," 244.

48. Ryan, "Theories of Etiology," 19–58.

49. Gail Ryan, "The Families of Sexually Abusive Youth," in *Juvenile Sexual Offending*, ed. Ryan Gail and Sandy Lane (San Francisco, CA: Jossey-Bass, 1997), 136–154.

50. Judith V. Becker, "Treating Adolescent Sexual Offenders," *Professional Psychology: Research and Practice* 21(5) (1990): 362–365; see generally Lin Shi and Jason Nichol, "Into the Mind of a Juvenile Sex Offender: A Clinical Analysis and Recommendation from an Attachment Perspective," *The American Journal of Family Therapy* 35(5) (2007).

51. Brandt Steele and Gail Ryan, "Deviancy: Development Gone Wrong," in *Juvenile Sexual Offending*, ed. Gail Ryan and Sandy Lane (San Francisco, CA: Jossey-Bass, 1997), 73.

52. Kim Bartholomew, "Avoidance of Intimacy: An Attachment Perspective," *Journal of Social and Personal Relationships* 7(2) (1990): 163.

53. Shi and Nichol, "Into the Mind of a Juvenile Sex Offender: A Clinical Analysis and Recommendation from an Attachment Perspective," 395–402.

54. William Marshall, "Intimacy, Loneliness, and Sexual Offenders," *Behavior Research and Therapy* 27(5) (1989): 498–499.

55. Ibid.

56. See generally: Alex R. Piquero, "Assessing the Relationships between Gender, Chronicity, Seriousness, and Offense Skewness in Criminal Offending," *Journal of Criminal Justice* 28(2) (2000).

57. See generally: Terrie E. Moffitt, "Adolescence-Limited and Life-Course-Persistent Antisocial Behavior: A Developmental Taxonomy," *Psychology Review* 100(4) (1993).

58. Nancy Calley, "Integrating Theory and Research: The Development of a Research-Based Treatment Program for Juvenile Male Sex Offenders," *Journal of Counseling and Development* 85(2) (2007): 131.

59. Judith V. Becker, Jerry Cunningham-Rathner, and Meg S. Kaplan, "Adolescent Sexual Offenders: Demographics, Criminal and Sexual Histories, and Recommendations for Reducing Future Offenses," *Journal of Interpersonal Violence* 1(4) (1987): 431–445.

60. Ibid.

61. Stephen Butler and Michael C. Seto, "Distinguishing Two Types of Adolescent Sex Offenders," *Journal of American Child Adolescent psychiatry* 41(1) (2002): 83–90.

62. See generally: Jan Chaiken and Marcia R. Chaiken, *Varieties of Criminal Behavior* (Santa Monica, CA: Rand, 1982).

63. Lynn O. Lightfoot and Howard E. Barbaree, "The Relationship between Substance Use and Abuse and Sexual Offending in Adolescents," in *The Juvenile Sex Offender*, ed. Howard E. Barbaree, William L. Marshall, and Stephen M. Hudson (New York: The Guilford Press, 1993): 203–224.

64. Weinrott, "Juvenile Sexual Aggression: A Critical Review," 2.

65. Salter, *Predators: Pedophiles, Rapists, and Other Sex Offenders*, 7–8.

66. Weinrott, "Juvenile Sexual Aggression: A Critical Review," 1.

67. Ibid., p. 2.

68. William L. Marshall, Stephen M. Hudson, and Sharon Hodkinson, "The Importance of Attachment Bonds in the Development of Juvenile Sex Offending," in *The Juvenile Sex Offender*, ed. Howard E. Barbaree, William L. Marshall, and Stephen M. Hudson (New York: The Guilford Press, 1993), 164–181.

69. Abel, Osborn, and Twigg, "Sexual Assault through the Life Span: Adult Offenders with Juvenile Histories," 104–117.

70. Becker, Cunningham-Rathner, and Kaplan, "Adolescent Sexual Offenders: Demographics, Criminal and Sexual Histories, and Recommendations for Reducing Future Offenses."

REFERENCES

Abel, Gene G., Candice A. Osborn, and Deborah A. Twigg. "Sexual Assault through the Life Span: Adult Offenders with Juvenile Histories." In *The Juvenile Sex*

Offender, edited by Howard E. Barbaree, William S. Marshall, and Stephen M. Hudson, 104–116. New York: The Guilford Press, 1993.

American Psychiatric Association. *Diagnostic and Statistical Manual of Mental Disorders, Fourth Edition*. Washington, DC: American Psychiatric Association, 1994.

Bartholomew, Kim. "Avoidance of Intimacy: An Attachment Perspective." *Journal of Social and Personal Relationships* 7(2) (1990): 147–178.

Becker, Judith V. "Treating Adolescent Sexual Offenders." *Professional Psychology: Research and Practice* 21(5) (1990): 362–365.

Becker, Judith V., Jerry Cunningham-Rathner, and Meg S. Kaplan. "Adolescent Sexual Offenders: Demographics, Criminal and Sexual Histories, and Recommendations for Reducing Future Offenses." *Journal of Interpersonal Violence* 1(4) (1987): 431–445.

Brownmiller, Susan. *Against Our Will: Men, Women, and Rape*. New York: Ballantine Books, 1975.

Burt, Martha R., and Rochelle Semmel Albin. "Rape Myths, Rape Definitions, and Probability of Conviction." *Journal of Applied Social Psychology* 11(3) (1981): 212–230.

Butler, Stephen, and Michael C. Seto. "Distinguishing Two Types of Adolescent Sex Offenders." *Journal of American Child Adolescent psychiatry* 41(1) (2002): 83–90.

Calley, Nancy. "Integrating Theory and Research: The Development of a Research-Based Treatment Program for Juvenile Male Sex Offenders." *Journal of Counseling and Development* 85(2) (2007): 131–142.

Chaiken, Jan, and Marcia R. Chaiken. *Varieties of Criminal Behavior*. Santa Monica, CA: Rand, 1982.

Denno, Deborah. "Considering Lead Poisoning as a Criminal Defense." *Fordham Urban Law Journal* 20(3) (1993): 377–400.

Edwards, Carla, and Rebecca Hendrix. "Traumagenic Dynamics in Adult Women Survivors of Childhood Sexual Abuse vs. Adolescent Male Sex Offenders with Similar Histories." *Journal of Offender Rehabilitation* 33(2) (2001): 33–45.

Goldstein, Arnold. *The Psychology of Group Aggression*. Chichester, UK: John Wiley & Sons, 2002.

Groth, Nicholas A., and Jean H. Birnbaum. *Men Who Rape: The Psychology of the Offender*. New York: Plenum Press, 1979.

Haney, Craig, Burtis Banks, and Philip Zimbardo. "Interpersonal Dynamics in a Simulated Prison." *International Journal of Criminology and Penology* 1(1) (1973): 74–150.

Hanna, Janan. "Teen Rape Suspect Could Face Adult Trial." *Chicago Tribune*, January 14, 1998, 1.

Hawley, Clyde, and Robert Buckley. "Food Dyes and Hyperkinetic Children." *Academy Therapy* 10(1) (1974): 27–32.

Hunter, John A., Judith.V. Becker, Meg S. Kaplan, and D.W Goodwin. "The Reliability and Discriminative Utility of the Adolescent Cognition Scale for Juvenile Sexual Offenses." *Annals of Sex Research* 4(3–4) (1991): 281–286.

Hunter, John A., Robert Hazelwood, and David Sleslinger. "Juvenile Perpetrated Sex Crimes: Patterns of Offending and Predictors of Violence." *The FBI Law Enforcement Bulletin* 69(3) (2000): 1–7.

Johnson, Cori. "Student Acceptance of Rape Myths." Paper presented at the annual meeting of the *Academy of Criminal Justice Services*, Cincinnati, OH: November, 2008.

Knight, Raymond A., and Robert A. Prentky. "Exploring Characteristics for Classifying Juvenile Sex Offenders." In *The Juvenile Sex Offender*, edited by Howard E. Barbaree, William L. Marshall, and Stephen M. Hudson, 45–83. New York: Guilford Press, 1993.

Lightfoot, Lynn O., and Howard E. Barbaree. "The Relationship between Substance Use and Abuse and Sexual Offending in Adolescents." In *The Juvenile Sex Offender*, edited by Howard E. Barbaree, William L. Marshall, and Stephen M. Hudson. New York: The Guilford Press, 1993.

Marshall, William L., and A. Eccless. "Issues in Clinical Practice with Sex Offenders." *Journal of Interpersonal Violence* 6(1) (1991): 68–93.

Marshall, William L. "Intimacy, Loneliness, and Sexual Offenders." *Behavior Research and Therapy* 27(5) (1989): 491–503.

Marshall, William L., Stephen M. Hudson, and Sharon Hodkinson. "The Importance of Attachment Bonds in the Development of Juvenile Sex Offending." In *The Juvenile Sex Offender*, edited by Howard E. Barbaree, William L. Marshall, and Stephen M. Hudson. New York: The Guilford Press, 1993.

McGuire, R., J. Carlisle, and B. Young. "Sexual Deviations as Conditioned Behaviour: A Hypothesis." *Behaviour Research and Therapy* 2 (1965): 185–190.

Moffitt, Terrie E. "Adolescence-Limited and Life-Course-Persistent Antisocial Behavior: A Developmental Taxonomy." *Psychology Review* 100(4) (1993): 674–701.

Muir, Grant, Kimberly Lonsway, and Diana Payne. "Rape Myth Acceptance among Scottish and American Students." *The Journal of Social Psychology* 136(2) (1996): 261–262.

Pavlov, Ivan. *Conditioned Reflexes*. Oxford: Clarendon Press, 1927.

Peterson, Zoe, and Charlene Muehlenhard. "Was It Rape? The Function of Women's Rape Myth Acceptance and Definitions of Sex in Labeling Their Own Experiences." *Sex Roles* 51(3–4) (2004): 129–144.

Piquero, Alex R. "Assessing the Relationships between Gender, Chronicity, Seriousness, and Offense Skewness in Criminal Offending." *Journal of Criminal Justice* 28(2) (2000): 103–115.

Rachmen, S. "Sexual Fetishisms: An Experimental Analogue." *Psychological Record* 16(3) (1966): 293–296.

Righthand, Sue, and Carlann Welch. "Juveniles Who Have Sexually Offended: A Review of the Professional Literature," 1–59. Washington, DC: Office of Juvenile Justice and Delinquency Prevention, 2001.

Ryan, Gail. "The Families of Sexually Abusive Youth." In *Juvenile Sexual Offending*, edited by Ryan Gail and Sandy Lane, 136–154. San Francisco, CA: Jossey-Bass, 1997.

———. "Theories of Etiology." In *Juvenile Sexual Offending*, edited by Gail Ryan and Sandy Lane, 19–58. San Francisco, CA: Jossey-Bass, 1997.

Salter, Anna. *Treating Child Sex Offenders and Victims: A Practical Guide*. Newbury Park, CA: Sage, 1988.

Salter, Anna C. *Predators: Pedophiles, Rapists, and Other Sex Offenders*. New York: Basic Books, 2003.

Scavo, Rebecca, and Bruce D. Buchanan. "Group Therapy for Male Adolescent Sex Offenders: A Model for Residential Treatment." *Residential Treatment for Children and Youth* 7(2) (1989): 59–74.

Schoenthaler, Stephen, and Walter Doraz. "Types of Offenses Which Can Be Reduced in an Institutional Setting Using Nutritional Intervention." *International Journal of Biosocial Research* 4(2) (1983): 74–84.

Schultz, Pamela. *Not Monsters: Analyzing the Stories of Child Molesters*. Oxford: Rowman & Littlefield Publishers, Inc., 2005.

Shi, Lin, and Jason Nichol. "Into the Mind of a Juvenile Sex Offender: A Clinical Analysis and Recommendation from an Attachment Perspective." *The American Journal of Family Therapy* 35(5) (2007): 395–402.

Smallbone, Stephen W., and Lynley Milne. "Associations between Trait Anger and Aggression Used in the Commission of Sexual Offenses." *International Journal of Offender Therapy and Comparative Criminology* 44(5) (2000): 606–617.

Steele, Brandt, and Gail Ryan. "Deviancy: Development Gone Wrong." In *Juvenile Sexual Offending*, edited by Gail Ryan and Sandy Lane, 59–76. San Francisco, CA: Jossey-Bass, 1997.

Sykes, Gresham, and David Matza. "Techniques of Neutralization: A Theory of Delinquency." *American Sociological Review* 22(6) (1957): 664–670.

Thornhill, Randy, and Craig T. Palmer. *A Natural History of Rape: Biological Bases of Sexual Coercion*. Cambridge, MA The MIT Press, 2000.

Trivers, Robert. "Parental Investment and Sexual Selection." In *Sexual Selection and the Descent Man, 1881–1971*, edited by B. Campbell. Chicago: Aldine, 1972.

Weinrott, Mark. "Juvenile Sexual Aggression: A Critical Review," 91–103. Portland, OR: Center for the Study and Prevention of Violence, 1996.

Williams, George. *Adaptation and Natural Selection*. Princeton: Princeton University Press, 1966.

Woodhams, Jessica. "Characteristics of Juvenile Sex Offending against Strangers: Findings from a Non-Clinical Study." *Aggression Behavior* 30(3) (2004): 243–253.

Worling, James R. "Personality-Based Typology of Adolescent Male Sexual Offenders: Differences in Recidivism Rates, Victim-Selection Characteristics, and Personal

Victimization Histories." *Sexual Abuse: A Journal of Research and Treatment* 13(3) (2001): 149–166.

Zgourides, George, Martin Monto, and Richard Harris. "Correlates of Adolescent Male Sexual Offense: Prior Adult Sexual Contact, Sexual Attitudes, and Use of Sexually Explicit Materials." *International Journal of Offender Therapy and Comparative Criminology* 41(3) (1997): 272–283.

Zolondek, Stacey O., Gene G. Abel, William F. Northey, and Alan D. Jordan. "The Self-Reported Behaviors of Juvenile Sex Offenders." In *Sexual Deviance*, edited by Christopher Hensley and Richard Tewksbury. Boulder, CO: Lynne Rienner Publishers, Inc., 2003.

3

High Profile Cases: How on Earth Did This Happen?

In our fast-paced, private world, we could all stand to *pay more attention* to others. When we don't, things are more likely to happen. We are not suggesting that we can stop every bad thing, but rather, that very bad things are not necessarily random. Thus, there are two goals to this chapter. The first is to offer examples of juvenile sex offenders about whom we should be concerned. In each case, paying careful attention, could have led to the necessary vigilance and assessment, which might have made a difference.

The second goal of the chapter is to present examples of how our reaction to juvenile sex offenders has gone awry. Given the range of what could be a "sex offense," it should be clear that the "one size fits all" approach that we have taken toward sex offenders is not in our best interest. A majority of juvenile sex offenders are really juveniles with behavior problems. They should be treated accordingly.

All of these cases garnered local or national attention. Some cases are of adult sex offenders; however, they are mentioned here because their sex offending began while they were juveniles. In some of the examples the juvenile offended with peers. Susceptibility to peer influence is another effect that has been attributed to the lesser-developed juvenile brain. Of course, in any of the cases below, a sex offender treatment specialist would make a more composite assessment of the juvenile sex offender than what is offered here.

THE IMPORTANCE OF VIGILANCE, ASSESSMENT, AND TREATMENT

Case 1: Albert Fish[1]

Albert Fish was executed at age 60, on January 16, 1936. Fish had been very religious (a trait common among adult sex offenders) and sadistic. His pathology began in childhood with an obsession for punishing himself. Fish married at least four times and had six children. In adulthood, he would beat himself or have friends or relatives beat him. He would stick needles in his groin, rose stems in his urethra and light fire in his anus using alcohol. He also mailed obscene letters (in more modern times, this might manifest as telephone scatologia), and consumed feces on occasion. He had illusions of being a biblical character ordered by God to castrate and, or to kill young children as a religious sacrifice.

In 1934 Fish was arrested for the murder of twelve-year-old Grace Budd. He befriended her family, gaining their trust. One day they permitted him to take her to someone's birthday party. She never returned. Six years later, Fish sent an anonymous message to the family that Grace had been strangled, dismembered, cooked, and eaten. He was traced via the message. Thereafter, he claimed to have killed three other children, but investigators believe him responsible for as many as fifteen murders. He admitted molesting about 400 children across twenty-three states.

Given what we know today—what warning signs existed about the young Albert Fish? Well, for starters, there was the presence of paraphilias indicative of a serious mental disorder, clearly accompanied by cognitive distortions and fantasy thinking. Additionally, his self-punishment is a characteristic of depression in children, something long ignored as a child ailment.

Case 2: Wesley Allan Dodd

Wesley Allan Dodd was known for his elaborate planning in abducting and torturing little boys. A loner as a juvenile, he began with exposing himself at age thirteen and molesting little boys by age fourteen. He was arrested at age twenty-eight for the attempted abduction of a six-year-old boy from a movie theater restroom. Thereafter, he confessed to killing two brothers, Cole and William Neer, ten and eleven years old respectively. Their bodies, tortured then stabbed were found in a park. A four-year-old, Lee Iseli, had also been murdered. As a result, Dodd was executed in Washington State in 1993.[2]

This is another case with possible "red flags" early on. Dodd was reportedly a loner as a youngster (indicative of his poor interpersonal skills with peers), and he reported a likelihood to re-offend sexually (indicative of a paraphilia involving sexual compulsion to deviance).

Case 3: John Joubert[3]

In September 1983, 20-year-old, John Joubert abducted and killed Danny Joe Eberle, a thirteen-year-old Bellevue, Nebraska, boy. His family grew concerned after realizing he was missing from his paper route. Joubert was eventually convicted of Eberle's murder

and that of another boy. Joubert began hurting others at age thirteen after realizing
that he enjoyed stabbing people with objects like pencils and razors. Thereafter, he sought
victims primarily through his volunteering with a Boy Scouts troop. His torture and
murder of children was a means of releasing his sexual tension.

Certainly most would agree that Joubert's violent behavior at age thirteen, his pleasure in another's pain, and his associated interpersonal trouble with peers were signs of something seriously wrong. Whatever did his parents, guardians, or school personnel do?

The juvenile sexual killer is rare, but a reality. In 1998 and 1999 per FBI data there were nine known sexual homicides of which one offender was a juvenile.[4] Generally, juveniles account for about 5.6 percent of all sex-related homicides but juveniles are more likely to be caught when they kill than adults.[5] This case was described in C. Wade Myers' book, *Juvenile Sexual Homicide*, published in 2002. The young killer, Ken was arrested at age twenty for the kidnapping, sexual battery, and murder of an adult female. However, detectives suspected that he killed at least once before while a teenager, possibly when in the military at age eighteen. Ken also admitted pursuing a woman at age sixteen when he flirted with the thought of kidnapping her to be his slave and to rape her. Ken fit the profile of such killers in that most are male, white, and less than thirty-five.

Case 4: Ken, the Juvenile Sexual Killer

In uteri, Ken was apparently malnourished, given a placenta problem. His mother
also had other pregnancy complications. Ken's father beat his mother, including while
she clutched Ken in her arms. Such violence may have had something to do with how
Ken came to associate violence with the warmth of a woman's affections. He was socially
awkward and a loner who abused drugs and alcohol. He attributed his social failings to a
poor self-image from having a deformed testicle and a hand wart problem. He grew up
with rage, setting fire to cats, viewing his father's pornography collection, and wetting
the bed until age eleven.

Like many other children, Ken read Nancy Drew mysteries voraciously at ages nine
and ten. But unlike many other children he noticed that he became sexually aroused when
reading that Nancy Drew was being held captive and helpless. At twenty, he decided to act
out a sex offense that he had planned for sometime. He got a drinking buddy to accompany
him. They went to a convenience store where Ken beat and kidnapped the woman. They
took her to a wooded area, tied her up, beat and raped her with objects, and forced her to
perform oral sex. Ken enjoyed hearing the woman beg for her life. He slowly strangled
her to death. He was caught when his vehicle got stuck leaving the scene.[6]

Note both Ken and John Joubert described early realizations of peculiar deviant sexually sadistic arousal (that is, being sexually aroused by the pain, humiliation, or domination of another). Being aroused by another's pain is not normal. Parents, remember the old days when such sexually sadistic pornographic images were available only in print? Today, they are a click away, on the Internet and in online games. There are also avatar worlds of virtual people where you can be anyone and do anything

Most juvenile sexual killers also have conduct disorder symptoms, for example assaulting adults, stealing, and lying. Less common is cruelty to animals. Their personalities might also be described as narcissistic or borderline in some cases. While sexual fantasies are a common part of sex, for those prone to violence the fantasies may be about turning "childhood trauma to adult triumph."[7] These killers are usually heterosexual, not psychotic, but anxious and paraphiliacs.[8]

There is also support here for the idea that proper prenatal care is significant in shaping who we become and that witnessing domestic violence can harm children. Often an abused woman will claim that she stayed in the violent relationship for her children's sustenance—but the harms may clearly outweigh any benefits as research indicates that exposing very young children to violence and abuse can change their brain chemistry making them prone to violence in later years.[9]

The *FBI Law Enforcement Bulletin* included the following report:

Case 5: In the Family—Brothers Gone Wild

In 1992, police arrested two brothers, ages 13 and 15, for the rape and attempted murder of a 36-year-old woman . . . After the rape, the victim asked the brothers if they planned to kill her. When the 13-year-old said yes, the victim asked if she could look at her mother's photograph first. The youngest offender removed the unframed photo from her dresser and tore it into small pieces in front of the kneeling victim. Then, for no apparent reason, he began cutting and stabbing her.[10]

Surely, these brothers did not manifest this violence suddenly. There were likely many signs of trouble. So who was not paying attention here—parents, guardians, social service agencies—including of course, juvenile justice with which they likely came in contact?

Case 6: Peers and a "Boys Will be Boys" Mentality

Among the people that you know there is probably someone to whom bad stuff tends to happen—so much so that you can almost predict it. If something goes down—there he or she is. Some people are more likely to be the victims of a crime or to be caught in the "wrong place at the wrong time"—largely because they are out and about more than the rest of us and their companions are willing to be deviant. The question then is—who are your child's peers?

Peers matter because a manifestation of the lesser-developed juvenile brain is a greater susceptibility to peer influence. Parents can affect this influence by the messages, in

particular, the values that they communicate to their children. Consider the messages that you might be communicating to the young people around you—particularly about the value of females. Are you also communicating how they should respond when under pressure? Often, parents endorse a "boys will be boys" mentality. This mentality is predictive of juvenile males who are more likely to commit a group rape and girls more likely to accept being sexually victimized by a group.[11]

Washington Post journalist Nathan McCall has an entire chapter "Trains" (referring to group rape) in his very acclaimed autobiography, *Makes Me Wanna Holler: A Young Black Man in America* (1994). In it, he vividly describes negative sexual beliefs that he acquired from his male peers when he was a juvenile. In part, McCall's miseducation about sex came from his parents' reluctance to discuss the topic—despite his efforts to gain information. Sexually active by age thirteen, he participated in a "train" on a female peer when he was fourteen. The victim, Vanessa was thirteen—a "nice girl," but "very naive." She had gone to a peer's home hoping to see a boy on whom she had a crush. Unbeknownst to her, she had been tricked into going to a house where the parents were away at work. She was ambushed, held captive, and asked to cooperate with her victimizers. When she refused, she was indirectly threatened with violence to intimidate her until she succumbed to the sexual assault. McCall concluded that many of these victims gave in out of shock and then remained silent about the attack out of shame.[12]

A juvenile sex offender could be anyone but most likely someone you know. Consider the following Ohio and Maryland cases, respectively:

Case 7: The Teenage Babysitter

"I trusted him. He used to live right down the street . . . " says Christina Ball, mother of five. Ball struggles as she tells how she learned her four-year-old daughter was molested by her 16-year-old cousin while he babysat. "My son said that my daughter and my cousin were kissing and hugging in the basement." My heart just dropped, Ball says.[13]

If this is the juvenile sex offender's only such offense and there are no paraphiliac tendencies, he is remorseful and he has family support, his prognosis to improve looks good. The following Maryland case suggests a bit more caution.

Case 8: The Teenage Babysitter Who We Thought We Knew

. . . before the Bethesda couple learned that their babysitter had been molesting their 5-year-old son, they had been "singing his praises" to the 15-year-old boy's parents . . . The victim made the startling revelation . . . during a casual conversation with his mother . . . the teenager also molested one of the 5-year-old's siblings and another boy he sat for . . . The teenager sat for the couple's three children—now 5, 7, and 9 years old—regularly for seven years. He repeatedly sodomized the 5-year-old for at least a year . . .[14]

The teenager pled guilty to sexually abusing the five-year-old. He appeared remorseful and ready to cooperate with treatment. The victims' parents spoke to other families for whom the teenager babysat. They were concerned that like themselves, others could be fooled by the "well-mannered, seemingly trustworthy teenager." The victim's parents also believed that their seven-year-old was victimized. The babysitter denied this. In all, the sitter molested at least two boys. He spent nine months in a juvenile treatment facility and was released. Like many cases of juvenile sex offending—this one happened when parents were not the ones supervising the juveniles; the victims also appear to not have talked about their victimization for some time—but, maybe they did. Five-year-olds are kindergarteners—they usually like to talk . . . but maybe we assume that they must have their story wrong, their words confused . . . so, we miss the signs and the messages. No—we are not blaming parents here. We are simply saying—PAY MORE ATTENTION! How well do you know your child's babysitter—really? Don't assume that you can identify a sex offender by the look, age, race, gender, class, demeanor, et cetera.

Our limited information about this case, particularly the victim and offender age gap and the fact that there were more than one victim suggest that this teenager is someone to watch (perhaps on a registry limited to law enforcement). On the other hand, some positives are that the juvenile seems to have evidenced some remorse and likely empathy for his victims and, he has a supportive family. Also good is that he has received therapy and he has been spared the public registry for now. These should facilitate his rehabilitation.

Okay—you did your thorough background check, called references, et cetera and you feel comfortable with your childcare provider. Careful . . . who does your trusted caregiver have around him or her? Will the caregiver step out for a moment leaving your child with a stranger?

Case 9: Third Party Access—The Daycare Provider's Son

A mother whose 6-year-old son was victimized said, "It blows your world apart. You can't believe this happened to your child." [Her] 6-year-old was molested by his daycare provider's 15-year-old son.[15]

FIXING THE MESS THAT WE HAVE MADE

By this, we should have a clearer idea of who the juvenile sex offenders are that concern us. Regarding other juveniles tagged as "sex offenders" who have been caught up by our policies made in ignorance—let us hasten to fix the mess that we have made. Here are some suggestions:

LET US AVOID LABELING JUVENILES WHO ARE WITHOUT A CLUE!

We need to be careful about mislabeling (or stigmatizing) child's play, playing doctor, "mooning," a kiss on the cheek, et cetera. One mother of a thirteen-year-old, tagged as a sex offender for touching his five-year-old cousin inappropriately told Arizona legislators, "He knows nothing about sex. There is no way to explain [the accusation of sexual harassment] to him." At that same meeting a father reported that his five-year-old son pinched a classmate on her behind and was subsequently accused of sexual harassment.[16]

Also consider the not uncommon scenario that got J. G. into national headlines in the mid-1990s.[17] J. G., a ten-year-old New Jersey boy, was found almost naked next to his five-year-old sister and an eight-year-old female cousin. Eventually the police became involved. Thinking there was penetration of the females J.G. was charged as a juvenile with two counts of aggravated sexual assault. J.G. was offered a suspended sentence that included attending therapy. The problem? New Jersey's Megan's Law required that J.G. be classified as a very serious tier-two offender. The law was written with adult sex offenders in mind, such that an adult penetrating a five- or eight-year-old child would certainly be horrific—but, although J.G. claimed intercourse with his victims, those who interrogated him concluded that he hadn't a clue. He thought lying on top of the girls while in underwear constituted sex. Had he received the least serious sex offender registration classification, only law enforcement would have had access to his registration information; but a tier-two classification meant schools and others had to be notified of his registration status. A big difference! Certainly, this is not what the American public had in mind!

Of course, given the follies of youth, there will always be the brazen prankster. Consider the following Illinois case:

> He's a high school senior . . . Making plans to go to college . . . a good kid who made a grave mistake at 13, ringing the doorbell of a neighbor's home and grabbing the breasts of a 13-year-old girl living there. He pleaded guilty to home invasion and sexual abuse, and registered . . . As a juvenile, his record was shielded from the public. But if a state law . . . is upheld, this 17-year-old's name and photograph could [be] public . . . until he's 24.[18]

Well, the good news for Illinois juveniles is that at least for now, juvenile sex offenders can avoid being on the state's public registry. If already on the registry, persons can petition to be removed. Otherwise, juvenile sex offenders will be on a registry limited to law enforcement, daycares, and schools.

LET US EDUCATE, TREAT, AND MONITOR "ROMEO AND JULIET" CASES INSTEAD OF PUNISHING THEM

The Genarlow Wilson Story

Genarlow Wilson, a senior at Douglas County High, was convicted of aggravated child molestation for having "consensual" oral sex with a fifteen-year-old classmate when he was seventeen. The incident, caught on video, appeared to have been initiated by the fifteen-year-old. It happened at a New Year's Eve party in 2003 near Atlanta, Georgia. Per Georgia law, a seventeen-year-old is an adult and a fifteen-year-old is a child; so, sexual contact between them is essentially statutory rape. Amazingly, Georgia law already had a sort of reduced sentence for a "Romeo and Juliet" scenario such that intercourse between them would have been a misdemeanor. However, oral sex between them amounted to a felony. There was some debate about whether the female agreed to the act (she appeared intoxicated on the video). Wilson refused to take a plea deal where pleading guilty would have gotten him out early but would have meant that he be placed on the sex offender registry for life. His sentence was a mandatory ten years in prison without parole. His case made national news with many calling the sentence extreme. Years later, October 26, 2007, the Supreme Court of Georgia agreed and Wilson was released within hours. As a result of the case, Georgia changed its laws making "consensual" oral sex in a Romeo and Juliet scenario a misdemeanor with a maximum sentence of twelve months in jail.

What do you think should have happened here? One positive is that an alleged sex offense against an African American female was taken seriously. Historically, when African American females have been sexually victimized it has been dismissed with ideas such as "those people live like that." A negative was that the press often touted the fact that Wilson was a high school football star, a homecoming king, and a 3.2 GPA student with potential scholarships to an ivy-league school.[19] This suggests that such a person could not be guilty of a sex offense—which is false. There are several cases of athletes, slightly older in tertiary institutions, who have committed forcible rape. There are also cases of people who are now veterinarians, attorneys, investment bankers, and international scholars who committed rape, including gang rape as juveniles. They were never prosecuted for it and for that reason only, they would not be named here. It would surprise you! Also note, juvenile sex offenders can be part of a family that does not appear dysfunctional. Genarlow Wilson has since received a scholarship to the prestigious Morehouse College.

Wilson's case ended well—but there are so many others that have not for both the juvenile sex offender and his or her family. Consider the following scenarios from Human Rights Watch:

Case 1: A 16-year old is convicted of statutory rape for "consensual" sex with a 14-year-old girlfriend whom he later married. He characterizes his situation thus: "We were in love. And now we are married. So it's like I am on the registry for having premarital sex. Does having premarital sex make me a danger to society? My wife doesn't think so."

Case 2: Dan M, a college student was convicted of the statutory rape of a 15-year-old girl when he was 17. He is required to register every three months. In college, his baseball coach was notified that Dan M. was a registered sex offender. His coach asked why he lied on his college application when he checked "no" to the inquiry about "ever having been convicted of a felony." Angry and embarrassed he explained that he had not lied. What happened to him was an adjudication. An adjudication means that the juvenile's case was heard in the juvenile justice system; thus, for any other type of offense, the juvenile's record would be sealed or expunged. Dan M. has found it frustrating to have to explain these circumstances ever so often.

When he travels to other states he is required to see what the local laws are regarding sex offenders and to inform the authorities of his presence. When he visits his parents in Arkansas for longer than a month his risk level must be assessed. This involves psychological testing of which Dan M. recounts, "I wanted to puke [the questions] were so disgusting. Is that the type of person people think I am? I am not attracted to children, or dead people. I would never rape anyone. I respect women; I have three sisters, a mother, grandmothers, aunt, and girlfriend who I love."

Let Us Continue to Offer Most Juveniles a Clean Slate When They Reach Adulthood

Should juvenile sex offenders have a clean slate when they become adults? We have been doing this for a long time with juvenile offenses in general. The idea is that this facilitates juvenile rehabilitation—by allowing juveniles to leave their transitory follies behind them. All states have had the practice of sealing and or expunging juvenile records. In recent years this has been changing. Consider the following case:

Amie Zyla of Waukesha, Wisconsin, was sexually assaulted at the age of eight by Joshua Wade who was fourteen. Wade was sent to a juvenile facility for treating juvenile sex offenders. Subsequently, he was re-arrested for sexual re-offending against other children. He then received a twenty-five-year prison sentence. Zyla has since campaigned for community notification about the presence of juvenile sex offenders.

Yes, some juveniles present a risk of re-offending. The best response here is to improve at predicting who these juveniles are—not to punish all the others (the 94 percent of juvenile sex offenders) who desist.

Let Us Avoid Unnecessary Transfers to the Adult Criminal Justice System

The next two cases are scenarios for which the juvenile suspects should not be transferred to the adult criminal justice system. Transferring a juvenile to the adult system is a big step—so much so that judges are not allowed to do it without a hearing specifically about the transfer. However, prosecutors and legislators can get around this requirement if permitted to do so by local laws. A transfer says to the juvenile—"you are so bad, we cannot treat you—so you will be punished." What a message to send to a young person. In the adult system, the judge may be lenient—thinking the offender too young for "hard time" in prison. However, if convicted, a prison sentence could subject the juvenile to abuse from older inmates. An adult conviction also carries a stigma that makes it difficult to get an education, rent a home, and to be employed.

The 12-Year-Old Rapist

A Family Court judge yesterday ruled that one of the two juveniles accused of raping an 11-year-old girl at gunpoint in a West Philadelphia alley will be tried as a juvenile— denying a prosecution request that he be tried as an adult. Assistant District Attorney Leon Goodman said the request was made because of the seriousness of the crime, the danger he poses to the community, and his previous delinquencies, including an assault . . . The rape occurred . . . in an alley behind 5910 Chestnut St. The juvenile and an older boy, a 15-year-old identified Tyrone Briggs, has been charged as an adult with rape, kidnapping and weapons offenses.[20]

Was the judge correct? The negatives here include the use of violence indicating an intent to harm, no mention of remorse, and the existence of a delinquency record. However, while this juvenile sounds like the type who might commit another offense in the future, the literature suggests that this re-offending will not be a sex offense. It sounds like the rape was an instrument of destructive action—when, another tool (besides rape) could have been utilized for a similar negative outcome. Of course, we would need more details to say all this with certainty. There is nothing in the details presented to suggest that the young suspect would be better off in the adult versus the juvenile justice system. Yes—there was a victim and the harm involved was grave. Certainly punishment can be a part of the rehabilitation regime—but it should not be the only aspect of our response.

TOWARD KEEPING JUVENILES IN THE JUVENILE JUSTICE SYSTEM: LET US REMOVE FROM PROSECUTORS THE POWER TO TRANSFER JUVENILES TO THE ADULT CRIMINAL JUSTICE SYSTEM

The following case is an example of why we should get prosecutors out of the mix. It is too tempting for prosecutors to build a name for themselves by taking advantage of vulnerable teens from less informed and less resourced families:

> *In Mesa, Arizona, fifteen-year-old Keimond Brown, a foster child, had sex with his guardian's thirteen-year-old daughter. The girl's mother reported the incident. Arizona allows such sexual activity to be direct filed or prosecuted in the adult system. Now twenty-four-years-old and the father of two daughters, Brown was recently jailed for disappearing while on probation. Because of his sex offender status while he was on probation he was not able to hold his daughters, wear shorts, use a computer, and any toys and movies he accesses must be approved by his probation officer. He is engaged and reportedly has been an excellent father. Many in the judicial system believe this an example of the law gone too far.[21]*

LET US TEACH JUVENILES WITH MALADIES TO SEEK HELP WHEN IN A CRISIS

One of the authors of this book has worked in different mental health facilities with schizophrenics. Some of these patients heard persuasive voices in their heads urging them to do things like pushing a stranger on to an active subway track. Notably, most of these patients would check themselves into a hospital when the voices became too much to bear. You see, these patients retained some sense of right versus wrong.

What did the others do? Well…there's a reason we don't excuse serial killers like Jeffrey Dahmer who killed and ate little boys. We could probably agree that he was crazy; however, his careful planning to evade capture indicates that he was sane enough to have gotten help for himself. Similarly, many of those sex offenders with the inclination to sexually *re-offend* likely have some sense that the behavior is wrong. After all, they do it in secret. This suggests that they have enough wits about them to get themselves some help. Yes, there are those cases of people who are too delusional to help themselves, but these are rare. The implication then, is that for the few juveniles with a paraphilia or urge to commit a sex offense, we teach them to get help when in a crisis. Consider the recent case of thirteen-year-old Adante Thornton in Washington State, tagged as a violent and chronic juvenile sex offender. He admitted to raping a five-year-old and a ten-year-old, plus three other boys. August 2007, Thornton had the good sense to check himself into juvenile detention in Mason County (where he could access treatment).[22]

The charge then, is to pay attention to the signs of trouble in the juveniles about us and to intervene as best as we can to help. We should also be as educated and as active as we can when it comes to communicating the laws that we would like to see enacted. Some things just don't make sense! Some things will harm more than they will heal. We should avoid labeling juveniles with sexual behavior problems as "criminals." Instead, we should educate, treat, and monitor "Romeos and Juliets," and children engaging in sexual pranks, et cetera. We can continue to offer most juvenile sex offenders (those *without* compulsion, a paraphilia, or predatory violence) a clean slate when they become adults. We can also avoid transferring juveniles to the adult criminal justice system where treatment is less likely to happen. Too often, by not thinking about the policies that we allow to happen, we recommend things for others not mindful that those others could be us, or our brothers, sisters, daughters, or sons. Such arrogance makes us vulnerable for we are all connected. It stands to reason that when we make life needlessly difficult for others we increase the risk to ourselves.

NOTES

1. Katherine Ramsland, "Albert H. Fish," *Tru TV* (2007): n.p., http://www.crimelibrary.com/serial_killers/notorious/fish/11.html (accessed November 15, 2007).

2. Camille Gibson, "Juvenile Sex Offenders," in *Youth Delinquency and Violence*, ed. Marilyn McShane and Frank P. Williams III (Westport, CT: Greenwood Praeger Publishing, 2007), 70.

3. Katherine Ramsland, "The Paper Boy," *Tru TV* (2007): n.p., http://www.crimelibrary.com/serial_killers/predators/john_joubert/index.html (accessed November 15, 2007).

4. Franklin Zimring, *An American Travesty: Legal Responses to Adolescent Sexual Offending* (Chicago: University of Chicago Press, 2004), 49.

5. Ibid., 62.

6. Wade C. Myers, *Juvenile Sexual Homicide* (London: Academic Press, 2002), 17–59.

7. Ibid., 24.

8. Ibid., 22.

9. Daniel Goleman, "Early Violence Leaves Its Mark on the Brain," *New York Times*, 1995, 1.

10. John A. Hunter, R. R. Hazelwood, and D. Sleslinger, "Juvenile Sexual Homicide," *The FBI Law Enforcement Bulletin* (2000): 1.

11. Anne Lacasse and Morton J. Mendelson, "Sexual Coercion among Adolescents: Victims and Perpetrators," *Journal of Interpersonal Violence* 22(4) (2007): 434.

12. Nathan McCall, *Makes Me Wanna Holler: A Young Black Man in America* (New York: Random House, 1994), 43–47.

13. WTOL11—News 11 WTOL—11 NEWS, http://www.wtol.com/global/story.asp?s=7415081&ClientType=Printable (accessed November 28, 2007).

14. Ernesto Londono, "Case of Juvenile Molester Sends Victim's Parents on Legislative Mission," *Washington Post*, August 7, 2006, B04.

15. 13WHAM.com, "These Sex Offenders Are Protected," (2007).

16. Human Rights Watch, No Easy Answers, 19 4G, http://hrw.org/reports/2007/us0907/7.htm#_Toc176672585 (September 2007) (accessed November 15, 2007), n.p.

17. Zimring, *An American Travesty: Legal Responses to Adolescent Sexual Offending*, 3–5.

18. Angela Rozas, "Do Young Sex Offenders Belong on Adult Register," *Chicago Tribune*, January 16, 2007, 1.

19. Wright Thompson, Outrageous Injustice: Genarlow Wilson (2007), http://sports.espn.go.com/espn/eticket/story?page=Wilson (accessed December 1, 2007).

20. Julie Shaw, "Rape Suspect 14, to Be Tried as a Juvenile," *The Philadelphia Inquirer*, July 20, 2006, B05.

21. Mary Reinhart, "Legislators Try to Ease Laws for Sex Crimes by Youths: Family Appeals Sway Conservative Lawmakers to Back Bills to Alter Statutes," *Knight Ridder Tribune Business News*, February 11, 2007, 1.

22. Travis Pittman, "13-Year-Old Sex Offender Voluntarily Returns To Custody" (August 31, 2007), http://www.king5.com (accessed November 15, 2007).

REFERENCES

13WHAM.com. "These Sex Offenders Are Protected" (accessed November 28, 2007).

Gibson, Camille. "Juvenile Sex Offenders." In *Youth Delinquency and Violence*, edited by Marilyn McShane and Frank P. Williams III. Westport, CT: Greenwood Praeger Publishing, 2007.

Goleman, Daniel. "Early Violence Leaves Its Mark on the Brain." *New York Times*, October 3, 1995, C1.

Human Rights Watch. "No Easy Answers." Human Rights Watch, 19, no. 4G. http://hrw.org/reports/2007/us0907/6.htm#_Toc176672576 (accessed November 15, 2007).

Human Rights Watch. "No Easy Answers." Human Rights Watch, 19, no. 4G. http://hrw.org/reports/2007/us0907/1.htm#_Toc176672549 (accessed November 15, 2007.)

Hunter, John A., R. R. Hazelwood, and D. Sleslinger. "Juvenile Sexual Homicide." *The FBI Law Enforcement Bulletin* (2000): 1–7.

Lacasse, Anne, and Morton J. Mendelson. "Sexual Coercion among Adolescents: Victims and Perpetrators." *Journal of Interpersonal Violence* 22(4)(2007): 424–437.

Londono, Ernesto. "Case of Juvenile Molester Sends Victim's Parents on Legislative Mission." *Washington Post*, August 7, 2006, 4.

McCall, Nathan. *Makes Me Wanna Holler: A Young Black Man in America*. New York: Random House, 1994.

Myers, Wade C. *Juvenile Sexual Homicide*. London: Academic Press, 2002.

Pittman, Travis. "13-Year-Old Sex Offender Voluntarily Returns to Custody" (August 31, 2007). http://www.king5.com (accessed November 15, 2007).

Ramsland, Katherine. "Albert H. Fish." *Tru TV* (2007).

———. "The Paper Boy." *Tru TV* (2007).

Reinhart, Mary. "Legislators Try to Ease Laws for Sex Crimes by Youths: Family Appeals Sway Conservative Lawmakers to Back Bills to Alter Statutes." *Knight Ridder Tribune Business News*, February 11, 2007, 1.

Rozas, Angela. "Do Young Sex Offenders Belong on Adult Register."*Chicago Tribune*, January 16, 2007, 1.

Shaw, Julie. "Rape Suspect 14, to Be Tried as a Juvenile." *The Philadelphia Inquirer*, July 20, 2006. WTOL11—News 11 WTOL—11 NEWS. http://www.wtol.com/global/story.asp?s=7415081&ClientType=Printable (accessed November 28, 2007).

Wright Thompson. "Outrageous Injustice: Genarlow Wilson. (2007)." http://sports.espn.go.com/espn/eticket/story?page=Wilson (accessed December 1, 2007).

Zimring, Franklin. *An American Travesty: Legal Responses to Adolescent Sexual Offending*. Chicago: University of Chicago Press, 2004.

4

Are All Juvenile Sex Offenders the Same?

A teenager who raped a 59-year-old... woman was sentenced Friday to 10 years. [The 16-year-old offender] entered the first-floor apartment of the victim during the... assault. The victim, who is disabled with a back injury, was held by the throat during the assault with such force that a small bone in her neck was broken, according to court testimony. Assistant Prosecutor Linda Lawhun filed a motion to have [the offender] tried as an adult due to the violence of the attack. [The offender] was arrested at Millville Senior High School's alternative school a few days after the attack. The break in the case came from the second of two surveillance tapes obtained from nearby properties. A porch-mounted camera on a house across the street from the victim's residence recorded the suspect trying to enter the premises. With the enhancement, the recording yielded a "clear photograph," according to the city police. In addition to the prison sentence, [the offender] will be subject to lifetime parole supervision and must register as a Megan's Law offender. He'll need to serve at least 8 $\frac{1}{2}$ years before he is eligible for parole under that state's No Early Release Act.[1]

Whether this is a "typical" juvenile sex offender is debatable; it could be argued the typical juvenile sex offender—if there is such a thing—does not choose an older person with a physical disability as a victim. Most of us would like to believe all sex offenders are the same—this would make identification of them a lot easier. The truth, however, is that sex offenders are a diverse group of offenders. The fact that they vary so much in their background, demographics, offense behaviors, and victim preferences means we cannot place sex offenders, even juvenile sex offenders, in one category.

The need to identify typologies of sex offenders is imperative. Given that sex offenders are a heterogeneous group of offenders, identifying subcategories of homogenous subsets would be helpful to those who need to recognize the characteristics of sex offenders, such as police officers, care providers, teachers, and parole/probation officers. For example, if a police officer, care provider, teacher, or parole/probation officer is familiar with only one or two types of sex offenders, he or she may not be able to recognize potential offenders when sexual abuse is reported. The same is true for probation and parole officers who often have regular contact with offenders already identified as sex offenders. Society, in general, needs to be aware of the different categories of adolescent sex offenders. The public serves as the eyes and ears and it is often individual people who alert police and social workers of potential abuse, rather than just the law enforcement agents. Also important, in the management of sex offenders who are living in the community and often court-ordered to treatment, treatment providers bear a great burden in assisting the offender to manage their sexual deviance. Once we know certain characteristics and behaviors are common to certain types of individuals, treatment plans can be specialized to that individual.

Also, one may presume that we should simply rely on expert opinion when it comes to assessing sex offenders, particularly young sex offenders. The experts in the social science field, for example, have accumulated many years of higher education—usually obtaining a Master's and/or Ph.D. in psychology, social work, or related fields. Additionally, they have usually worked many years with sex offenders and those with a wide range of mental abnormalities. Would it not make more sense that they would know exactly how to treat such offenders? Not necessarily so. Professionals in this area make judgments about their clients at a rate that is only slightly better than guessing.[2] The truth is that we are simply at the beginning of empirically assessing sex offenders. While a good foundation of research exists, we have a great deal more to learn. Typologies are essential; we must first be able to identify and describe this population in order to determine causality and develop sophisticated treatment plans.

Several researchers have created a juvenile sex offender typology. Even though several individual and groups of researchers have developed their own classification systems, a great deal of overlap exists among the different systems. Because the typologies created by different researchers vary in the number of categories and characteristics, it does not mean one classification system is better than the next. In fact, each classification is based on different characteristics and assessment techniques. Some are based on socialization deficits, while others are based on their persistence of offending, psychological factors, and/or victim characteristics. Each typology can provide some unique facet into the understanding of this group of offenders.

Most classifications include factors categorized as either static or dynamic. Static factors refer to factors that typically do not change; this would include:

past psychiatric history, sexual history, family history, number of prior sexual offenses characteristics of prior sexual offenses, prior victim selection, and prior nonsexual antisocial behavior.[3] When someone sits down with an offender and assesses these factors, they are not likely to change. While the number of prior offenses can change in the future, the number at the time of the interview is not likely to change. The other factors, dynamic factors, do in fact change within a short amount of time. This would include such factors as motivation, acceptance of responsibility, level of victim empathy, quality of peer relationships, level of sexual self-regulation, current substance abuse, and current symptoms of mental illness. Most typologies include a host of both static and dynamic factors. Many of these factors, static and dynamic, are also used to assess risk for re-offense.

A common characteristic discussed in many of the typologies is antisocial personality disorder. Antisocial Personality Disorder, as defined by the American Psychiatric Association, includes a pervasive pattern of disregard for others and must include at least three of the following characteristics: (1) committing crimes; (2) lying/conning others for his or her own gain; (3) inability to plan ahead/impulsivity; (4) aggressive behavior; (5) no regard for others' safety or their own; (6) not able to sustain work; and (7) no remorse for harming others.[4] Typically these behaviors must persist for an extended period of time and usually are present during adolescence (usually since age fifteen). Also, those who show these behaviors before the age of fifteen are labeled as having Conduct Disorder, rather than Antisocial Personality Disorder.

So who gets to decide what groups constitute a typology and how did they go about creating the typology? Those who work with sex offenders and study them create typologies in different ways. For example, one pair of researchers relied on their expert knowledge and experience in treating adolescent sex offenders to create their categories.[5] Another compiled prior research to summarize their categories.[6] Others have used psychological assessment tools to identify unique characteristics within a population of young male sex offenders.[7]

Researchers vary in what key characteristics they have or are interested in for inclusion into a typology. For example, those who develop a typology for the purpose of identifying those who have a high risk of re-offending would likely want to include recidivism rates and assess which characteristics are predictive of re-offending. Treatment providers may want to establish types of treatment that should be used with each category of treatment. For example, those who offend against siblings may need different treatment than those who assault strangers or acquaintances. The bottom line is that there is no single "right" typology.

TYPOLOGIES BASED ON RESEARCHERS' PRIOR EXPERIENCE

One way to develop a typology is to intuitively create groups based on one's own experience. As treatment providers come into contact with dozens of teenage sex offenders, oftentimes they see similarities and differences and begin to conceptualize the different groups by merely noting the salient characteristics. In this section, we describe several researchers who have years and sometimes decades of experience in working with this group of offenders. We also describe each of their typologies created with explanations and examples.

O'BRIEN AND BERA'S TYPOLOGY

These researchers were one of the first to develop a formal classification of juvenile sex offenders. Until the 1980s, researchers had only attempted to classify adult sex offenders. Each of the researchers had worked with sex offenders for over ten years at the time they created the typology. Michael O'Brien was the founder of a treatment center for adolescents. Walter Bera worked with both victims and offenders of sexual abuse. One of the purposes of their typology was to assess the best treatment option, given the juvenile's offending characteristics and background experiences. While treatment issues are fully discussed in Chapter 6, this section includes a brief explanation of the suggested treatment plans, given each group's characteristics.[8]

Based on their experience the two researchers and treatment providers identified seven categories of juvenile sex offenders: *naïve experimenters, undersocialized child exploiters, sexual aggressives, sexual compulsives, disturbed impulsives, group influenced,* and *pseudosocialized child exploiters.* The behaviors range from exposing one's self to another to raping someone. Their social skills range from underdeveloped to savvy and their family backgrounds range from functional to dysfunctional.[9]

The *naïve experimenter* includes juveniles who are sexually naïve, but have fairly healthy relationships with average social skills. This offender is usually between eleven and fourteen years old with a victim who is usually between two and six years old. This offender typically does not have a history of acting out. The abuse usually occurs in a situation that allows for a certain degree of privacy allowing sexual behavior. For example, he may be babysitting, camping, or at some other family function. The following is a case study presented by the researchers in their explanation of a *naïve experimenter*:

> *Johnny is a 13-year-old boy who had been asked to babysit a neighbor girl, age 5, named Nicky. Johnny had been babysitting for only a short time and the situation was still new to him. While there he discovered a Playboy magazine hidden under the couch and Johnny found the explicit photographs arousing. While helping Nicky change into her pajamas he wanted to see what it was like to kiss and touch her in the way depicted in the photograph. After a short time he felt guilty and stopped. Later that week Nicky told her mother and Johnny was arrested for criminal sexual misconduct.*[10]

There are several noteworthy characteristics in this scenario; first, the teenager in this situation is relatively young and after exposed to some sort of sexual stimuli (e.g., *Playboy* magazine), he touches a younger child inappropriately. While sexual exploration is considered part of normal sexual development during this age range, the young teenager chooses someone who is younger than himself. If he had simply engaged in the same type of exploration with someone who was within the same age-range, it would not have been criminal. This type of sexual molestation, therefore, involves normal behavior, with the exception of the age of the victim. Additionally, there is some sort of acknowledgement on the offender's part that this behavior was inappropriate due to the fact that he indicated he felt guilty and subsequently ceased the behavior.

One of the researcher's key purposes of identifying salient groups of young sex offenders was for treatment purposes. The authors suggested short-term intensive treatment is usually sufficient for the *naïve experimenter*. The treatment, however, should include a strong educational component that distinguishes sexuality from sexual abuse. The educational component should also include the child along with his parents. In fact, family communication should be open; discussions of sexuality should occur for the purpose of minimizing inappropriate behavior.[11]

Another type of juvenile sex offender identified by these researchers is the *undersocialized child exploiters*. While the researchers do not describe the specific ages of the victim or the offender, a case study of a sixteen-year-old victimizing "considerably younger children." This type of offender, lacking socialization with appropriate-aged peers, often forms friendships with younger children. He relies on children for companionship, which later evolves into sexual abuse. This type of individual often spends time alone and has few friends who are close to his own age. The offender often has feelings of inadequacy and insecurity; the victim often has admiration for the older boy. While he does not have a history of acting out, his family dynamics are not healthy. The mother is typically overinvolved and the father is distant. The victim, similar to the *naïve experimenter*, is someone who is accessible in the context of family gatherings, playing in the neighborhood, or babysitting. The offender often uses tricks or manipulation to gain access to the child. The following case scenario is provided as an example of this type of offender:

> *Jerry, age 16, had no close peer relationships and only a few school acquaintances. He could be considered a loner, and he spent a good portion of his time watching television or playing video games at home. He was well-liked by his parents and was no trouble at home or at school. When playing outside he was often by himself or with considerably younger children. In the course of playing with younger children he became involved with them sexually and required fondling and oral-genital contact as an initiation rite for membership in a club he had formed. No threats or force were used, but he did maintain secrecy with the children by telling them not to tell their parents. One of the children told a teacher and Jerry was arrested for criminal sexual conduct.*[12]

This type of offender has used games or tricks to gain access to the child. Similar to the *naïve experimenter*, this type of offender does not use force or threat of force to touch and molest the children. This type of offender, however, is older, and is slightly savvier than the naïve experimenter in that he uses more manipulation—forming a "secret society" to gain victim cooperation.[13]

Treatment for this type of offender also should involve the family. Any member who is abnormally dependent needs to be worked with to become more independent. The problem is that the offender is focused on family, rather than his peers. Changes need to be made in how the family communicates with each other. In addition to family therapy, individual therapy and peer-age therapy need to occur. This should include social skills so the offender can learn to establish and maintain relationships with peers who are the same age. The treatment can be community-based, but if the victim involves a sibling living in the same household, the offender needs to be removed, at least temporarily, from the home.[14]

Another identified category is the *pseudosocilaized child exploiter*. This type of offender is an older adolescent who molests a younger child. He lacks remorse; the abuse usually occurs over a long period of time—up to several years. He also lacks insight into his behavior, often perceiving the abuse as something the victim wants to do, and perhaps enjoys. He views the molestation as an intimate exchange, rather than abuse. He, therefore, lacks any guilt. The abuse is described as a "narcissistic exploitation of a vulnerable child to gain sexual pleasure."[15] Unfortunately there are not necessarily any telltale signs in the offender's previous behaviors, as the authors who identified this category note this type of offender does not have any history of acting out and typically has good social skills. The following excerpt is the example given by the authors to describe the pseudosocialized child exploiter:

> *Norm was a 17-year-old boy, the youngest of six children. He was an exceptional achiever: An A student and in the top bracket of students completing the SAT. This religious and college-bound youth had also engaged in kissing, oral-genital sex and penis vaginal rubbing with a niece 6 years younger than he.*
>
> *The abuse events occurred regularly over a three-year period and it appeared he had trained her into a victim role and coaxed her to remain silent. Vaginal redness led to the questions by the girl's physician and her final disclosure. The entire family was grievously shocked when Norm was arrested for criminal sexual conduct.*[16]

Compared to the two previous categories, this one involves more serious abuse in that the abuse occurs over a substantial period of time and involves more than a slight boundary violation. While there is evidence that the offender knew the behavior was wrong (i.e., encouraging the victim to not tell), the offender engages in such behavior with the notion it is mutually consenting and does not have any insight into the child's inability to dissuade or refuse participation.

The authors describing this type of offender acknowledge that treatment of this kind of sexual offender is difficult, if not impossible. They note that this type of offender's desire to truly change is lacking. Their participation is often superficial and the therapist's goal should be to break through this superficial level of compliance to deal with the underlying issues. Residential treatment should be provided if he does not comply with community-based individual, peer-group, and family therapy. This type of offender can become a lifelong offender without appropriate intervention and treatment.[17]

Another type of young sex offender described includes the *sexual aggressives*. While the researchers gave no specific age range for the offender, their case study included a fifteen-year-old teenager. The victim, however, can be an adult, someone who is peer-aged, or a child. This type of offender usually comes from a dysfunctional family where abuse is usually present. The offender usually exhibits antisocial behavior, low impulse-control, engages in fights with family and peers, and has a history of drug abuse. The abuse itself usually involves threats of violence or actual violence. The purpose of the abuse is usually to gain power. They are usually angry and dominate and/or humiliate their victims. In some cases, the sexual abuse may be learned; violence in and of itself results in sexual arousal. Violence and sexual pleasure become enmeshed in the offender's mind. A case example of this type of offender is presented here:

> *Troy, age 15, was a victim of severe abuse at the hands of his stepfather, his mother's third husband. The mother was passive and often suffered from physical beatings from her husband as well. Troy had a history of fire-setting, theft, vandalism, and truancy over several years. Very social and flamboyant, he took a 14-year-old girl out on a date and when she refused to "go all the way," Troy slapped her and forced her to perform oral sex by threatening her with a screwdriver. When Troy released her, she made her way home and told her mother what happened. Troy was arrested later that evening by police for first-degree criminal sexual conduct.[18]*

A notable characteristic of this type of juvenile sex offender is his antisocial traits. Those with Antisocial Personality Disorder, by definition, often have a general disregard for others' feelings.[19] In fact, they lack the ability to empathize with others. They put their feelings and desires (e.g., want to have sex) ahead of other's feelings. They often do not have long-term plans and are unable to delay gratification. It is important to note that while many career criminals are antisocial, not all those with antisocial personalities are sex offenders.

The treatment recommendations for this type of offender are long-term and residential based; it should include intensive individual, group, and family therapy (if possible). With regard to the family member's role, their behaviors need to be addressed as they often serve to undermine the goals established in treatment for the offender. Anger management also needs to be a focus of therapy, as the offender should learn how to express anger in a more socially appropriate manner. With regard to his social and intimate needs, he should learn how to meet such needs in an appropriate way as well.[20]

Another type of sex offender is the *sexual compulsives*. This type of offender often engages in repetitive obsessive behaviors ranging from exhibitionism, voyeurism (e.g., looking through windows at unsuspecting victims as they disrobe), and obscene phone calling. This offender may also have fetishes, such as stealing women's underwear. The behaviors, therefore, are often repetitive and obsessive. Their families are often rigid and lack emotional expressions. The offender does not openly express any negative emotion. The following is an example of a *sexual compulsive*:

> *David, age 16, was a football player and a good student. His mother was a traditional homemaker and his father was often gone, working two shifts in a hospital. David committed a series of exposing incidents in front of high school girls near his school and was identified and arrested by the police. In the course of therapy it was discovered that he*

had exposed himself numerous times to his older sister who kept it a secret and just yelled at him. The total abuse history spanned a two-year period.[21]

One of the most distinguishing characteristics of this type of offender is that the offender engages in hands-off offenses; that is, he does not force a victim to touch him nor does he actually touch his victim. While some may not see this as serious, it is an indication of sexual deviancy, which may promulgate hands-on offenses later.

The researchers who identified this category suggested a treatment program similar to the treatment of any other type of obsessive behaviors, including nonsexual obsessive behavior. As they note, "They include specifying the cognitive-emotional-behavioral sequence that makes up the deviant change of events and developing numerous interventions in that sequence that can be practiced in individual, group, and family therapy."[22]

Obsessive-compulsive disorders are usually earmarked by obsessive thoughts, which are defined as "recurrent and persistent thoughts, impulses, or images that are experienced, at some time during the disturbance, as intrusive and inappropriate and that cause marked anxiety and distress."[23] The thoughts are not justified by genuine worries about experiences or problems the individual is experiencing. Additionally, the thoughts do not go away, even when the person tries to ignore them or engage in some sort of activity to divert the thoughts. Compulsions are defined as repetitive behaviors, such as hand-washing, or mental acts, such as counting over and over in one's mind. Usually the behaviors or acts are the result of trying to reduce anxiety or a stressful situation and cause some sort of distress to the individual. Compulsions, therefore, are the result of the individual's need to act on their obsessions.[24]

While medication can be used to treat obsessive-compulsive disorders, behavior therapy has shown to be quite effective. In fact, it has been found 80 to 90 percent of those treated for obsessive-compulsive behavior disorders had decreased symptoms after receiving behavior treatment.[25] Treatment is rather short, usually only lasting approximately ten weeks. Typically the individual is exposed to the object they obsess about and they are taught an anxiety-reducing ritual until the patient learns not to react to the object that causes the obsessive-compulsive thoughts and behaviors—a technique known as systematic desensitization.

The sixth category of adolescent sex offender described is the *disturbed impulsive*. This type of offender has serious psychological problems, including serious learning problems. Family dysfunction is present and also usually includes substance abuse. The sexual abuse can be a one-time unexpected anomaly or it may be a pattern of activity. The victim can be a child, peer, or adult.

Chemical abuse or a thought disorder may serve as precursors to the abuse. The following scenario exemplifies such an offender:

> *Bill, age 15, was living with his father who had won custody of him and his sister after bitter divorce proceedings. He had grown up in a house where there was always tension and anxiety as a result of the marital discord, and he generally learned to keep to himself. One day while taking the vacuum cleaner from his sister's closet he turned to his sister who was sitting in her underwear and grabbed her, tore off her underwear and attempted to mount her while she screamed, "Stop! Stop!" Finally she pushed him off and he seemed to "come to his senses," grabbed the vacuum cleaner and left to complete his household chores. Because of the family tension the sister kept the event quiet. A second incident occurred with a girlfriend of his sister's, whom Bill accosted suddenly while ice skating with her, grabbing her breast and buttocks. This incident was reported to the police and he was questioned and left to the custody of his father. He was finally arrested after accosting an adult female in the laundry room of his mother's apartment building. Again, the assault was sudden and unpredictable. He was subsequently placed in a psychiatric hospital.[26]*

This particular offender appears to engage in a series of escalating behavior; for example, one incident in and of itself may not constitute psychological maladies, yet given that each incident seemed to escalate in seriousness and, taken as a whole, constituted a serious problem.

The suggested treatment for such offenders includes conducting a battery of psychological exams, including obtaining individual and family history information. The offender should be placed in a residential treatment facility for adolescent sex offenders or in an inpatient psychiatric facility. Community-based treatment should only be used if the psychological symptoms can be treated with medication.[27]

The seventh group of juvenile offenders is called *group influenced*. This type of offender is usually a younger teen and the sexual abuse usually occurs in the context of a group and he usually knows his victim. He is either reacting to pressure or expectations from his peers or trying to gain approval from his friends by exhibiting leadership qualities. He usually does not have prior contact with the criminal justice system. An example is as follows:

> *Greg, age 13, was a lonely boy whose only friend was Travis, age 14. One evening they went to a neighbor's house after the parents had left. While there, Travis encouraged the group that included Greg, a 12-year-old boy and his 11-year-old sister to engage in a game of "strip poker." The boys began kissing and fondling the girl when her brother went to the bathroom. Both boys told her not to tell but the next morning she told her parents. Both Travis and Greg were arrested for criminal sexual conduct.[28]*

This incident involves an offender and victim with a two-and three-year age difference and also included fondling, making it more serious than simple experimentation. Also, the activity occurred under a cloak of secrecy, indicating the boys did not want others to know what they did. They also did this only when the victim's brother was not present.

When these types of offenders are in therapy together, they should be separated immediately. Their stories should be examined closely to determine the role of each of the participants. The leader of the abuse may meet the criteria for another category of sex offenders and may need residential treatment, while the others need to take responsibility for their role, which can usually be accomplished through outpatient treatment.[29]

Overall, this typology is quite appealing; it is based on firsthand experiences and it has a great deal of face validity, meaning it appears to be as accurate as its basic logic. No one, however, has tested this typology to assess its application to all groups of juvenile sex offenders.[30] This typology, nevertheless, provides a great deal of detail and provides case studies that are useful. When others read about the individual cases, they may be able to relate to the case—they may notice similarities in other reported incidents of sexual abuse or they may have firsthand knowledge of such cases.

PRENTKY, HARRIS, FRIZZELL, AND RIGHTHAND'S TYPOLOGY

Prentky and his colleagues proposed a typology with six categories of juvenile offenders: *child molesters, rapists, sexually reactive children, fondlers, paraphilic offenders*, and *unclassifiable*. The authors created this typology based on their own knowledge of what they had experienced in their work. This typology most resembles the adult typologies that exist. A common delineation in many adult typologies is the delineation between *child molesters* and *rapists*. A child molester, by definition, chooses victims to sexually molest. It is often someone who has groomed their victim, meaning they have spent time with the child and they coerce them into sexual behavior by slowing eroding personal boundaries. A rapist, however, chooses an adult victim and sexually assaults the victim by force, threat of force, or manipulation.[31]

With regard to Prentky and his colleagues' typology of juvenile sex offenders, the *child molester* typically chooses a victim younger than twelve years old and is at least five years younger than him. The *rapist* chooses someone who is twelve years old and is no more than five years younger than he.[32]

Those who are *sexually reactive* are relatively young; they are younger than eleven years old. Their victims are also younger than eleven years old. For the *fondlers*, the age difference between the victim and offender was less than five years. Their sexual behaviors include fondling, caressing, touching, and rubbing (without one's consent). While these are all hands-on offenses, none involve penetration. Those who were *paraphilic offenders* have no hands-on offenses; instead their offenses include exhibitionism and obscene phone calls. Additionally, those who are *unclassifiable* do not fit any of the previously described categories.[33]

STATISTICALLY DERIVED TYPOLOGIES

As noted earlier, there are several ways to develop typologies. In addition to relying on one's own experience and intuitively creating groups, researchers can also gather information from different groups of known offenders and rely on statistical programs to identify the similarities and differences among the offenders to place them in salient groups. A common method to developing a typology of sex offenders is to use a method called cluster analysis. After key characteristics of a group of offenders are gathered and entered into a dataset, a statistical procedure identifies the two most similar offenders and assigns them to a group. At the same time, any other similar cases are assigned to their own group. Afterwards, the next most similar individual is assigned to the group. This is a repetitious process where at each stage the most similar cases are linked to a group, until all of the offenders eventually are in one group. Essentially at the beginning, each offender is in his own group and at the last stage, everyone is in the same group. It is up to the researcher to find a point where there are several developed groups in which the groups are the most similar, yet they are distinguishable from the other groups. There are several other statistical procedures to identify at one point this occurs.[34] In the following section, we describe several typologies that have relied on statistical measures to create typologies of sex offenders.

GRAVES'S TYPOLOGY

In 1996, Roger B. Graves published research based on his doctoral dissertation that identified three types of adolescent sex offenders.[35] His findings were based on 16,000 adolescent sex offenders who appeared in earlier research. When a researcher gathers previous research findings and relies on several studies to make some sort of conclusion, it is called a meta-analysis. When one study is completed using a small sample of adolescent sex offenders it is not known whether the findings are true for all adolescent sex offenders. For example, if someone examines thirty adolescent sex offenders from a small treatment facility in a rural part of the country, the characteristics of the group may not be similar to those in a different part of the country or in a different type of facility. By relying on all studies published on the topic, a comprehensive perspective is provided of what is currently known about that particular population.

The result of Graves analysis research was three identified groups of offenders: *pedophilic, sexual assault,* and *undifferentiated.* Just as the name suggests, pedophilic sex offenders consistently molest children who are comparatively much younger; in fact, their victims are at least three years younger than the offender. This group often lacks confidence and they tend to be socially isolated.[36]

This group is clearly distinguishable from the other groups by its sexual interest in those who are several years younger than themselves. Pedophilia is a disorder that is usually characteristic of adults, however. In fact, the *Diagnostic and Statistical Manual for Mental Disorders, IV,* which is a book developed by the American Psychiatric Association to identify all recognized mental disorders, defines pedophilia as involving sexual activity "with a prepubescent child (generally age thirteen years or younger). The individual with pedophilia must be at least sixteen years old and at least five years older than the victim. For individuals in late adolescence with pedophilia, no precise age difference is specified, and clinical judgment must be used; both the sexual maturity of the child and the age difference must be taken into account."[37] Thus, while the *Manual* does not recognize pedophilia as something teenagers or children experience, Graves' research shows there are children who have a sexual orientation to children.

Those who fit the criteria for *sexual assault* have peers or older females as victims.[38] According to most states' legal definition, sexual assault typically involves forcing one's self on another. Force, threat of force, or lack of consent is typically required.[39]

The third group, *undifferentiated,* engages in both hands-on and hands-off offenses. The hands-off offenses, for example, can include exhibitionism. Their abnormal sexual behaviors usually begin when the offenders were relatively young. They usually have the most severe psychological issues and come from dysfunctional families.[40]

WEINROTT'S TYPOLOGY

Although this typology was not published, the findings were presented at a national conference on child abuse.[41] Four broad categories of juvenile sexual offenders were identified: (1) those who sexually abuse; (2) those who have deviant arousal; (3) those who are psychopathic; and (4) others who just need appropriate rules set for sexual behavior.[42] Although, details of each type are not published, the four types are consistent with other typologies in that there are those who are simply experimenting, albeit inappropriately, and simply need some boundaries through acute treatment. Others, however, have underlying problems (i.e., psychopathic traits) or have developed sexual deviancy and likely need treatment.

WORLING'S TYPOLOGY

James Worling has worked with a sexual abuse treatment program in Toronto, Canada. His typology is based on 112 sex offenders who were twelve to nineteen years old. All were convicted or had acknowledged their sexual offenses. The offenders were administered a psychological assessment called the California Psychological Examination, which is considered a reliable tool in assessing interpersonal and intrapersonal function. Additionally, a twelve-item scale measured exposure to abuse and incidents such as spanking, hitting, kicking, and choking.[43]

The authors note that their results of the typology were similar to a previous identified typology (not presented here),[44] which used a different battery of psychological examinations. Given that they are so similar, this suggests the categories proposed are likely to be accurate and reliable. Worling's typology included re-arrest rates for approximately six years; thus, the typology can provide information about those who are most likely to be re-arrested for a sexual offense. Worling's typology yielded four categories of sex offenders: *antisocial/impulsive*, *usual/isolated*, *overcontrolled/reserved*, and *confident/aggressive*.[45]

The most common group was the *antisocial/impulsive* who, as the name suggests, exhibit antisocial and impulsive tendencies. This group was the most likely to have sexual assault charges and most likely to have experienced prior abuse in the form of physical discipline from their parents. The link between harsh parental discipline and later developing antisocial behaviors has been noted by several experts.[46] This group had the second highest of subsequent arrests for violent, including sexual, offenses during the six-year follow-up period. The *unusual/isolated* group is described as socially awkward with poor interpersonal skills lacking basic social, such as skills introducing one's self, starting a conversation, listening, and asking a question. The group had the highest rate of arrests for any offense, sexual offenses, and violent offenses. They were also the least likely to have their parents still married and living together.[47]

The third group, *overcontrolled/reserved*, was the most likely to have a male victim and the most likely to have their parents living together and still married. They, however, were the least likely to have a re-arrest for any type of offense, for violent offenses, or for a sexual re-offense. The most notable characteristic of the fourth group, *confident/aggressive*, was that they were the most likely to have reported being victimized as a child. They were the second most likely to have experienced sexual abuse as a child. The third and fourth groups are described as the "relatively healthier" groups. They were most likely to have their parents still living together and married. The more pathological groups, *antisocial/impulsive* and *unusual/isolated* offender were the most likely to have a subsequent arrest.[48]

Given that two of the groups had lower rates of re-arrests suggests different responses to treatment. For example, those who had higher rates of re-arrests, long-term residential treatment may be most appropriate. The groups with lower rates of re-arrests may need only short-term treatment.

OXNAM AND VESS'S TYPOLOGY

One of the most recent typologies of adolescent sex offenders was developed by Paul Oxnam and James Vess. These researchers worked together when Paul was working on his Master's degree at Victoria University of Wellington, located in New Zealand. Jim (James) Vess was his supervising professor at the time. They used a sophisticated psychological tool called the Millon Adolescent Clinical Inventory (MACI). The scientific community has deemed this assessment tool as reliable and valid. It is a test that adolescents take, which includes 160 true-false items. It assesses personality patterns, clinical symptoms, and any of their significant personal concerns. More specifically, it assesses personality disorders that are recognized disorders by the American Psychiatric Association. It assesses the following personality characteristics: borderline behaviors, conforming, doleful, dramatizing, egotistic, forceful, inhibited, introversive, oppositional, self-demeaning, submissive, and unruly. The personal concerns scale assesses the individual's perceptions of self, including such factors as body and self-image, sexual discomfort, prior abuse, family problems, and social insensitivity. Clinical symptoms include eating dysfunctions, susceptibility to substance abuse, a predisposition to delinquency and emotional problems such as anxiety, impulsivity, depression, and suicide.[49]

After the tests were administered to twenty-five known adolescent sex offenders, the researchers identified (through statistical analysis) three distinct groups based on their psychological test results: *antisocial*, *inadequate*, and *normal range*. Those in the *antisocial* group scored high on the unruly and oppositional scales. They also scored high on the following clinical syndrome scales: delinquent predisposition, family discord, and impulsive propensity. Their personality assessment showed they were more likely than the other to act out aggressively and unpredictably. They do not form close intimate relationships with others. Their scores also suggested high rates of delinquency and susceptibility to drug and alcohol abuse.[50]

Those in the *inadequate* group exhibited higher than normal scores on several scales indicating they were generally inhibited, introverted, and often engaged in self-demeaning thoughts and behaviors. Their clinical symptoms indicated high rates of experiencing childhood abuse, depression, peer insecurity, and low self-esteem. They suffer from cognitive, emotional, and behavioral problems. Chronic depression is common among this group. They often have a pessimistic attitude and view themselves in a negative way. They have experienced childhood abuse at a substantially higher rate than those in the other groups. Their abuse involved family members, sometimes including their parents, who verbally, physically, and sexually abused them.[51]

For those in the *normal* group, none of their scores suggested unusual elevations on personality patterns, symptoms, or concerns. They have only a slight elevation on the sexual discomfort scale, suggesting confusion of sexual issues and sexual maturation development problems. The researchers describe these adolescents as having a desire to meet other's expectations and follow rules. They also exhibited slightly elevated scores on the anxiety scale, indicating they are slightly anxious.[52]

One of the most noteworthy findings from Oxnam and Vess's proposed typology is that there is a group of adolescent sex offenders who do not exhibit symptoms of clinical significance—meaning if you or I came across this particular youth, we would not have any immediate warning signs that he is abnormal in any way. This is true regardless of our psychological knowledge or experience. As Oxnam and Vess note, they are no different on any of the tested scales to those adolescents who have not sexually offended. This provides support for the notion that some—not all—but some offenders are psychologically normal and they offend out of curiosity or experimentation as opposed to responding to their own psychological maladies.

DISTINGUISHING JUVENILE SEX OFFENDERS BY ONE CRITICAL FACTOR

Instead of developing typologies, which are based on several factors, some have attempted to identify a single factor. Researchers have attempted to distinguish juvenile sex offenders by their prior sexual victimization and their likelihood to recidivate as a key factor; we discuss both of these factors in this section.

Sexual Abuse Victim as a Critical Factor

A key factor identified previously has been the exposure of adolescent sex offenders to prior sexual abuse, meaning the offenders were victims of sexual abuse prior to becoming offenders. In a comparison of adolescent sex offenders with a history of sexual victimization to those without a history of sexual victimization, only 21 of the 107 adolescents reported experiencing sexual victimization, making it difficult to make meaningful comparisons. The researchers, however, did find that the two groups of adolescents differed slightly with regard to their educational background. Those with a history of sexual abuse began school later and their performance was worse than those without a history of sexual abuse. Also, those with a history of sexual abuse were more likely to report feeling isolated beyond the age of fourteen. Aside from this finding, few differences were found.[53]

An important finding from this study is that there are a large number of sex offenders who have not been sexually abused. While it may make sense to most of us—or it may be easier to deal with sex offenders if we perceive them as victims—this research indicates sexual abuse is only one of many factors related to committing sexual offenses.

Recidivism as a Distinguishing Factor

Once a sex offender, always a sex offender. Right? Maybe. The answer may not be so simple. It would be easy to respond to such offenders if this were true: once someone sexually offended, we could incarcerate him (or her) for the rest of his (or her) life. The problem, however, is that not all adolescents who sexually offend continue to do so. Several researchers have also identified prior arrest record as a critical factor in predicting future arrests. One of the most straightforward typologies in fact, includes three possible paths of offending: continued delinquency (in general), continued sexual offending, and no further offending.[54] These findings highlight the fact that not all who sexually offend continue to sexually offend. It has been found by other researchers that approximately half of adolescent sex offenders do not have arrests for nonsexual crimes and the other half do have such arrests.[55] Prior criminal histories have been used to assess future likelihood of additional arrests.[56] Assessing patterns of arrests throughout one's life can be useful in determining others' risk level.

On the flip side of this argument, it is important to note that many adult sex offenders began sexually offending during their adolescence.[57] The following dialogue occurred between a psychologist and one of her clients:

> *I created my first victim when I was thirteen, a female victim . . . Sally was six I was thirteen, and I raped and molested Sally by forcing my hands and fingers on her vulva and in her vagina and forcing objects into her vagina. Sally is my only female victim, my one female victim. I created my first male victim when I was fifteen, and I have been victimizing male children virtually nonstop until my incarceration . . .*
>
> *Q. How many total victims did you have?*
>
> *A. I have eleven male rape victims, one female rape victim and I have approximately 1,250 male molest victims, and I say approximately because I really don't know.*[58]

In this dialogue the adult sex offender says he began offending during his adolescence. Theoretically if someone knew of his first victim and intervened, a potential outcome is that approximately 1,000 victims could have been prevented. Suppose several adolescents who were on this track could be stopped in their offending careers during early on—how many thousands of victims could be prevented by just intervening in just a few dozen or so cases? The implications of this are far-reaching.

As noted by several researchers, though, many of the adolescents are not going to continue offending. If someone were to intervene in those cases, would it cause more harm than good? While many of these theoretical situations cannot be fully explored, we know that properly assessing adolescents for their potential offending is imperative.

Along this line of thinking, two researchers assessed the differences between adolescents with and without a history of nonsexual arrests. In an assessment of a group of adolescent sex offenders with and without a history of nonsexual offenses, the sex offender group with a history of other nonsexual offenses (i.e., general crime), had significantly more current behavior problems, fewer prosocial attitudes/beliefs, and higher expected risk of committing sexual offenses. The researcher concluded that their history of nonsexual offenses is a critical factor when assessing their potential risk for committing additional offenses and should be included as a factor in developing a typology of adolescent sex offenders.[59]

DISCUSSION OF TYPOLOGIES

In order for a typology to accurately describe the groups of sex offenders that really exist, it must be tested on groups of sex offenders other than the one that produced that typology. Thus, while a specific sample used by each of the researchers generated the typology proposed, it is imperative to apply the typology on a separate group of young sex offenders; if the typology fits the sample, it is likely to be valid. Developing typologies for young sex offenders is relatively new and unfortunately no tests of any of the proposed typologies could be found. Nevertheless, the review of the typologies that have been developed for juvenile (and sometimes even younger) sex offenders show a great number of commonalities and similar categories created among the different typologies. This is indicative of groups of young sex offenders that are in fact accurate depictions of what can be found among this population. In the following section, we identify the overlapping categories of sex offenders that exist among the different proposed typologies.

PEDOPHILES AND RAPISTS

A common distinction among adult male sex offenders is whether they choose victims who are also adults, *rapists*, or whether they choose children, *pedophiles*.[60] It is clear several of the typologies for young sex offenders used a similar distinction. For example, one researcher[61] specifically noted the adolescents choose either peers, *pedophillic* group, or those who are peer-aged or adults, *sexual assault* group. Likewise, O'Brien and Bera identified a group of adolescent sex offenders, *sexual aggressives*, who have victims of any age, including adults.[62] They also identified another group, *undersocialized child exploiters*, which teenagers often choose victims that are much younger than themselves. Another group of researchers, Prentky and his colleagues, also noted two groups of adolescent offenders, *child molesters* and *rapists* that are distinguishable primarily between the age difference between themselves and their victim.[63]

YOUTH WITH SLIGHT BOUNDARY ISSUES

Several of those who developed typologies indicated there is a group of offenders who only exhibited slight boundary issues in expressing their sexuality. Many of the youth, therefore, could be treated with short-term therapy based on developing appropriate boundaries. For example, O'Brien and Bera identified a group of youth, *naïve experimenters*, who usually engage in inappropriate touching of a younger child in the context of some sort of activity allowing privacy, such as camping or babysitting.[64] Weinrott also identified a group of those who need appropriate rules established for their sexual behavior. Again, this group includes offenders who inappropriately touch their victim.[65]

Several groups were also identified involving youth that had poorly developed social skills. One pair of researchers, for example, identified *undersocialized child exploiters*.[66] This group of offenders will often develop friendships with younger youth—playing games with them and relying on them for their own self-confidence. Eventually he sexually abuses the youth. Another researcher also identified *unusual/isolated* offenders who are described as socially awkward, having difficulties with the most basic social situation, such as introducing oneself.[67] Another pair of researchers also identified a group called *inadequate*, who are often introverted and usually have experienced childhood abuse.[68] It is clear that these youth with social deficits rely on children for sources of comfort and fulfilling their sexual needs in lieu of healthy relationships with those who are the same age as them. These youth therefore have not been properly socialized; perhaps this group of offenders has parents who are also socially ill-equipped or have not spent time socializing the youth.

Several researchers noted a group of youth who were involved in obsessive-compulsive, repetitive type behavior.[69] It usually involved hands-off offenses, such as exhibitionism—exposing one's self to another person. One researcher described them as having deviant sexual arousal.[70] This group of offenders, therefore, often exhibits fetishes—sexual attraction to inanimate objects (e.g., women's shoes or clothing items). These offenders are often provided with the same type of treatment as those with any other type of obsessive-compulsive behavior. Such treatment is usually short-term and highly effective.

YOUTH WITH PSYCHOLOGICAL PROBLEMS

Categories of youth who exhibit serious psychological problems were also identified. One researcher identified this group as *disturbed impulsives*, often having learning problems along with family dysfunction.[71] Another researcher also described a group of offenders who had psychopathic traits.[72] Thus, there is a group of offenders who show severe psychological problems, but again, this is only one group—not all sex offenders exhibit such problems.

ANTISOCIAL YOUTH

The term antisocial is usually used to describe those who are defiant, lack remorse, lack the ability to empathize, and often disregard rules.[73] It is important to note that not all youth who are antisocial commit sexual offenses; however, portions of those who commit sexual offenses exhibit antisocial characteristics. A pair of researchers identified a group of young sex offenders who scored high on antisocial characteristics.[74] Another researcher also identified a group of offenders who were described as antisocial.[75]

PSYCHOLOGICALLY NORMAL YOUTH

While it is hard to believe that anyone would use the word "normal" to describe a sex offender, researchers have found some sex offenders are relatively normal in regard to psychological maladies. One researcher[76] and subsequently, a group of researchers[77] administered different psychological examinations to a group of sex offenders and found they did not exhibit any unusual psychological characteristics. In fact, one researcher identified two of the four groups of sex offenders were relatively psychologically healthy as compared to the other two identified groups.[78] While these groups exhibit normal psychological factors, it is clear their behavior warrants psychological treatment.

YOUTH WHO EXPERIENCED PRIOR ABUSE

Several of the researchers included at least one group of offenders who had prior exposure to abuse.[79] For example, Oxnam and Vess indicated those who were *inadequate* were the most likely to have been exposed to previous abuse; however, Worling noted those who were *confident/aggressive* and *antisocial/impulsive* were the most likely among his sample to have experienced abuse. O'Brien and Bera describe a category of offenders, *pseudosocialized child exploiters*, who are also likely to have experienced prior abuse. This group often lacks remorse and has little to no insight into their behavior; they do not see their actions as abusive.

It is clear from all of the identifying features of the salient groups of offenders that many of the typologies overlap. It is possible, for example, that youth who experience prior sexual abuse can also fit into other categories. All of this information, although complicated, leads one to the simple conclusion that even among a small portion of the adolescent/young offenders, they vary a great deal in their characteristics and offending patterns. Such offenders should never be placed in a one-size-fits-all approach when attempting to provide treatment.

COMPARISON OF JUVENILE/YOUTH TYPOLOGIES TO ADULT TYPOLOGIES

In a recent review of all the typologies that have been created for sex offenders, it was noted that aside from typologies of adult males, there are typologies for juvenile sex offenders, female sex offenders, and cyber offenders.[80] Within each of those categories, additional subcategories exist. Thus, it shows that sex offenders are an extremely heterogeneous group. Some of the first typologies created were in fact for adult males, as they drew the most attention from the public after several cases of sexual abuse and murder were highly publicized in the 1980s and 1990s.

ADULT CLASSIFICATION

Most classification systems for adult males were broadly divided into rapists and child molesters. Rapists, by definition, typically sexually assault an adult. Rapists are also a heterogeneous group. Several identified subtypes of adult sex offenders include: *compensatory*, *sadistic*, and *power/control*. For example, someone who uses only as much force as necessary during the act to achieve sexual gratification is known as *compensatory rapists*. These types of rapists are often described as "gentleman rapists," denoting their behavior during the rape. They often feel inadequate and have a type of courtship disorder, meaning they are not able to initiate and maintain an intimate relationship with others.[81]

Sadistic rapists are often psychopaths; hallmarks of psychopaths include poor impulse control, manipulation, lack of empathy, and they do not experience guilt at the same levels others do (not to be confused with psychosis, which occurs when someone cannot distinguish between what is real and what is not [e.g., hallucinations and delusions]). They receive sexual gratification by torturing and eliciting fear from their victims. These types of rapists may eventually kill their victims after raping them, becoming serial rapist-murderers. While the compensatory and sadistic rapist have primary sexual motivations, the next two types do not have primary sexual motivations. Although they receive sexual gratification from the event, it is motivated by other factors.[82]

The *power/control* rapists, for example, have a strong desire to overpower and dominate their victim. They will often humiliate and degrade the victim. This offender usually has an angry disposition. Similarly, the *opportunistic rapist* usually engages in impulsive type behavior and the rape usually occurs while they are engaging in another offense. For example, he may break into someone's home to burglarize it, but realize there is someone home. He simply takes advantage of the situation by raping the unsuspecting victim.[83]

The other broad category of sex offenders is pedophiles. Unlike rapists, pedophiles are sexually attracted to children. There are two broad types of pedophiles: *fixated* and *regressed*. *Fixated offenders* have primary sexual interest in children; they usually do not find peer-age individuals attractive. Their attraction to children is persistent, usually never having an "appropriate" intimate relationship. This type of behavior typically emerges during their adolescence.[84]

Those who are regressed *pedophiles* typically have a normal sexual history. Sometimes they are even married or in committed relationships. The attraction to children is usually triggered by a stressful event, such as the loss of a friend or family member, or divorce. Typically the offenders have encountered an experience that leads to them doubting their own self-confidence. The abuse itself stems from a desire to meet sexual needs and the behavior usually doesn't appear until their adulthood.[85]

Several researchers have further classified several subtypes of pedophiles and rapists, which show the diverse range in behaviors and motivations for their actions. Additionally, many of the categories include similar factors as the juveniles (i.e., low self-esteem, inadequacies, inappropriate expression of sexual desires), many of the juvenile categories of sex offenders are dissimilar. We know that many adult sex offenders began their sexual deviancy during their adolescence, yet we have no clear evidence or research that shows which type of juvenile sex offender matures into which type of adult sex offender category.[86]

WHAT DO TYPOLOGIES TELL US ABOUT JUVENILE SEX OFFENDERS?

At the beginning of this chapter, a media report was presented of a teenage male who broke into an elderly woman's home and raped her. This case involved several serious factors: (1) he did not know his victim; (2) he committed breaking and entering to commit the rape; (3) he did not choose a victim who was younger, yet he still chose someone who was vulnerable (the victim was disabled); and (4) he used violence to commit the rape. While additional details were not presented that would allow someone to identify a specific category of juvenile sex offenders proposed in the typologies, we do know it involves one of the rape categories and not the molestation (or pedophile) categories. Also, most juvenile sex offenders do not use violence or force to commit their rape; this case included several "rare" features. Most media reports, in fact, include odd or unusual cases. This is an important fact to keep in mind; when we read the newspaper or hear a news report, we must keep in mind, the cases presented are not the usual or typical offender.

Also, the media report indicated the teenager was facing a long-term prison sentence and lifetime registration on a public sex offender registry. Given this, we know the consequences of committing such an offense impact the offender for the rest of his life. It becomes imperative, therefore, to identify and treat sexual deviance and that too, hopefully, before one escalates to such serious behavior.

While all of the typologies present shed a slightly different light on juveniles who sexually offend, they all reinforce the finding that sex offenders are a heterogeneous group of offenders; they differ in their social skills, levels of manipulation, choice of victims, family background, and types of sexual behavior. This does not necessarily mean all such offenders are extremely unique, but rather a middle ground should be found—there are several subsets of juvenile sexual offenders who share similar characteristics. Identifying commonalities is crucial. After juveniles are identified by their subset, treatment plans can be developed accordingly. For example, those who engage in less serious forms of deviancy (e.g., exposing one's self), require different treatment than those who break into one's house to commit rape.

NOTES

1. Miles Jackson, "Teen Sentenced to 10 Years for Sex Assault," *The Daily Journal*, September 22, 2007, 1.

2. R. Karl Hanson and Monique T. Bussière, "Predicting Relapse: A Meta-Analysis of Sexual Offender Recidivism Studies," *Journal of Consulting and Clinical Psychology* 66(2) (1998): 4–5.

3. R. Karl Hanson, "Introduction to the Special Section on Dynamic Risk Assessment with Sex Offenders," *Sexual Abuse: A Journal of Research and Treatment* 14(2) (2002): 99.

4. American Psychiatric Association, *Diagnostic and Statistical Manual of Mental Disorders*, Fourth Edition (Washington, DC: American Psychiatric Association, 1994), 649–650.

5. Michael O'Brien and Walter Bera, "Adolescent Sexual Offenders: A Descriptive Typology," *National Family Life Education Network* 1(3) (1986): 1–4; Robert Prentky, Bert Harris, and Sue Righthand, "An Actuarial Procedure for Assessing Risk with Juvenile Sex Offenders," *Sexual Abuse: A Journal of Research and Treatment* 12(2) (2000): 76.

6. Roger Graves et al., "Demographic and Parental Characteristics of Youthful Sexual Offenders," *International Journal of Offender Therapy and Comparative Criminology* 40(4) (1996): 305–306.

7. See genrally Paul Oxnam and James Vess, "A Personality-Based Typology of Adolescent Sexual Offenders Using the Million Adolescent Clinical Inventory," *New Zealand Journal of Psychology* 35(1) (2006).

8. O'Brien and Bera, "Adolescent Sexual Offenders: A Descriptive Typology," *National Family Life Education Network* 1(3) (1986): 1–4.

9. Ibid.

10. Ibid., 2.

11. Ibid.

12. Ibid., 2.

13. Ibid.

14. Ibid.

15. Ibid., 3.

16. Ibid.

17. Ibid.

18. Ibid.

19. American Psychiatric Association, *Diagnostic and Statistical Manual of Mental Disorders*, Fourth Edition, 649–650.

20. O'Brien and Bera, "Adolescent Sexual Offenders: A Descriptive Typology," 1–4.

21. Ibid., 3.

22. Ibid., 4.

23. American Psychiatric Association, *Diagnostic and Statistical Manual of Mental Disorders*, Fourth Edition, 422.

24. Ibid.

25. Melinda A. Stanley and Samuel M. Turner, "Current Status of Pharmacological and Behavioral Treatment of Obsessive-Compulsive Disorder," *Behavior Therapy* 26(1) (1995): 171.

26. O'Brien and Bera, "Adolescent Sexual Offenders: A Descriptive Typology," 4.

27. Ibid.

28. Ibid., 4.

29. Ibid.

30. Righthand and Welch, "Juveniles Who Have Sexually Offended: A Review of the Professional Literature," 13.

31. Prentky, Harris, Frizzell and Righthand, "An Actuarial Procedure for Assessing Risk with Juvenile Sex Offenders," 88.

32. Ibid., 76.

33. Ibid.

34. See generally James Worling, "Personality-Based Typology of Adolescent Male Sexual Offenders: Differences in Recidivism Rates, Victim Selection Characteristics, and Personal Victimization Histories," *Sexual Abuse: A Journal of Research and Treatment* 13(3) (2001): 150. Oxnam and Vess, "A Personality-Based Typology of Adolescent Sexual Offenders Using the Million Adolescent Clinical Inventory," 39.

35. Graves et al., "Demographic and Parental Characteristics of Youthful Sexual Offenders," 300–317.

36. Ibid.

37. American Psychiatric Association, *Diagnostic and Statistical Manual of Mental Disorders, Fourth Edition*, 527.

38. Graves et al., "Demographic and Parental Characteristics of Youthful Sexual Offenders," 305–311.

39. Ibid.

40. Ibid.

41. Righthand and Welch, "Juveniles Who Have Sexually Offended: A Review of the Professional Literature," 21–22.

42. Ibid.

43. Worling, "Personality-Based Typology of Adolescent Male Sexual Offenders: Differences in Recidivism Rates, Victim Selection Characteristics, and Personal Victimization Histories," *Sexual Abuse: A Journal of Research and Treatment* 13(3) (2001): 149–166.

44. The authors were referring to the following study: Wayne R. Smith and Caren Monastersky, "Assessing Juvenile Sexual Offenders' Risk for Reoffending," *Criminal Justice and Behavior* 13(2) (1986).

45. Worling, "Personality-Based Typology of Adolescent Male Sexual Offenders: Differences in Recidivism Rates, Victim Selection Characteristics, and Personal Victimization Histories," 149–166.

46. See generally: Kenneth Dodge et al., "Social Information-Processing Patterns Partially Mediate the Effect on Early Physical Abuse on Later Conduct Problems," *Journal of Abnormal Psychology* 104(4) (1995): 632; David Fergusson and Michael Lynskey, "Physical Punishment/Maltreatment during Childhood and Adjustment in Young Adulthood," *Child Abuse & Neglect* 21(7) (1997): 627–628.

47. Worling, "Personality-Based Typology of Adolescent Male Sexual Offenders: Differences in Recidivism Rates, Victim Selection Characteristics, and Personal Victimization Histories."

48. Ibid.

49. Oxnam and Vess, "A Personality-Based Typology of Adolescent Sexual Offenders Using the Million Adolescent Clinical Inventory," 36–44.

50. Ibid.

51. Ibid.

52. Ibid.

53. Peter Hummel, Volker Thomke, and Hartmut Oldenburger, "Male Adolescent Sex Offenders against Children: Similarities and Differences between Those Offenders with and Those without a History of Sexual Abuse," *Journal of Adolescence* 23(3) (2000): 313–314.

54. Becker, Cunningham-Rathner, and Kaplan, "Adolescent Sexual Offenders: Demographics, Criminal and Sexual Histories, and Recommendations for Reducing Future Offenses," *Journal of Interpersonal Violence* 1(4) (1987): 431–445.

55. Gail Ryan et al., "Trends in a National Sample of Sexually Abusive Youths," *Journal of the American Academy of Child and Adolescent Psychiatry* 35(1) (1996): 335–336.

56. Butler and Seto, "Distinguishing Two Types of Adolescent Sex Offenders," *Journal of American Child Adolescent Psychiatry* 41(1) (2002): 83–90.

57. Janis F. Bremer, "Serious Juvenile Sex Offenders: Treatment and Long-Term Follow-Up," *Psychiatric Annals* 22(6) (1992), as cited in L. Shi and J. Nicol, "Into the Mind of a Juvenile Sex Offender: A Clinical Analysis and Recommendation from an Attachment Perspective." *The American Journal of Family Therapy*, 35(5) (2007): 395.

58. Anna C. Salter, *Predators: Pedophiles, Rapists, and Other Sex Offenders* (New York: Basic Books, 2003), 26.

59. Butler and Seto, "Distinguishing Two Types of Adolescent Sex Offenders," 83–84.

60. Gina Robertiello and Karen Terry, "Can We Profile Sex Offenders? A Review of Sex Offenders Typologies," *Aggression and Violent Behavior* 12(5) (2007), 508.

61. Graves et al., "Demographic and Parental Characteristics of Youthful Sexual Offenders," 305–306.

62. O'Brien and Bera, "Adolescent Sexual Offenders: A Descriptive Typology," 3.

63. Robert Prentky et al., "An Actuarial Procedure for Assessing Risk with Juvenile Sex Offenders," *Sexual Abuse: A Journal of Research and Treatment* 12(2) (2000): 76.

64. O'Brien and Bera, "Adolescent Sexual Offenders: A Descriptive Typology," 2.

65. Righthand and Welch, "Juveniles Who Have Sexually Offended: A Review of the Professional Literature."

66. O'Brien and Bera, "Adolescent Sexual Offenders: A Descriptive Typology," 2.

67. Worling, "Personality-Based Typology of Adolescent Male Sexual Offenders: Differences in Recidivism Rates, Victim Selection Characteristics, and Personal Victimization Histories," 162–163.

68. Oxnam and Vess, "A Personality-Based Typology of Adolescent Sexual Offenders Using the Million Adolescent Clinical Inventory," 41.

69. Prentky, Harris, and Righthand, "An Actuarial Procedure for Assessing Risk with Juvenile Sex Offenders," 89.

70. Righthand and Welch, "Juveniles Who Have Sexually Offended: A Review of the Professional Literature," 22.

71. O'Brien and Bera, "Adolescent Sexual Offenders: A Descriptive Typology," 4.

72. Graves et al., "Demographic and Parental Characteristics of Youthful Sexual Offenders," 312.

73. American Psychiatric Association, *Diagnostic and Statistical Manual of Mental Disorders*, Fourth Edition, 649–650.

74. See generally Oxnam and Vess, "A Personality-Based Typology of Adolescent Sexual Offenders Using the Million Adolescent Clinical Inventory."

75. See generally Worling, "Personality-Based Typology of Adolescent Male Sexual Offenders: Differences in Recidivism Rates, Victim Selection Characteristics, and Personal Victimization Histories."

76. Ibid.

77. See generally Oxnam and Vess, "A Personality-Based Typology of Adolescent Sexual Offenders Using the Million Adolescent Clinical Inventory."

78. Worling, "Personality-Based Typology of Adolescent Male Sexual Offenders: Differences in Recidivism Rates, Victim Selection Characteristics, and Personal Victimization Histories," 161.

79. See generally O'Brien and Bera, "Adolescent Sexual Offenders: A Descriptive Typology"; Worling, "Personality-Based Typology of Adolescent Male Sexual Offenders: Differences in Recidivism Rates, Victim Selection Characteristics, and Personal Victimization Histories"; Oxnam and Vess, "A Personality- Based Typology of Adolescent Sexual Offenders Using the Million Adolescent Clinical Inventory."

80. Robertiello and Terry, "Can We Profile Sex Offenders? A Review of Sex Offenders Typologies," 508.

81. For a description of typologies, see generally Robertiello and Terry, "Can We Profile Sex Offenders? A Review of Sex Offenders Typologies."

82. Ibid.

83. Ibid.

84. Ibid.

85. Ibid.

86. Ibid.

REFERENCES

"5th-Graders Accused of Having Sex in Class." *Chicago Tribune*, April 5, 2007, 6.

Abel, Gene G., Candice A. Osborn, and Deborah A. Twigg. "Sexual Assault through the Life Span: Adult Offenders with Juvenile Histories." In *The Juvenile Sex Offender*, edited by Howard E. Barbaree, William S. Marshall, and Stephen M. Hudson. New York: The Guilford Press, 1993.

American Psychiatric Association. *Diagnostic and Statistical Manual of Mental Disorders, Fourth Edition*. Washington, DC: American Psychiatric Association, 1994.

Associated Press. "Woman, 19, Charged in Online Sex Ring." CBS News. http://www.cbsnews.com/stories/2007/07/12/national/printable3052371.shtml.

Bartholomew, Kim. "Avoidance of Intimacy: An Attachment Perspective." *Journal of Social and Personal Relationships* 7(2) (1990): 147–178.

Becker, Judith V. "Treating Adolescent Sexual Offenders." *Professional Psychology: Research and Practice* 21(5) (1990): 362–365.

Becker, Judith V., Jerry Cunningham-Rathner, and Meg S. Kaplan. "Adolescent Sexual Offenders: Demographics, Criminal and Sexual Histories, and Recommendations for Reducing Future Offenses." *Journal of Interpersonal Violence* 1(4) (1987): 431–445.

Brantlinger, Ellen. "Mildly Mentally Retarded Secondary Students' Information about and Attitudes toward Sexuality and Sexuality Education." *Education and Training of the Mentally Retarded* 20(2) (1985): 99–108.

Bremer, Janis F. "Serious Juvenile Sex Offenders: Treatment and Long-Term Follow-Up." *Psychiatric Annals* 22(6) (1992): 326–332.

Brownmiller, Susan. *Against Our Will: Men, Women, and Rape*. New York: Ballantine Books, 1975.

Bumby, Kurt M., and Nancy H. Bumby. "Adolescent Females Who Sexually Perpetrate: Preliminary Findings." Paper presented at the 12th Annual Research and Treatment Conference of the Association for the Treatment of Sexual Abusers, Boston, MA, 1993.

Bumby, Nancy H., and Kurt M. Bumby. "Adolescent Sexual Offenders." In *The Sex Offender: New Insights, Treatment, Innovations, and Legal Developments*, edited by K. B. Schwartz and R. H. Cellini, 10.1–10.16. Kingston, NJ: Civic Research Institute, Inc., 1997.

Burt, Martha R., and Rochelle Semmel Albin. "Rape Myths, Rape Definitions, and Probability of Conviction." *Journal of Applied Social Psychology* 11(3) (1981): 212–230.

Butler, Stephen, and Michael C. Seto. "Distinguishing Two Types of Adolescent Sex Offenders." *Journal of American Child Adolescent psychiatry* 41(1) (2002): 83–90.

Calley, Nancy. "Integrating Theory and Research: The Development of a Research-Based Treatment Program for Juvenile Male Sex Offenders." *Journal of Counseling and Development* 85(2) (2007): 131–142.

Chaiken, Jan, and Marcia R. Chaiken. *Varieties of Criminal Behavior*. Santa Monica, CA: Rand, 1982.

Chow, Eva W. C., and Alberto L. Choy. "Clinical Characteristics and Treatment Response to SSRI in a Female Pedophile." *Archives of Sexual Behavior* 31(2) (2002): 211–215.

CNN.com. "Letourneau Says She and Former Student Are Engaged," October 12, 2004.

Crawford, Selwyn. "Girl's 15-Year Sentence in Fort Worth Rape Case Called Harsh." *The Dallas Morning News*, January 13, 1995, 27A.

Davis, Glen E., and Harold Leitenberg. "Adolescent Sex Offenders." *Psychology Bulletin* 101 (1987): 417–427.

Denno, Deborah. "Considering Lead Poisoning as a Criminal Defense." *Fordham Urban Law Journal* 20(3) (1993): 377–400.

Denov, Myriam S. *Perspectives on Female Sex Offending: A Culture of Denial*. Burlington, VT: Ashgate Publishing Company, 2004.

Dodge, Kenneth, Gregory Pettit, John Bates, and Ernest Valente. "Social Information-Processing Patterns Partially Mediate the Effect on Early Physical Abuse on Later Conduct Problems." *Journal of Abnormal Psychology* 104(4) (1995): 632–643.

Edwards, Carla, and Rebecca Hendrix. "Traumagenic Dynamics in Adult Women Survivors of Childhood Sexual Abuse vs. Adolescent Male Sex Offenders with Similar Histories." *Journal of Offender Rehabilitation* 33(2) (2001): 33–45.

Fehrenbach, Peter A., and Caren Monastersky. "Characteristics of Female Adolescent Sexual Offenders." *American Journal of Orthopsychiatry* 58(1) (1988): 148–151.

Fehrenbach, Peter A., Wayne Smith, Caren Montastersky, and Robert W. Deisher."
Adolescent Sexual Offenders: Offenders and Offense Characteristics." *American Journal of Orthopsychiatry* 56(2) (1986): 225–231.

Fergusson, David, and Michael Lynskey. "Physical Punishment/Maltreatment during Childhood and Adjustment in Young Adulthood." *Child Abuse & Neglect* 21(7) (1997): 617–630.

Fromuth, Mary Ellen, and Victoria E. Conn. "Hidden Perpetrators: Sexual Molestation in a Nonclinical Sample of College Women." *Journal of Interpersonal Violence* 12(3) (1997): 456–465.

Gilby, Rhonda, Lucille Wolf, and Benjamin Goldberg. "Mentally Retarded Adolescent Sex Offenders. A Survey and Pilot Study." *Canadian Journal of Psychiatry* 34 (1989): 542–548.

Goldstein, Arnold. *The Psychology of Group Aggression*. Chichester, UK: John Wiley & Sons, 2002.

Goldston, Linda. "Children Who Molest Children: Today's Victims May Become the Aggressors of Tomorrow." *The Dallas Morning News*, June 23, 1987.

Graves, Roger, Kim Openshaw, Frank Ascoine, and Susan Ericksen. "Demographic and Parental Characteristics of Youthful Sexual Offenders." *International Journal of Offender Therapy and Comparative Criminology* 40(4) (1996): 300–317.

Gray, Alison, Aida Busconi, Paul Houchens, and William D. Pithers. "Children with Sexual Behavior Problems and Their Caregivers: Demographics Functioning, and Clinical Patterns." *Sexual Abuse: A Journal of Research and Treatment* 9(4) (1997): 267–290.

Groth, Nicholas A., and Jean H. Birnbaum. *Men Who Rape: The Psychology of the Offender*. New York: Plenum Press, 1979.

Haney, Craig, Burtis Banks, and Philip Zimbardo. "Interpersonal Dynamics in a Simulated Prison." *International Journal of Criminology and Penology* 1(1) (1973): 74–150.

Hanna, Janan. "Teen Rape Suspect Could Face Adult Trial." *Chicago Tribune*, January 14, 1998, 1.

Hanson, R. Karl. "Introduction to the Special Section on Dynamic Risk Assessment with Sex Offenders." *Sexual Abuse: A Journal of Research and Treatment* 14(2) (2002): 99–101.

Hanson, R. Karl, and Monique T. Bussière. "Predicting Relapse: A Meta-Analysis of Sexual Offender Recidivism Studies." *Journal of Consulting and Clinical Psychology* 66(2) (1998): 348–362.

Hart, Timothy C., and Callie Rennison. "Reporting Crime to the Police, 1992–2000." Washington, DC: U.S. Department of Justice, Bureau of Justice Statistics (2003).

Hawley, Clyde, and Robert Buckley. "Food Dyes and Hyperkinetic Children." *Academy Therapy* 10(1) (1974): 27–32.

Hetherton, Jacquie. "The Idealization of Women: Its Role in the Minimization of Child Sexual Abuse by Females." *Child Abuse and Neglect* 23(2) (1999): 161–174.

Hislop, Julia. *Female Sex Offenders: What Therapists, Law Enforcement and Child Protective Services Need to Know*. Washington: Issues Press, 2001.

Hummel, Peter, Volker Thomke, and Hartmut Oldenburger. "Male Adolescent Sex Offenders against Children: Similarities and Differences between Those Offenders with and Those without a History of Sexual Abuse." *Journal of Adolescence* 23(3) (2000): 305–317.

Hunter, John A. "Understanding Juvenile Sex Offenders: Research Findings and Guidelines for Effective Management and Treatment." In *Juvenile Justice Fact Sheet*. Charlottesville, VA: Institute of Law, Psychiatry, and Public Policy, 2000.

Hunter, John A., Judith V. Becker, Meg S. Kaplan, and D. W. Goodwin. "The Reliability and Discriminative Utility of the Adolescent Cognition Scale for Juvenile Sexual Offenses." *Annals of Sex Research* 4(3–4) (1991): 281–286.

Hunter, John A., Robert Hazelwood, and David Sleslinger. "Juvenile Perpetrated Sex Crimes: Patterns of Offending and Predictors of Violence." *The FBI Law Enforcement Bulletin* 69(3) (2000): 1–7.

Hunter, John A., Jr., L. J. Lexier, D. W. Goodwin, P. A. Browne, and C. Dennis. "Psychosexual, Attitudinal, and Developmental Characteristics of Juvenile Female Sexual Perpetrators in a Residential Treatment Setting." *Journal of Child and Family Studies* 2(4) (1993): 317–326.

Jackson, Miles. "Teen Sentenced to 10 Years for Sex Assault." *The Daily Journal*, September 22, 2007.

Johnson, Cori. "Student Acceptance of Rape Myths." In *Academy of Criminal Justice Services*. Cincinnati, OH, 2008.

Johnson, Toni Cavanagh. "Female Child Perpetrators: Children Who Molest Other Children." *Child Abuse and Neglect* 13(4) (1989): 571–585.

Knight, Raymond A., and Robert A. Prentky. "Exploring Characteristics for Classifying Juvenile Sex Offenders." In *The Juvenile Sex Offender*, edited by Howard E. Barbaree, William L. Marshall, and Stephen M. Hudson, 45–83. New York: Guilford Press, 1993.

Kubik, K. Elizabeth, Jeffrey E. Hecker, and Sue Righthand. "Adolescent Females Who Have Sexually Offended: Comparison with Delinquent Adolescent Female Offenders and Adolescent Males Who Sexually Offend." *Journal of Child Sexual Abuse* 11(3) (2002): 63–83.

Letourneau, Elizabeth J., Sonja K. Schoenwald, and Ashli J. Sheidow. "Children and Adolescents with Sexual Behavior Problems." *Child Maltreatment* 9(1) (2004): 49–61.

Lightfoot, Lynn O., and Howard E. Barbaree. "The Relationship between Substance Use and Abuse and Sexual Offending in Adolescents." In *The Juvenile Sex Offender*, edited by Howard E. Barbaree, William L. Marshall, and Stephen M. Hudson. New York: The Guilford Press, 1993.

Marshall, W. L., and A. Eccless. "Issues in Clinical Practice with Sex Offenders." *Journal of Interpersonal Violence* 6(1) (1991): 68–93.

Marshall, William. "Intimacy, Loneliness, and Sexual Offenders." *Behavior Research and Therapy* 27(5) (1989): 491–503.

Marshall, William L., Stephen M. Hudson, and Sharon Hodkinson. "The Importance of Attachment Bonds in the Development of Juvenile Sex Offending." In *The Juvenile Sex Offender*, edited by Howard E. Barbaree, William L. Marshall, and Stephen M. Hudson. New York: The Guilford Press, 1993.

Mathews, Ruth, J. A. Hunter, Jr., and Jacqueline Vuz. "Juvenile Female Sexual Offenders: Clinical Characteristics and Treatment Issues." *Sexual Abuse: A Journal of Research and Treatment* 9(3) (1997): 187–199.

Mathews, Ruth, Jane Kinder Matthews, and Kathleen Speltz. *Female Sexual Offenders: An Exploratory Study*. Brandon, VT: The Safer Society Press, 1989.

Mathis, James L. *Clear Thinking about Sexual Deviations: A New Look at an Old Problem*. Chicago, IL: Nelson-Holt, 1972.

Mayer, Adele. *Women Sex Offenders*. Holmes Beach, FL: Learning Publications, Inc., 1992.

McCarty, Loretta M. "Investigation of Incest: Opportunity to Motivate Families to Seek Help." *Child Welfare* 60 (1981): 679–689.

McGuire, R., J. Carlisle, and B. Young. "Sexual Deviations as Conditioned Behaviour: A Hypothesis." *Behaviour Research and Therapy* 2 (1965): 185–190.

Moffitt, Terrie E. "Adolescence-Limited and Life-Course-Persistent Antisocial Behavior: A Developmental Taxonomy." *Psychology Review* 100(4) (1993): 674–701.

Muir, Grant, Kimberly Lonsway, and Diana Payne. "Rape Myth Acceptance among Scottish and American Students." *The Journal of Social Psychology* 136(2) (1996): 261–262.

National Center for Child Abuse and Neglect. "Study Findings: National Study of Incidence and Severity of Child Abuse and Neglect," edited by NCCAN. Washington, DC: DHEW, 1981.

National Task Force on Juvenile Sexual Offending. *Juvenile and Family Court Journal*, 1993.

O'Brien, Michael, and Walter Bera. "Adolescent Sexual Offenders: A Descriptive Typology." *National Family Life Education Network* 1(3) (1986): 1–4.

Oxnam, Paul, and James Vess. "A Personality-Based Typology of Adolescent Sexual Offenders Using the Million Adolescent Clinical Inventory." *New Zealand Journal of Psychology* 35(1) (2006): 36–44.

Parks, Gregory A., and David E. Bard. "Risk Factors for Adolescent Sex Offender Recidivism: Evaluation of Predictive Factors and Comparison of Three Groups Based upon Victim Type." *Sexual Abuse: A Journal of Research and Treatment* 18(4) (2006): 319–342.

Pavlov, Ivan. *Conditioned Reflexes*. Oxford: Clarendon Press, 1927.

Peterson, Zoe, and Charlene Muehlenhard. "Was It Rape? The Function of Women's Rape Myth Acceptance and Definitions of Sex in Labeling Their Own Experiences." *Sex Roles* 51(3–4) (2004): 129–144.

Piquero, Alex R. "Assessing the Relationships between Gender, Chronicity, Seriousness, and Offense Skewness in Criminal Offending." *Journal of Criminal Justice* 28(2) (2000): 103–115.

Prentky, Robert, Bert Harris, Kate Frizzell, and Sue Righthand. "An Actuarial Proce-dure for Assessing Risk with Juvenile Sex Offenders." *Sexual Abuse: A Journal of Research and Treatment* 12(2) (2000): 71–93.

Prentky, Robert, Bert Harris, and Sue Righthand. "An Actuarial Procedure for Assess-ing Risk with Juvenile Sex Offenders." *Sexual Abuse: A Journal of Research and Treatment* 12(2) (2000): 71–93.

Rachmen, S. "Sexual Fetishisms: An Experimental Analogue." *Psychological Record* 16(3) (1966): 293–296.

Ray, Jo Ann, and Diana J. English. "Comparison of Female and Male Children with Sexual Behavior Problems." *Journal of Youth and Adolescence* 24(4) (1995): 439–451.

Righthand, Sue, and Carlann Welch. "Juveniles Who Have Sexually Offended: A Re-view of the Professional Literature," 1–59. Washington, DC: Office of Juvenile Justice and Delinquency Prevention, 2001.

Robertiello, Gina, and Karen Terry. "Can We Profile Sex Offenders? A Review of Sex Offenders Typologies." *Aggression and Violent Behavior* 12(5) (2007): 508–518.

Rosencrans, Bobbie. *The Last Secret: Daughters Sexually Abused by Mothers.* Orwell, VT: Safer Society Press, 1997.

Rowe, William, Sandra Savage, Mark Ragg, and Kay Wigle. *Sexuality and the Devel-opmentally Handicapped: A Guidebook for Health Care Professionals.* New York: Edwin Mellen, 1987.

Ryan, Gail. "The Families of Sexually Abusive Youth." In *Juvenile Sexual Offending*, edited by Ryan Gail and Sandy Lane, 136–154. San Francisco, CA: Jossey-Bass, 1997.

———. "Theories of Etiology." In *Juvenile Sexual Offending,* edited by Gail Ryan and Sandy Lane, 19–58. San Francisco, CA: Jossey-Bass, 1997.

Ryan, Gail, Thomas J. Miyoshi, Jeffrey L. Metzner, Richard D. Krugman, and George E. Fryer. "Trends in a National Sample of Sexually Abusive Youths." *Journal of the American Academy of Child and Adolescent Psychiatry* 35(1) (1996): 17–25.

Salter, Anna. *Treating Child Sex Offenders and Victims: A Practical Guide.* Newbury Park, CA: Sage, 1988.

Salter, Anna C. *Predators: Pedophiles, Rapists, and Other Sex Offenders.* New York: Basic Books, 2003.

Sarrel, Phillip M., and William H. Masters. "Sexual Molestation of Men by Women." *Archives of Sexual Behavior* 11(2) (1982): 117–131.

Scavo, Rebecca, and Bruce D. Buchanan. "Group Therapy for Male Adolescent Sex Of-fenders: A Model for Residential Treatment." *Residential Treatment for Children and Youth* 7(2) (1989): 59–74.

Schoenthaler, Stephen, and Walter Doraz. "Types of Offenses Which Can Be Reduced in an Institutional Setting Using Nutritional Intervention." *International Journal of Biosocial Research* 4(2) (1983): 74–84.

Schultz, Pamela. *Not Monsters: Analyzing the Stories of Child Molesters.* Oxford: Rowman & Littlefield Publishers, Inc., 2005.

Shi, Lin, and Jason Nichol. "Into the Mind of a Juvenile Sex Offender: A Clinical Analysis and Recommendation from an Attachment Perspective." *The American Journal of Family Therapy* 35(5) (2007): 395–402.

Smallbone, Stephen W., and Lynley Milne. "Associations between Trait Anger and Aggression Used in the Commission of Sexual Offenses." *International Journal of Offender Therapy and Comparative Criminology* 44(5) (2000): 606–617.

Smith, Wayne R., and Caren Monastersky. "Assessing Juvenile Sexual Offenders' Risk for Reoffending." *Criminal Justice and Behavior* 13(2) (1986): 115–140.

Stanley, Melinda A., and Samuel M. Turner. "Current Status of Pharmacological and Behavioral Treatment of Obsessive-Compulsive Disorder." *Behavior Therapy* 26(1) (1995): 163–186.

Steele, Brandt, and Gail Ryan. "Deviancy: Development Gone Wrong." In *Juvenile Sexual Offending*, edited by Gail Ryan and Sandy Lane, 59–76. San Francisco, CA: Jossey-Bass, 1997.

Stermac, Lana, and Frederick Matthews. "Issues and Approaches to the Treatment of Developmentally Disabled Sexual Offenders." In *The Juvenile Sex Offender*, edited by Howard E. Barbaree, William L. Marshall, and Stephen M. Hudson. New York: The Guilford Press, 1987.

Stermac, Lana, and Peter Sheridan. "The Developmentally Disabled Adolescent Sex Offender." In *The Juvenile Sex Offender*, edited by Howard E. Barbaree, William L. Marshall, and Stephen M. Hudson. New York: The Guilford Press, 1993.

Syed, Fariya, and Sharon Williams. "Case Studies of Female Sex Offenders." Ottawa, ON: Correctional Service of Canada, 1996.

Sykes, Gresham, and David Matza. "Techniques of Neutralization: A Theory of Delinquency." *American Sociological Review* 22(6) (1957): 664–670.

Tardif, Monique, Nathalie Auclair, Martine Jacob, and Julie Carpentier. "Sexual Abuse Perpetrated by Adult and Juvenile Females: An Ultimate Attempt to Resolve a Conflict Associated with Maternal Identity." *Child Abuse & Neglect* 29(2) (2005): 153–167.

Thornhill, Randy, and Craig T. Palmer. *A Natural History of Rape: Biological Bases of Sexual Coercion*. Cambridge, MA: The MIT Press, 2000.

Trivers, Robert. "Parental Investment and Sexual Selection." In *Sexual Selection and the Descent of Man, 1881–1971*, edited by B. Campbell. Chicago: Aldine, 1972.

Turner, Marcia T. *Female Adolescent Sexual Abusers: An Exploratory Study of Mother-Daughter Dynamics with Implications for Treatment*. Brandon, VT: The Safer Society Press, 1994.

U.S. Department of Justice. *Uniform Crime Reports, 2005*. Washington, DC: Government Printing Office, 2006.

Vandiver, Donna M, Kelly A. Cheeseman, and Robert Worley. "A Qualitative Assessment of Registered Sex Offenders: Characteristics and Attitudes toward Registration." Paper presented at the Annual Meeting of the Southwestern Association of Criminal Justice, Fort Worth, TX, 2006.

Vandiver, Donna M. "A Prospective Analysis of Juvenile Male Sex Offenders: Characteristics and Recidivism Rates as Adults." *Journal of Interpersonal Violence* 21(5) (2006): 673–688.

———. "Female Sex Offenders." In *Sex and Sexuality*, edited by Richard D. McAnulty and M. Michele Burnette, 47–80. Westport, CT: Praeger, 2006.

Vandiver, Donna M., and Jeremy Braithwaite. "Juvenile Female Sex Offenders: A Longitudinal Study of Recidivism Rates." Paper presented at the Annual Meeting of the American Society of Criminology, Atlanta, GA, 2007.

Vandiver, Donna M., and Glen Kercher. "Offender and Victim Characteristics of Registered Female Sexual Offenders in Texas: A Proposed Typology of Female Sexual Offenders." *Sexual Abuse: A Journal of Research and Treatment* 16(2) (2004): 121–137.

Vandiver, Donna M., and Raymond Teske, Jr. "Juvenile Female and Male Sex Offenders: A Comparison of Offender, Victim, and Judicial Processing Characteristics." *International Journal of Offender Therapy and Comparative Criminology* 50(2) (2006): 148–165.

Vick, Jennifer, Ruth McRoy, and Bobbie Matthews. "Young Female Sex Offenders: Assessment and Treatment Issues." *Journal of Child Sexual Abuse* 11(2) (2002): 1–23.

Waite, Dennis, Adrienne Keller, Elizabeth L. McGarvey, Edward Wieckowski, Relana Pinkerton, and Gerald L. Brown. "Juvenile Sex Offender Re-Arrest Rates for Sexual, Violent Nonsexual and Property Crimes: A 10-Year Follow-Up." *Sexual Abuse: A Journal of Research and Treatment* 17(3) (2005): 313–331.

Weinrott, Mark. "Juvenile Sexual Aggression: A Critical Review," 91–103. Portland, OR: Center for the Study and Prevention of Violence, 1996.

Welldon, Estele V. *Mother, Madonna, Whore: The Idealization and Denigration of Motherhood.* London: Free Association Book, 1988.

Williams, George. *Adaptation and Natural Selection.* Princeton: Princeton University Press, 1966.

Witt, Philip H., Jackson T. Bosley, and Sean P. Hiscox. "Evaluation of Juvenile Sex Offenders." *The Journal of Psychiatry & Law* 30 (2002): 569–592.

Woodhams, Jessica. "Characteristics of Juvenile Sex Offending against Strangers: Findings from a Non-Clinical Study." *Aggression Behavior* 30(3) (2004): 243–253.

Worling, James. "Personality-Based Typology of Adolescent Male Sexual Offenders: Differences in Recidivism Rates, Victim Selection Characteristics, and Personal Victimization Histories." *Sexual Abuse: A Journal of Research and Treatment* 13(3) (2001): 149–166.

WSBTV.com. "3 Young Boys Arrested in Rape Case." Action News 2, WSBTV, November 19, 2007.

Zgourides, George, Martin Monto, and Richard Harris. "Correlates of Adolescent Male Sexual Offense: Prior Adult Sexual Contact, Sexual Attitudes, and Use of Sexually Explicit Materials." *International Journal of Offender Therapy and Comparative Criminology* 41(3) (1997): 272–283.

Zolondek, Stacey O., Gene G. Abel, William F. Northey, and Alan D. Jordan. "The Self-Reported Behaviors of Juvenile Sex Offenders." In *Sexual Deviance*, edited by Christopher Hensley and Richard Tewksbury. Boulder, CO: Lynne Rienner Publishers, Inc., 2003.

5

Unusual Populations of Juvenile Sex Offenders: Females, Developmentally Disabled, and Very Young Sex Offenders

Five 5th Graders, ages 11 to 13, face charges after authorities said four of them had sex in front of other students in an unsupervised classroom. The three boys and two girls were arrested Tuesday at the Spearsville school in rural north Louisiana authorities said. They said one of the boys was posted as the lookout for teachers during the March 27th incident (*Chicago Tribune*, April 5, 2007).[1]

The above media report of a sexual incident leaves one with more questions than answers. For example, was this normal experimentation or was it in fact sexual abuse. Also, questionable, what role did the females have—were they victims or were they consenting partners? Perhaps such stories pique our curiosity and raise more questions than answers. We will cover the most up-to-date research findings in this chapter to answer some of the questions regarding female sex offenders. Additionally, other special populations of juvenile sex offenders are examined, such as those who are very young (i.e., younger than twelve), and those who have developmental disabilities. These groups of juvenile sex offenders are in fact an oddity in that they make up a very small portion of this population of sex offenders. This particular chapter, therefore, should not leave one with the impression that sexual abuse is so pervasive that a large number of girls, those younger than twelve, and those with developmental disabilities, commit such offenses. Rather, one should recognize that such populations rarely commit sexual offenses.

JUVENILE FEMALE SEX OFFENDERS

While it is difficult to imagine any young person sexually abusing another, it is even more difficult to imagine a young girl sexually abusing someone. The truth is—it is not very common. The Federal Bureau of Investigation (FBI) estimates juvenile girls accounted for only 60 of the 14,924 (less than 1 percent) rape perpetrators reported to the police in 2005. Additionally, girls only accounted for 1,000 of the 48,112 (2 percent) other sexual offenses committed by juveniles.[2] Although sexual abuse is often underreported to the police and difficult to prosecute,[3] most experts agree that females simply do not comprise a substantial portion of sex offenders.[4]

Additional sources of information also indicate the number of young female juveniles who sexually offend is rather low. Even though it was not until the 1980s that studies began to appear on the topic, those studies reveal a similar trend: there aren't very many sex offenders who are juvenile and female. One of the most recognizable names in child abuse and sexual abuse research is David Finkelhor. In the early 1980s, he and a colleague reassessed two prior studies to assess the extent of (adult and juvenile) females who commit sexual offenses. They concluded 13 percent of sexual abusers were female and that number may be too high.[5] Thus, the numbers of females, juvenile and adult, who sexually abuse is relatively low. Most, if not all, experts agree that adult men make up the majority of sex offenders.

Another research study included a survey of slightly more than 500 female college students at a southeastern college.[6] The anonymous survey included questions about prior sexual behavior and attitudes. From the results it was estimated that 4 percent (twenty-two of the women) reported an incident that meets the criteria for sexual molestation. Only 2 percent reported sexual fantasies involving young girls and only 3 percent reported sexual fantasies involving young boys. This study is important in that it included information *not* reported to the police. One may argue (and rightfully so) that we cannot place a great deal of weight on the FBI's numbers, because they do not include the full scope of sexual abuse. Individual research projects have shown that sexual abuse by young females is relatively low.

How can a female abuse a male?

Many may believe it is virtually impossible for a female to rape a male; as one author asked, "What harm can be done without a penis?"[7] Lacking a penis, therefore, would theoretically lend one powerless to sexually abuse another person. Sexual abuse, however, is not limited to the typical scenario of a stranger leaping from a heavily wooded area to hold a woman down while he forces her to have sex with him. Sexual abuse includes both rape and molestation. With regard to molestation, it is well known that sexual abuse often occurs under the veil of slowly eroding personal boundaries until a victim allows someone to touch him or her inappropriately. It is in fact possible for a young female to talk a (usually younger) victim into cooperating into sexual behavior. The term grooming is often used to describe this process of an offender slowly gaining the trust and confidence of their victim. For example, an offender may begin by establishing a friendship where the two spend time together. Over time, they engage in different games or activities in which the offender touches the victim—perhaps just tickling them. The behavior eventually escalates to the point where the victim allows the offender to touch their private parts. While the following example includes an adult male rather than a juvenile, it shows how a child can be groomed.

> *When a person like myself wants to obtain access to a child, you don't just go up and get the child and sexually molest the child. There's a process of obtaining the child's friendship and, in my case, also obtaining the family's friendship and their trust. When you get their trust, that's when the child becomes vulnerable, and you can molest the child. . . . As far as the children goes, they're kind of easy. You befriend them. You take them places. You buy them gifts . . . Now in the process of grooming the child, you win his trust and I mean, the child has a look in his eyes—it's hard to explain—you just have to kind of know the look. You know when you've got that kid. You know when that kid trusts you.*[8]

There are many cognitive barriers one must overcome in order to recognize girls' capacity to engage in sexual deviance. While it is relatively easy for anyone to believe a boy may engage in sexual deviancy, it is not so easy for someone to believe a girl may do the same. There are many stereotypes regarding sexually appropriate behavior for both girls and boys and most include a passive female and an aggressive female. A therapist who studied the barriers of acknowledging females who sexually offended made the following note:

> *I had reached a point in my work where I naively thought I had seen and heard everything, and that nothing that a client disclosed could possibly surprise me. All of this changed when one of my clients disclosed that he had been sexually abused by his mother. I had never before heard of sexual abuse by women and that the training that I received in both social work and criminology had never mentioned or even insinuated that women could be perpetrators of sexual abuse . . . I sought out more experienced professionals for information and advice on the topic . . . Many of the professionals I consulted not only questioned whether it was possible for a woman to commit a sexual offense, but also questioned whether sexual abuse by a woman would be harmful to the victim.*[9]

The therapist later came to the conclusion that a female can in fact sexually abuse and many, even those in social work, hold stereotypes about men and women preventing them from recognizing such behavior. For example, she states it is "apparent that female sex offending challenges traditional sexual scripts concerning 'appropriate' female behaviour."[10] This is evident in examining the laws regarding sexual abuse. Although many states have reworded their laws to include gender-neutral terms where the offender and the victim can be either male or female, the FBI still recognizes rape very narrowly: "the carnal knowledge of a female, forcibly and against her will." It is evident the definition assumes only females could be victims of rape; one may claim it indirectly assumes the offender can only be male.

Sexual abuse by a female can involve a wide range of behavior. Their behavior, for example, may be only passive. For example, the Fort Worth Bureau of *The Dallas Morning News* reported a fourteen-year-old girl lured a seventeen-year-old friend to an apartment where she knew four gang members were waiting to rape her.[11] The girl received a fifteen-year sentence for her role in the rape. It has also been found that female juveniles engage in more active abuse, such as touching the victim's genital, kissing, and hugging (in a sexual manner), oral-genital contact, and sexual intercourse.[12] Thus, while their role may be ancillary in some cases, there are cases in which their role is much more involved. For example, a juvenile who sexually offended described molesting her nine-year-old nephew:

> *The sexual abuse started when I was raped. I never told anyone what happened, and I exploded at times. I began to take it out on [the victim]. It began with touching his penis, then it led to oral sex . . . He would be playing with cards, Legos or listening to music . . . I would then reach over . . . would put my hands inside his pants, then I'd ask him to take his pants off. He would. I would ask him to lay down. He would. I would then suck on his penis. He would get scared and tense. He would get an erection, but no ejaculation or orgasm.*[13]

These cases present two very different situations. It shows that the role girls have in sexual offenses can range in very active participation to just assisting in a rape by having no physical contact with the victim, yet remain instrumental in the commission of the rape or molestation.

In another case, a woman also described a very active role in molesting a boy and a girl when she was fifteen years old. The boy was someone whom she babysat and when he misbehaved she pushed him and "began rubbing up and down on top of him."[14] She said she stopped when she realized what she was doing. Later, however, she was removed from her mother's home to stay with her aunt. She was jealous of her cousin, Sarah. She said that she "had mixed feelings about [Sarah]" and she described what she did to Sarah:

> *When I felt bad, I started to touch Sarah's breasts and vagina and she'd touch mine. It began three months after I moved in and happened when alone with her, babysitting. I'd be nice to her and ask her to scratch my back. If she didn't do what I asked, I'd hit her. I would guide her hand when I wanted her to touch me.*[15]

The molestation included kissing, vaginal finger penetration, and sucking on breasts. The abuse lasted for almost two years and ceased only when the offender was removed from the home.

Most would agree these cases do in fact involve sexual abuse perpetrated by a girl. In order to recognize such abuse, one must challenge their own assumptions about gender role expectations for girls and boys. It takes a certain degree of introspection to admit we all have assumptions about what is and is not appropriate based on the person's gender, but most would agree after reading these cases that girls are in fact capable of molestation.

RESEARCH ON JUVENILE FEMALE SEX OFFENDERS

Because the number of juvenile females is relatively low, only about a dozen of studies have been conducted specifically on this subgroup of sex offenders and each of those studies includes only a small number of offenders, making it difficult to draw conclusions about all juvenile females who sexually offend. Studying this subgroup of offenders poses a unique problem: in order to produce accurate results, at least thirty are needed for a sample. Because so few commit these types of offenses, however, it becomes practically impossible for a researcher to find that many girls who have committed sexual offenses. The studies that have been done, however, do provide a snapshot of what we currently know about young girls who sexually offend. There are a few studies that include fewer than thirty girls and there are several of those studies that include sample sizes between thirty and sixty-seven.[16] The case studies often provide more details of specific cases and the cases with more than thirty girls are helpful in providing information about the range of behavior and general characteristics of this group of offenders.

Age & Race. The average age of females who sexually offend is approximately fourteen or fifteen years old.[17] In the study asking college women about their previous sexual behaviors, and of the twenty-two who sexually offended, the majority of offenses occurred between the ages of ten and fourteen. Thus, these studies indicate juvenile girls who sexually abuse, usually do so in their early teen years.

With regard to race, most of the juvenile girls are Caucasian, with only a small portion including minority races.[18] Official data sources, such as the FBI's Uniform Crime Report, also reports that most sex offenders (regardless of juvenile or adult status) are Caucasian. It is not known whether sex offenders are more prevalent among Caucasians or whether Caucasians are more likely to report such offenses to the police. It is known that most offenders choose victims who are of the same race as themselves, which means if Caucasians were more likely to report being victimized, it would make sense that most of the offenders are Caucasian as well.

Prior Sexual Victimization: The Most Prevalent Characteristic. Prior sexual victimization has been identified as the most prevalent characteristic defining this group of sex offenders.[19] Several studies reveal that more than half of the victims were sexually victimized prior to committing the abuse. A study of twenty-eight girls found that half reported a history of being sexually abused.[20] In another sample of eleven child sex offenders who were in the custody of the Department of Corrections, 64 percent reported sexual victimization.[21] Of the twenty-two college students who reported molesting when they were younger, 70 percent reported they were sexually abused as a child.[22] Another found that 78 percent of the sixty-seven girls were sexually abused.[23] Another reported that 94 percent of thirty-four girls were sexually abused.[24] All of these ten girls, examined in an in-patient facility, were sexually abused.[25] There was one study, however, which reported only 10 percent were identified as being either sexually or physically abused.[26] The findings with this study are not consistent with the finding of the majority of the studies. It is concluded, therefore, that a substantial portion of juvenile girls who sexually abuse were in fact victims of sexual abuse.

What are the Circumstances of Females Who Sexually Abuse? With regard to young girls who sexually abuse, it is problematic for anyone to imagine (1) that a young person can sexually offend and (2) that a sex offender could be female. Many, however, have heard of adult females who sexually abuse. For example, there was a great deal of attention received by Mary Kay Latournou, a Seattle teacher who had a sexual relationship with her sixth grade student, Vili Fualaau.[27] Despite being jailed for six months for this crime, she proceeded to have two children with the young boy and after he reached the age of twenty-one, the two married. This was not the only case of a teacher having sex with a child. Debra LaFave, in Florida, was also convicted of having sex with a student. Researchers of adult female sex offenders have noted this is one of the most common types of situations of sexual abuse when the perpetrator is a female.[28] Given that this is what we know about adult women who sexually offend, it can be said such situations do not apply to juvenile girls who sexually offend. While there is no typology or formal typologies specific to only juvenile girls, there is anecdotal evidence that many of the young girls who sexually offend do so in the context of babysitting.[29]

Recently, in an examination of adult sex offenders, two researchers[30] noted that the type of women who were having sex with their students, a category previously identified as *teacher-lover*,[31] may be too narrow a description. The researchers later provided a case study where a woman who was not a teacher, but worked at a youth facility, reported details of abusing a teenage boy.[32] While this type of sex offender may not be directly applicable to describing juvenile girls who engage in sexual abuse, a similar category may exist where a juvenile girl abuses someone whom she is babysitting. Several researchers have reported girls in their study who abused in the context of a babysitting situation.[33] For both juveniles and adults, the girls/women assume some sort of caretaking role and use that situation to gain access to the victim. While as an adult, there are feelings that the perpetrator describes, such as love, belongingness, et cetera. However, for juveniles, it may simply be an extension of experimenting with one's sexuality.

Another situation that has been identified is incest, particularly with a juvenile girl abusing a younger sibling. Most studies of juvenile females show high rates of abusing a relative. In one study that included twenty-two girls who had sexually abused, 70 percent molested a family member. The victim was typically younger than the offender, between the ages of five and seven. The victims included primarily male cousins and siblings. One of the hallmarks of this study is that it did not involve a sample of girls in treatment; it included a sample of college students who were asked about their previous sexual experiences.[34]

It is highly likely that babysitter and incestual abuse are not the only circumstance or likely situations involving juvenile female perpetrators, yet these are the clearly identified situations outlined in previous research efforts. The media has reported other incidents where females are involved as accomplices to rape where they have assisted another person (male) by setting up a situation where a victim can be raped. As noted in the earlier mentioned Dallas Fort Worth, newspaper, a girl led her friend to an apartment where she knew she would be raped as a part of a gang initiation.[35] Another situation reported in the news involved girls recruiting others for prostitution. The *Associated Press* reported the following:

> *A 19-year-old woman faces federal charges of recruiting minors for prostitution, af-*
> *ter some teenage girls told investigators she was actively recruiting clients for a sex*
> *ring she allegedly operated out of a motel where she worked. Investigators believe [the*
> *offender] . . . advertised in the "erotic services" section of the Web site Craigslist.org, and*
> *more recently on the "Live Links" telephone chat line, according to a statement by [an]*
> *FBI agent . . . [the] Police Detective started the investigation in December after a girl*
> *who allegedly worked for [the offender] confided in him. "I work at one of the schools, so*
> *the victim felt pretty comfortable in talking to me about what was going on" . . . It kind of*
> *snowballed on the state level, and it turned into a federal investigation once we found that*
> *the Internet was used and that the victims were underage . . . The offender[the mother of*
> *a 14-month-old girl] was charged June 14 in federal court with recruiting minors for a*
> *prostitution ring . . . According to the court documents and statement [from others] that*
> *the offender was recruiting high school girls to work for her as prostitutes at a town house*
> *she rented in Burnsville.*[36]

While the accused in this situation did not engage in a "hands-on" offense in the victim's exposure to sexual abuse, her role was in fact an active one in orchestrating the sexual interaction. It was likely in the course of prostitution that these girls were encouraged to have sex with older men. Due to their status as juveniles, this likely constitutes sexual molestation.

CRIMINAL JUSTICE INVOLVEMENT AND RESPONSE

Most juvenile females are rarely reported to the police. The fact is, regardless of the gender of the offender, sexual abuse is one of the least reported offenses to the police. One measure of sexual offenses that is not based on police reports is the National Crime Victimization Survey (NCVS). This survey involves a large sample of people from across the United States. It involves a large survey of whether those who are twelve years or older have been victims of all types of crimes, including sexual offenses. Information from this source and other individual studies show that only one-third of sexual assault victims report it to the police.[37] The problem is even worse for those who are molested by a female. NCVS shows that 32 percent of those who are molested by a male report the incident, compared to only 13 percent when the perpetrator is female.[38] No reliable sources were found to assess the reporting rates when the offender is both female and juvenile.

Most of the research conducted shows formal involvement of the criminal justice system is nonexistent or minimal. For example, one team of researchers found that none of the twenty-two girls who molested someone were reported to the police.[39] As noted earlier, however, many of the research efforts have relied upon a clinical sample. Additionally, as researchers note, females who sexually abuse are often presented to the treatment center as in need of psychological/psychiatric assistance (as opposed to needing the attention of law enforcement).[40]

In an examination of those who were registered sex offenders in Texas, it was shown that the females were most likely to receive a probation sentence.[41] Approximately three-fourths of that sample (of sixty-one) received probation and the other one-fourth were placed in a residential facility. Most received a sentence requiring slightly less than three years of supervision (either on probation or at the residential facility).

WHO ARE THE VICTIMS OF YOUNG FEMALE SEXUAL OFFENDERS?

Young females who sexually abuse typically have between two to three identifiable victims. Again, an attempt to measure the true extent of their abuse is very difficult, if not impossible, to ascertain. The victims are almost always a friend or relative; rarely are strangers victimized. This has substantial implications: people should not be fearful that their child would be attacked and sexually abused by a stranger. The girls who commit such offenses do not target strangers. Thus, if a juvenile female sexually victimized someone, it is likely they have close contact with the offender.[42]

The victims are often even younger than the offender. Prior research indicates almost all of the victims were under the age of twelve and their average age is usually between five and eight.[43] What this means is that these young girls often choose a victim who is younger than herself—and usually much younger.

Why Would a Female Sexually Abuse? In one of the first public acknowledgments that females could be the perpetrators of sexual abuse, it was noted that a motivating factor was not sexual gratification.[44] While this may be hard to grasp, as a sexual offense is in fact "sexual," other motives have been identified, such as dysfunctional families,[45] negative emotions (e.g., loneliness, revenge, and anger),[46] and prior sexual abuse.[47]

Poor family structure and support appear to be common denominators in many of the cases of young female sexual abuse. Many of the young females who sexually abused in one study had families in which the caretakers have only a modicum of information about sexual issues; they have difficulty in expressing feelings associated with their sexual desire. In many instances the mother discusses her own sexual desires with her young daughter(s). The mother often has successive relationships with different males and sexually molests her daughter when no male is present. These types of behavior may be linked to the young female later sexually abusing.[48]

Another more specific explanation that has been explored is an attempt for the girls to resolve a conflict associated with maternal identity.[49] This explanation has its roots in psychological theory. In an examination of fifteen juvenile female sex offenders and thirteen adult female sex offenders, evidence was found to support this notion. It was found 93 percent of the adults had a maternal link with their victim; the victims were their daughters, sons, nephews, or nieces. Also 60 percent of the juvenile females reported a strained relationship with their mother. In many of these cases the juveniles may choose a younger sibling to focus their aggression toward. Approximately three-quarters (73 percent) of the juveniles reported their parents separated, abandoned, or died during their childhood. Approximately half (47 percent) had no contact with their father. Seventy-eight percent were sexually abused before the age of twelve, and most of those were by an uncle. The authors who explored this theory relied on prior research[50] that proposed incestuous relationships occur when a rival child is perceived by the aggressor as somehow responsible for a deprivation that persists. The mother holds a unique power over the child. Perhaps the abuse is a way to retaliate.

Anger and jealously have been recognized as possible motivators in one study. Many of the young sex offenders abused a sibling who had not been abused previously and was described as the "favored" child in the family. This type of behavior may be explained as a way to get back at her parents. The sexual abuse, therefore, appeared to be a way these young sex offenders express anger.[51]

One of the most commonly explored theories about why someone engages in sexual abuse is that perhaps they were abused themselves. This theory is often called the cycle of violence theory. It poses that when someone is the victim of sexual abuse they will often experience a host of negative feelings and consequences. Later, that individual trying to make sense of the behavior somehow tries to identify with his or her abuser and engage in the same behavior by abusing someone else. This theory was initially very popular. Also, it is easier for society to address this individual. Most people, for example, are OK with the notion of treating a "victim" of sexual abuse as opposed to an "offender."[52] Thus, if this person can be thought of as a victim, we can move past what they have done and treat them as a person, rather than an offender.

Support for this theory has not been strong. It was found that many sexual offenders claimed to have been victims of such abuse, but when offenders were given a polygraph, the number of victims-turned-victimizer dramatically reduced.[53] One could draw the conclusion that many offenders claimed to have been abused to gain sympathy from those around them. Research regarding whether the cycle of violence theory can be applied to young females has not been tested. The research that has been done on this group of offenders suggests the theory should be looked at further. Several studies have shown many of the juvenile girls were sexually abused as children. While each study differs in how they measure this, most include substantial documentation of such abuse. The rate of sexual abuse is extremely high, with most studies reporting anywhere from approximately 70 percent to 100 percent of the young girls were sexually abused.[54] Also, when female juveniles who sexually offended were compared to those who had not sexually offended, those who sexually offended were much more likely to have reported being the victims of sexual abuse. While it is possible that the cycle of violence theory may not apply to all sex offenders, it may be a significant factor for juvenile females.

An alternative explanation of the cycle of violence theory, aside from the psychological process that occurs, is that perhaps when someone is abused, and they are particularly young, it is a learned behavior. The offender is simply acting out her own sexual abuse.[55] Young children assume this is an act of love and caring. When they want to express such feelings to someone else, perhaps a younger sibling, they will engage in such behavior. It has also been found in some cases the child identifies with the aggressor.[56] This explanation is possibly a plausible one, especially when very young children act out sexually. Most children prior to reaching puberty do not normally engage in behaviors seeking sexual stimuli. A noted expert in sexual abuse described such instances: "I'm treating a little 4-year-old now who was anally raped . . . He gets a 3-year-old down on the floor and tries to repeat the same thing. And this is very common, especially the younger the child, and the less able they are to really understand or make sense of what happened to them . . . "[57]

It has also been reported that in many of the families of the juvenile female sex offender, sexual abuse is pervasive and may engage in the behavior on a younger sibling because it is inevitable they will be abused. If the juvenile female sex offender is the abuser, the abuse may be less severe as compared to being victimized by an older member of the family.[58]

Are They Just Mentally Ill? Intuitively, it could be presumed these girls who engage in sexual abuse must suffer from mental illness. This conclusion, however, is only partly true. To fully assess this question, researchers must rely on a representative sample—that is, the sample must include those in the general population and not just those who are known to be mentally ill. If one went to a mental health facility and assessed which of the young girls had molested someone, all of the girls would have a mental health problem. They would not have been included in the sample if they did not have a mental health problem. Most of the studies on adolescent sex offenders have in fact relied on clinical or mental health samples. The studies that show high rates of mental illness among this group of offenders typically have relied on a clinical sample. Thus, most studies do show a high rate of mental illness, yet those studies relied upon a mental health population initially.

One interesting point to many of those studies is that the types of mental illness one may suspect—psychosis—is simply not prevalent. Psychosis refers to having a break with reality, meaning the person cannot distinguish between what is real and not real, usually characterized by delusions (false thoughts) or hallucinations (seeing things that are not real). The type of mental illness these girls exhibit includes mood disorders and personality disorders. One study, for example, revealed that half of the approximately seventy girls were diagnosed with posttraumatic stress disorder (PTSD) and the other half suffered from some sort of mood disturbance such as depression and/or anxiety.[59] Posttraumatic stress disorder (PTSD) is typically the result of witnessing atrocious events, such as killing in wars or witnessing genocide; however, therapists have also found those who suffered severe abuse also suffer from PTSD. Other studies have also reported high rates of anxiety, depression, and PTSD.[60]

A more accurate measurement of mental illness includes an assessment of those who have molested to those who have not. It was reported in one study (relying on a college sample) that there were no significant differences between the abusers and non-abusers with regard to psychological adjustment.[61] Thus, while much of the research has identified high rates of mental illness, it may simply be because most studies have relied upon clinical samples.

Family Background. Another common finding among juvenile girls who sexually offend is that they come from dysfunctional families and are exposed to other risk factors. It has been found, for example, that adolescents who have been exposed to violence between the parents are often involved in illegal behaviors themselves.[62] The mother has often been found to have poor boundaries, suffer from depression and low self-esteem, and exhibit dependent personalities.[63] The mother often abused drugs while their biological father was described as volatile, emotionally and physically abusive, and emotionally distant from the family. Physical and sexual abuse was also prevalent in many of these families.[64]

Male/Female Differences. Females who sexually offend do not necessarily mirror their male counterparts. Research has found substantial differences between these two groups of sexual offenders. Several studies show that girls were younger than the boys when they committed sexual offenses. Usually the age difference was about a year or two. For example, one study revealed girls were 11.6 years of age and the boys were 13.2.[65] Girls were much more likely to be younger than twelve years old when compared to the boys. If girls are offending at younger ages, this may again provide evidence that girls are being sexually victimized and acting out more so than their male counterparts. This, however, would need to be tested to support this claim.

The age that someone begins such abuse is a critical factor. Many criminological theorists contend that while many juveniles and young adults engage in some form of deviance and/or criminality, they typically age out of such behavior.[66] For those who begin offending at a very young age, before their teens, they are likely to persist such behavior throughout their life. While tests of whether this applies to sexual crime has not been well-tested, it can be presumed that those who begin sexually offending at a young age are in need of treatment in order to reduce repeated sexual abuse.

Girls are more likely than males to have experienced sexual abuse. For example, one study found the juvenile females who sexually offended had an average of 4.5 people who had sexually abused them compared to males who reported only 1.4 persons, on average, who had sexually abused them.[67] Also, the abuse usually began earlier for girls. Approximately 64 percent of the girls were abused before the age of five compared to only 26 percent of the boys. Other studies have reported similar findings,[68] indicating this finding is more likely than not to be true.

Girls were far more likely than their male counterparts to exhibit behavior problems.[69] Girls were significantly more likely to exhibit temper tantrums while under agency supervision. They were also more likely to steal and be truant from school. Girls were also more likely than the boys to be treated as victims.

One may presume that the abuse that young girls engage in just isn't as serious as young boys. This isn't necessarily so—studies show that girls have just as many victims (an average of three). Additionally, the type of sentences males and females received has been found to be comparable[70] suggesting their crimes are comparable. The only exception to this is that males received a slightly longer sentence on average than their female counterparts.

Continued Behavior? No research has been published on whether juvenile girls who engage in sexual molestation are likely to continue such behavior into their adulthood. One study, not yet published, however, indicates girls who commit sexual offenses when they are juveniles, may not necessarily continue such behavior after they reach adulthood. The study was presented at a national criminal justice conference in 2007 and was conducted by one of the authors of this book and her colleague (Donna Vandiver and Jeremy Braithwaite).[71] The study included all female sex offenders who were registered in Texas as of April 27, 2001, and had committed a sexual offense when they were younger than seventeen. At that time, sixty-one met this criterion. The cohort was followed for an average of five years after they turned seventeen years old, which is adult status in Texas. Of all of the females, only three were re-arrested for a sexual offense; however, almost half (46 percent) were arrested for a nonsexual offense. A few conclusions can be drawn from these findings, but first some of the limitations of this study need to be noted.

Personally, I am always skeptical when someone tells me how low risk sex offenders are—those people or studies usually support such claims by citing their low arrest rates. Using arrest rates as a measure of continued sexual behavior happens to be one of the weakest measures. Why is this? Well, sexual offenses are rarely reported to law enforcement and when they are, arrests must be preceded by a moderate degree of support. Unfortunately, sexual offenses often leave behind little evidence, especially if the victim waits any length of time before reporting the abuse. We also know that most victims know their offenders and often fear retaliation. Thus, many sexual offenses never result in an arrest and are not included in official government statistics.

So why do we include such measures—why not use other measures? Unfortunately, there are few other ways to measure recidivism. The primary use of such numbers, however, should not be used to determine the true number of recidivists, but rather to gain information from those whom we know have been re-arrested. If we can assess those who are re-arrested, then information or critical characteristics can be identified that indicate a propensity to continue offending.

The findings from this study showed few were re-arrested for a sexual offense and almost half were re-arrested for a nonsexual offense. This indicates that when a juvenile is arrested for a sex offense, they have a high likelihood of continued (nonsexual) offending. The behavior should not be ignored or thought of as "normal deviance" during their developmental stage of adolescence. Intervention is critical.

Anecdotal evidence also shows that girls who sexually abused someone when they were younger do not grow up to continue such abuse. In fact, in one study, it was found that the sexual abuse they engaged in when they were young was a one-time incident.[72]

Another way to assess whether those who commit sex offenses as juveniles and continue on in their adulthood is to look at the female adult sexual offenders and assess whether they began offending as juveniles. There is anecdotal evidence of adult female sex offender who report sexually abusing when they were juveniles. For example, one woman who was convicted for sexual assaulting two young girls she was babysitting described an earlier sexual molestation when she was still a teenager, eighteen years old:

Her first victim was the 4-year-old daughter of a friend. Ms. A had become sexually aroused while watching adult, heterosexual pornographic videos with her adult boyfriend earlier in the evening. While bathing the 4-year-old girl, she became further aroused by the touching of the girl. After the bath, she took the girl into a bedroom, spread her legs, and licked the child's vaginal area for a few minutes. This was sexually gratifying to [the offender]. She recalled the girl squirmed around in the bed, but she did not believe that the child resisted her actions. She then returned to the living room and engaged in sexual intercourse with her boyfriend . . . [the boyfriend] was not aware of, and did not participate in her sexual acts with the child.[73]

The truth is that not enough research exists to fully answer the question of whether juvenile girls who sexually offend continue to abuse. Initial studies show that those who sexually abuse may not necessarily continue such behavior, yet more research is needed to support this claim. It may be presumed, however, juvenile females who sexually offend are more likely to have run-ins with the law after they reach adulthood.

How Harmful is Sexual Abuse by a Juvenile Female? As a professor and a sex offender researcher, one of the most common reactions that I receive when I mention girls or women who sexually abuse is that the victim must have been "lucky." Recently, in a class of forty undergraduate college students, I discussed a case where a female had sex with a younger teenage boy and I heard one student giggle and say "man he must have been lucky." Evidence from within the treatment community indicates even professionals focus more so on male on female abuse rather than female on male/female abuse.[74] However, evidence exists that shows those who experience sexual abuse suffer emotionally for years afterward.[75]

One case study report included a sister-brother incest case involving a fourteen-year-old girl who began molesting her ten-year-old brother; the abuse occurred for two years.

She stimulated him manually and orally and then inserted his penis into her vagina. At first he only felt frightened and did not understand what was happening. She usually threatened to beat him or attack him with a knife if he told anyone. He does not recall if he ejaculated. He was too frightened to tell his parents.[76]

Later his sister went to a psychiatric treatment; the victim later became suicidal and he too was placed in psychiatric treatment. He married later and entered treatment when he was unable to consummate his marriage.

This case study indicates sexual abuse by an adolescent female, although both are young, can still have a negative impact on the victim for years to come. The abused ten-year-old carried the emotional burden into his adulthood, affecting his relationship with his wife. While it is not known if all victims suffer such emotional turmoil, it cannot be ruled out.

In addition to the effects experienced by the victim, secondary victims also exist. This includes the effects felt by family members.[77] The family of the offender can be affected emotionally, socially, and even financially. In addition to these effects, society bears the burden in most instances of absorbing the costs of incarceration, if in fact the offender is incarcerated. The entire community is affected because that offender lives in someone's neighborhood; they are also someone's classmate when they return to school. A large number of people can be affected by one incident of sexual abuse.

Are Juvenile Females Different from Adult Females Who Sexually Abuse?
There is some evidence that the characteristics of adult females are similar to juvenile females who sexually offend. Approximately seven individual and groups of researchers have created a typology of adult female sex offenders[78] and several categories exist that may apply to some of the descriptions of juvenile females who have sexually offended. It should be noted, however, that no typologies have been developed specifically for juvenile sex offenders. This is likely due to the relatively small samples of such offenders. In order to develop a typology, a fairly large sample is needed.

In the adult female typologies, two separate teams of researchers have identified a group of offenders who sexually abuse those that they are babysitting.[79] Such incidents have also been found among the juvenile female population.[80] All but one of the researchers who developed an adult typology identified a category of offenders who offends with another person. This included a variety of combinations, such as male-female offenders and females acting with a family member and females acting with a nonfamily member. Although females acting with another female were identified, a female acting with a male partner was the more common combination. With regard to the juvenile females, a female acting with a male (or group of males) was found when a young girl coaxed her friend to a certain location to be sexually abused by gang members as part of their initiation.[81]

Most of the researchers, six of the seven, reported a type of offender who offends against a family member (i.e., incest).[82] A prevalent characteristic among this group was being sexually abused themselves. Sexual victimization among juvenile female sex offenders was actually described as one of most distinguishing characteristics of this group.

Two researchers identified a group of adult females who were described as "criminal," exhibiting antisocial behavior, and having a high number of arrests and re-arrests. This category may be applicable to some of the juveniles, given that some of the girls showed acting out behaviors, inability to succeed in school, and having antisocial tendencies.

One researcher identified a group of adult females who were psychologically disturbed and had a substantial history of emotional problems.[83] As noted earlier, few exhibited psychotic episodes, but many had a history of personality disorders, such as posttraumatic stress disorder.

There were two broadly identified categories in the adult female samples that do not necessarily apply to juveniles. Several of those who developed a typology included a category of a woman raping a man or another woman. The victim is usually raped after they are physically constrained or threatened.[84] The incident could be described as a stereotypical rape that occurs in reverse: a woman, without any notice, attacks a man or woman and forces herself upon the victim. One researcher, however, suggested that the act was motivated by anger.[85] While, anger has been identified as a motivating factor for juveniles, it is difficult to compare this group of women to juvenile girls. Additionally, another category of women offenders that was identified includes women with homosexual tendencies who molest a child.[86]

VERY YOUNG (MALE AND FEMALE) SEX OFFENDERS

The average or typical age of the females in these studies shows us that the girls are usually around the age of fourteen or fifteen. Incidents, however, involving younger offenders have been brought to the attention of the public by the media. While these cases are by no means common, they do exist. In the following news report, three young boys in Georgia were accused of rape.

Police say they've arrested three young boys on charges they kidnapped and raped an 11-year-old-girl in the woods near an Acworth apartment complex. Police say the boys—who are 8 and 9 years old—are in a Cobb County youth detention center but could face adult criminal charges. "Reportedly two 9-year-old boys and one 8-year-old boy took the girl into the woods against her will where she was raped," said Capt. Wayne Bennard of the Acworth Police Department. Police reports show the girl went to authorities Saturday for the alleged attack, which she says happened Thursday. The victim told police they had been playing outside the West Ridge Apartments before the attack. She told her mother the boys forced her into the woods after threatening her with a rope. The girl told her mother about the alleged attack on Saturday. "When she started telling me I didn't know how to react," said the victim's mother. "I was shocked, I didn't expect it," "It's unbelievable they're starting at such a young age now," she added. You would think something like that at 14, 13; maybe a teenager, but their ages is really bothering me." The suspects are being held at the Cobb County Youth Detention Center. "The three boys have been charged with crimes ranging from rape, sexual assault, kidnapping and false imprisonment," said Bennard. "The reaction is dismay." The father of one of the suspects told WSB-TV Channel 2 Action News his son denies the rape happened. "Word had got back to her parents what she did and she hanged her story around and said she was raped," said Brandon LeBlanc. "That's when they took her to the hospital and get rape kit and that's why they interrogating all these boys on these charges." Prosecutors had not received the case report from police on Monday, nor had they decided whether to try the suspects as adults. "That decision hasn't been made," Said Kathy Watkins, a spokeswoman for the Cobb County District Attorney's office. She had no further comment.[87]

Given that this incident involved an alleged offense, it is difficult to say what actually happened and whether someone as young as eight years old is capable of committing rape. It could perhaps be a false accusation or it could be that the three young boys held the girl against her will and raped her. If that is in fact the case, it brings up so many questions, such as whether the defendants should face adult charges. It is difficult to imagine an eight-year-old and two nine-year-olds facing such serious charges. There are relatively few cases of very young male offenders included in empirical research studies. Also, we could only find one study including involving very young female sex offenders.

One such study focused on sex offender treatment program for child perpetrators, which included thirteen female offenders between the ages of four and thirteen.[88] It is difficult for anyone to imagine someone as young as four engaging in aggressive sexual behavior; this, however, was the case. All of the girls in the reported study met strict criteria that excluded normal child-play (i.e., "I'll show you mine if you show me yours"). In fact, an eight-year-old adopted girl, Jenny, had intercourse with her nine-year-old brother, also adopted. Regarding the interview, a clinician made the following statements:

Jenny was a highly sexualized and manipulative child whose thoughts and actions were pervaded by sexual themes. She masturbated frequently and openly and frequently attempted to touch the genitals of adults and children around her. Mark, with whom she had intercourse, was a passive, dependent, and frightened child, who stated in the interview, "If I didn't do what she wanted, she would get mad at me. She would make faces at me, wouldn't talk to me, and would look so sad. I didn't want to do it [have intercourse] because I knew it was wrong and our parents would be mad.[89]

Additionally, some of the cases involved excessive force. In the following note, the use of force is evident:

Four girls who were cousins participated in the abuse of the brother of one of the girls. The male child was 18 months old. They restrained him and orally copulated him. The abuse was so severe that he required medical attention.[90]

In the above example, the young girls had been abused themselves and were forced to have oral sex with their father or uncle.

While it is not typical for girls to sexually abuse prior to puberty, such case studies show that it is not impossible for very young girls to begin abusing young. In all of these cases, the young girls had experienced pervasive sexual abuse.[91] Additionally, all of them molested a younger sibling, unless they did not have a younger sibling. Thus, only those without siblings molested someone other than a sibling.

JUVENILE OFFENDERS (MALE AND FEMALE) WITH DEVELOPMENTAL DISABILITIES

Very few studies have been conducted on juveniles with developmental disabilities who have sexually offended.[92] In fact only one study and one book chapter could be found on the topic.[93] It has been found, however, that 21 percent of those in treatment for developmental disabilities had sexual related problems;[94] while this does not tell us how many juveniles with developmental disabilities in and out of treatment sexually offend, it does provide an indication that the number is at least equal to nondevelopmentally disabled juveniles.

The one study conducted on this group of sex offenders was conducted in 1989.[95] The developmentally disabled sex offenders were more likely to engage in "inappropriate, non-assaultive 'nuisance' behaviors such as public masturbation exhibitionism and voyeurism"[96] when compared to nondevelopmentally disabled juveniles who engaged in sexual offenses. Additionally, the disabled group was less discriminating in their choice of sexual partner by choosing both same-sex and opposite-sex partners, and adult and child victims. The disabled group was also less likely to engage in other forms of delinquency when compared to the nondisabled group.

Although developmentally disabled juvenile sex offenders show some similar deficits as nondisabled juvenile sex offenders (i.e., lack of sexual knowledge, poor anger control, sexual impulsivity,[97] poor social and assertiveness skills,[98] low self-esteem, social isolation, and deviant sexual arousal patterns).[99] Those with developmental disabilities are four times more likely than the nondisabled to have been sexually abused.[100] Additionally, those with a disability lack a solid foundation of sexual knowledge.[101] Another disadvantage this group is faced with is the lack of an outlet to express themselves sexually. For instance, many of those with a developmental disability are not encouraged to date, marry, or express their sexual needs.[102]

WHAT DO WE KNOW ABOUT SPECIAL POPULATIONS OF SEX OFFENDERS?

We know most sex offenders are adult and male; however, very small proportions are young females. In fact, juvenile females account for less than 10 percent of the known sex offender population. With regard to the young females, we know some are very young. Those who work at treatment facilities have found female offenders to be as young as four years old. Two of the most pervasive features of young and juvenile females are that they have likely been victims of sexual abuse prior to becoming offenders and they often come from dysfunctional families. The context in which the victims abuse includes babysitter abuse, incest, and some engage in hands-off offenses, assisting in a rape or recruiting others for prostitution. These girls often exhibit behavior problems and experience depression. There are relatively few studies specifically conducted on female sex offenders and none have been published regarding whether young girls who sexually offend grow up to be adult sex offenders. Preliminary reports indicate rather low numbers.

We also know there are similarities between the characteristics of juvenile sex offenders and the typologies of adult female sex offenders. For example, both have sexually offended in the context of a caretaking or mentor-type role (i.e., babysitting and teacher-student relationship). Both groups, also, have certain offenders who have chosen family members as victims, exhibited criminal characteristics, and exhibited severe emotional problems. The research in this field is in fact developing. There are still a substantial number of questions about this particular group of offenders.

In addition to juvenile females, there is also another group of offenders that make up another small proportion of sex offenders, those with developmental disabilities. It has been shown that those with a developmental disability are no more likely to sexually offend than their nondevelopmentally disabled counterparts. While this group was no more likely than those without a developmental disability to have social deficits, they were more likely to engage in public masturbation, yet they were less discriminatory in their victim choices. This group is at a substantial disadvantage in that their opportunities to express themselves is sexually is limited.

All of these groups pose unique problems to the treatment professionals. Their needs and motivations for sexually offending differ from other sex offenders; thus, treatment geared toward the "typical" sex offender does not necessarily apply to this group of offenders. Treatment guidelines and criminal justice responses must take into consideration the special needs of these groups in order to prevent additional victims.

NOTES

1. "5th-Graders Accused of Having Sex in Class," *Chicago Tribune*, April 5, 2007, 6.

2. U.S. Department of Justice, *Uniform Crime Reports, 2005* (Washington, DC: Government Printing Office, 2006).

3. Jacquie Hetherton, "The Idealization of Women: Its Role in the Minimization of Child Sexual Abuse by Females," *Child Abuse and Neglect* 23(2) (1999): 163.

4. National Center for Child Abuse and Neglect (1981), as cited in: Toni Cavanagh Johnson, "Female Child Perpetrators: Children Who Molest Other Children," *Child Abuse and Neglect* 13(4) (1989).

5. Ibid., 571.

6. Mary Ellen Fromuth and Victoria E. Conn, "Hidden Perpetrators: Sexual Molestation in a Nonclinical Sample of College Women," *Journal of Interpersonal Violence* 12(3) (1997): 456–465.

7. Julia Hislop, *Female Sex Offenders: What Therapists, Law Enforcement and Child Protective Services Need to Know* (Washington, DC: Issues Press, 2001), 11.

8. Anna C. Salter, *Predators: Pedophiles, Rapists, and Other Sex Offenders* (New York: Basic Books, 2003), 42.

9. Myriam S. Denov, *Perspectives on Female Sex Offending: A Culture of Denial* (Burlington, VT: Ashgate Publishing Company, 2004), ix.

10. Ibid., 5.

11. Selwyn Crawford, "Girl's 15-Year Sentence in Fort Worth Rape Case Called Harsh," *The Dallas Morning News*, January 13, 1995, p. 27A.

12. Fromuth and Conn, "Hidden Perpetrators: Sexual Molestation in a Nonclinical Sample of College Women," 460.

13. Ruth Mathews, Jane Kinder Matthews, and Kathleen Speltz, *Female Sexual Offenders: An Exploratory Study* (Brandon, VT: The Safer Society Press, 1989), 17.

14. Ibid., 18.

15. Ibid.

16. See generally: Ibid. (Sample size = 67), Jo Ann Ray and Diana J. English, "Comparison of Female and Male Children with Sexual Behavior Problems," *Journal of Youth and Adolescence* 24(4) (1995) (Sample size = 34); Donna M. Vandiver and Raymond Teske, Jr., "Juvenile Female and Male Sex Offenders: A Comparison of Offender, Victim, and Judicial Processing Characteristics," *International Journal of Offender Therapy and Comparative Criminology* 50(2) (2006): 148–165 (Sample size = 61).

17. See generally: Nancy. H. Bumby and Kurt M. Bumby, "Adolescent Sexual Offenders," in *The Sex Offender: New Insights, Treatment, Innovations, and Legal Developments*, ed. Barbara K. Schwartz and Henry R. Cellini (Kingston: Civic Research Institute, Inc., 1997); Peter A. Fehrenbach et al., "Adolescent Sexual Offenders: Offenders and Offense Characteristics," *American Journal of Orthopsychiatry* 56(2) (1986); John A. Hunter, Jr., et al., "Psychosexual, Attitudinal, and Developmental Characteristics of Juvenile Female Sexual Perpetrators in a Residential Treatment Setting," *Journal of Child and Family Studies* 2(4) (1993); Elizabeth J. Letourneau, Sonja K. Schoenwald,

and Ashli J. Sheidow, "Children and Adolescents with Sexual Behavior Problems," *Child Maltreatment* 9(1) (2004); Mathews, Hunter, and Vuz, "Juvenile Female Sexual Offenders: Clinical Characteristics and Treatment Issues"; Vandiver and Teske, "Juvenile Female and Male Sex Offenders: A Comparison of Offender, Victim, and Judicial Processing Characteristics."

18. See generally: Johnson, "Female Child Perpetrators: Children Who Molest Other Children"; Letourneau, Schoenwald, and Sheidow, "Children and Adolescents with Sexual Behavior Problems"; Ray and English, "Comparison of Female and Male Children with Sexual Behavior Problems"; Mathews, Hunter, and Vuz, "Juvenile Female Sexual Offenders: Clinical Characteristics and Treatment Issues"; Vandiver and Teske, "Juvenile Female and Male Sex Offenders: A Comparison of Offender, Victim, and Judicial Processing Characteristics."

19. Jennifer Vick, Ruth McRoy, and Bobbie Matthews, "Young Female Sex Offenders: Assessment and Treatment Issues," *Journal of Child Sexual Abuse* 11(2) (2002): 3.

20. Peter A. Fehrenbach and Caren Monastersky, "Characteristics of Female Adolescent Sexual Offenders," *American Journal of Orthopsychiatry* 58(1) (1988): 150.

21. Elizabeth K. Kubik, Jeffrey E. Hecker, and Sue Righthand, "Adolescent Females Who Have Sexually Offended: Comparison with Delinquent Adolescent Female Offenders and Adolescent Males Who Sexually Offend," *Journal of Child Sexual Abuse* 11(3) (2002): 71.

22. Fromuth and Conn, "Hidden Perpetrators: Sexual Molestation in a Nonclinical Sample of College Women," 460.

23. Mathews, Hunter, and Vuz, "Juvenile Female Sexual Offenders: Clinical Characteristics and Treatment Issues," 191–192.

24. Ray and English, "Comparison of Female and Male Children with Sexual Behavior Problems," 442.

25. Hunter et al., "Psychosexual, Attitudinal, and Developmental Characteristics of Juvenile Female Sexual Perpetrators in a Residential Treatment Setting," 321.

26. Letourneau, Schoenwald, and Sheidow, "Children and Adolescents with Sexual Behavior Problems," 56.

27. CNN.com, "Letourneau Says She and Former Student Are Engaged," October 12, 2004, n.p.

28. See generally: Mathews, Hunter, and Vuz, "Juvenile Female Sexual Offenders: Clinical Characteristics and Treatment Issues"; Donna M. Vandiver, "Female Sex Offenders," in *Sex and Sexuality*, ed. Richard D. McAnulty and M. Michele Burnette (Westport, CT: Praeger, 2006).

29. Mathews, Hunter, and Vuz, "Juvenile Female Sexual Offenders: Clinical Characteristics and Treatment Issues," 188, 95.

30. Donna M. Vandiver and Glen Kercher, "Offender and Victim Characteristics of Registered Female Sexual Offenders in Texas: A Proposed Typology of Female Sexual Offenders," *Sexual Abuse: A Journal of Research and Treatment* 16(2) (2004): 123.

31. Mathews, Hunter, and Vuz, "Juvenile Female Sexual Offenders: Clinical Characteristics and Treatment Issues," 32–33.

32. Donna M. Vandiver, Kelly A. Cheeseman, and Robert Worley, "A Qualitative Assessment of Registered Sex Offenders: Characteristics and Attitudes toward Registration." Paper presented at the Annual Meeting of the Southwestern Association of Criminal Justice, Fort Worth, TX, 2006), n.p.

33. Mathews, Hunter, and Vuz, "Juvenile Female Sexual Offenders: Clinical Characteristics and Treatment Issues," 195; Fehrenbach and Monastersky, "Characteristics of Female Adolescent Sexual Offenders," 150.

34. Fromuth and Conn, "Hidden Perpetrators: Sexual Molestation in a Nonclinical Sample of College Women," 456–465.

35. Crawford, "Girl's 15-Year Sentence in Fw Rape Case Called Harsh," 1.

36. Associated Press, "Woman, 19, Charged in Online Sex Ring," CBS News, http://www.cbsnews.com/stories/2007/07/12/national/printable3052371.shtml.

37. Timothy C. Hart and Callie Rennison, "Reporting Crime to the Police, 1992–2000," Washington, DC: U.S. Department of Justice, Bureau of Justice Statistics (2003), 1.

38. Ibid.

39. Fromuth and Conn, "Hidden Perpetrators: Sexual Molestation in a Nonclinical Sample of College Women," 459.

40. Ray and English, "Comparison of Female and Male Children with Sexual Behavior Problems," 446.

41. Vandiver and Teske, "Juvenile Female and Male Sex Offenders: A Comparison of Offender, Victim, and Judicial Processing Characteristics," 148–165.

42. Kurt M. Bumby and Nancy H. Bumby, "Adolescent Females Who Sexually Perpetrate: Preliminary Findings." Paper presented at the 12th Annual Research and Treatment Conference of the Association for the Treatment of Sexual Abusers, Boston, 1993), n.p. Ray and English, "Comparison of Female and Male Children with Sexual Behavior Problems," 439–451, Johnson, "Female Child Perpetrators: Children Who Molest Other Children," 571–585.

43. See generally: Vandiver and Teske, "Juvenile Female and Male Sex Offenders: A Comparison of Offender, Victim, and Judicial Processing Characteristics"; Fehrenbach et al., "Adolescent Sexual Offenders: Offenders and Offense Characteristics"; Fromuth and Conn, "Hidden Perpetrators: Sexual Molestation in a Nonclinical Sample of College Women"; Johnson, "Female Child Perpetrators: Children Who Molest Other Children"; Hunter et al., "Psychosexual, Attitudinal, and Developmental Characteristics of Juvenile Female Sexual Perpetrators in a Residential Treatment Setting."

44. See generally: Nicholas A. Groth and Jean H. Birnbaum, *Men Who Rape: The Psychology of the Offender* (New York: Plenum Press, 1979); Johnson, "Female Child Perpetrators: Children Who Molest Other Children."

45. Johnson, "Female Child Perpetrators: Children Who Molest Other Children," 579, 81–82.

46. Mathews, Hunter, and Vuz, "Juvenile Female Sexual Offenders: Clinical Characteristics and Treatment Issues," 196.

47. Daniel Salter et al., "Development of Sexually Abusive Behavior in Sexually Victimised Males: A Longitudinal Study," *The Lancet* 361 (2003): 471–476.

48. Johnson, "Female Child Perpetrators: Children Who Molest Other Children," 571–585.

49. Monique Tardif et al., "Sexual Abuse Perpetrated by Adult and Juvenile Females: An Ultimate Attempt to Resolve a Conflict Associated with Maternal Identity," *Child Abuse & Neglect* 29(2) (2005): 153–167.

50. See generally: Estele V. Welldon, *Mother, Madonna, Whore: The Idealization and Denigration of Motherhood* (London: Free Association Book, 1988).

51. Johnson, "Female Child Perpetrators: Children Who Molest Other Children," 582.

52. ,72–75.

53. Ibid.

54. See generally: Fromuth and Conn, "Hidden Perpetrators: Sexual Molestation in a Nonclinical Sample of College Women"; Johnson, "Female Child Perpetrators: Children Who Molest Other Children"; Mathews, Hunter, and Vuz, "Juvenile Female Sexual Offenders: Clinical Characteristics and Treatment Issues"; Ray and English, "Comparison of Female and Male Children with Sexual Behavior Problems."

55. Johnson, "Female Child Perpetrators: Children Who Molest Other Children," 582.

56. See generally: Marcia T. Turner, *Female Adolescent Sexual Abusers: An Exploratory Study of Mother-Daughter Dynamics with Implications for Treatment* (Brandon, VT: The Safer Society Press, 1994).

57. Linda Goldston, "Children Who Molest Children: Today's Victims May Become the Aggressors of Tomorrow," *The Dallas Morning News*, June 23, 1987, 1.

58. Turner, *Female Adolescent Sexual Abusers: An Exploratory Study of Mother-Daughter Dynamics with Implications for Treatment.*

59. Mathews, Hunter, and Vuz, "Juvenile Female Sexual Offenders: Clinical Characteristics and Treatment Issues," 191.

60. See generally: Johnson, "Female Child Perpetrators: Children Who Molest Other Children"; Mathews, Hunter, and Vuz, "Juvenile Female Sexual Offenders: Clinical Characteristics and Treatment Issues."

61. Fromuth and Conn, "Hidden Perpetrators: Sexual Molestation in a Nonclinical Sample of College Women," 461.

62. Alison Gray et al., "Children with Sexual Behavior Problems and Their Caregivers: Demographics Functioning, and Clinical Patterns," *Sexual Abuse: A Journal of Research and Treatment* 9(4) (1997): 267–290.

63. Johnson, "Female Child Perpetrators: Children Who Molest Other Children," 581.

64. See generally: Fehrenbach and Monastersky, "Characteristics of Female Adolescent Sexual Offenders"; Mathews, Hunter, and Vuz, "Juvenile Female Sexual Offenders: Clinical Characteristics and Treatment Issues"; Ray and English, "Comparison of Female and Male Children with Sexual Behavior Problems."

65. Ray and English, "Comparison of Female and Male Children with Sexual Behavior Problems," 441–442.

66. See generally: Alex R. Piquero, "Assessing the Relationships between Gender, Chronicity, Seriousness, and Offense Skewness in Criminal Offending," *Journal of Criminal Justice* 28(2) (2000).

67. Mathews, Hunter, and Vuz, "Juvenile Female Sexual Offenders: Clinical Characteristics and Treatment Issues," 192.

68. See generally: Kubik, Hecker, and Righthand, "Adolescent Females Who Have Sexually Offended: Comparison with Delinquent Adolescent Female Offenders and Adolescent Males Who Sexually Offend"; Fromuth and Conn, "Hidden Perpetrators: Sexual Molestation in a Nonclinical Sample of College Women."

69. Ray and English, "Comparison of Female and Male Children with Sexual Behavior Problems," 444.

70. Vandiver and Teske, "Juvenile Female and Male Sex Offenders: A Comparison of Offender, Victim, and Judicial Processing Characteristics," 157–158.

71. Donna M. Vandiver and Jeremy Braithwaite, "Juvenile Female Sex Offenders: A Longitudinal Study of Recidivism Rates." Paper presented at the Annual Meeting of the American Society of Criminology, Atlanta, GA, 2007)," n.p.

72. Fromuth and Conn, "Hidden Perpetrators: Sexual Molestation in a Nonclinical Sample of College Women," 459.

73. Eva W. C. Chow and Alberto L. Choy, "Clinical Characteristics and Treatment Response to SSRI in a Female Pedophile," *Archives of Sexual Behavior* 31(2) (2002): 212.

74. See generally: Bobbie Rosencrans, *The Last Secret: Daughters Sexually Abused by Mothers* (Orwell, VT: Safer Society Press, 1997).

75. Phillip M. Sarrel and William H. Masters, "Sexual Molestation of Men by Women," *Archives of Sexual Behavior* 11(2) (1982): 125.

76. Ibid., 125.

77. Philip H. Witt, Jackson T. Bosley, and Sean P. Hiscox, "Evaluation of Juvenile Sex Offenders," *The Journal of Psychiatry & Law* 30 (2002): 587.

78. Vandiver, "Female Sex Offenders," 55–56.

79. Mathews, Hunter, and Vuz, "Juvenile Female Sexual Offenders: Clinical Characteristics and Treatment Issues," 195; Sarrel and Masters, "Sexual Molestation of Men by Women," 122–123.

80. Mathews, Hunter, and Vuz, "Juvenile Female Sexual Offenders: Clinical Characteristics and Treatment Issues," 195.

81. Crawford, "Girl's 15-Year Sentence in Fort Worth Rape Case Called Harsh," 27A.

82. Vandiver, "Female Sex Offenders," 55–56.

83. Loretta M. McCarty, "Investigation of Incest: Opportunity to Motivate Families to Seek Help," *Child Welfare* 60 (1981): 679–689.

84. See generally: Adele Mayer, *Women Sex Offenders* (Holmes Beach, FL: Learning Publications, Inc., 1992), 120; Sarrel and Masters, "Sexual Molestation of Men by Women," 1982.

85. Fariya Syed and Sharon Williams, "Case Studies of Female Sex Offenders," Ottawa, ON: Correctional Service of Canada, 1996, n.p.

86. Mayer, *Women Sex Offenders*, 30–35.

87. WSBTV.com, "3 Young Boys Arrested in Rape Case," Action News 2, WSBTV.

88. Johnson, "Female Child Perpetrators: Children Who Molest Other Children," 571.

89. Ibid., 576

90. Ibid., 578.

91. Ibid.

92. Lana Stermac and Peter Sheridan, "The Developmentally Disabled Adolescent Sex Offender," in *The Juvenile Sex Offender*, ed. Howard E. Barbaree, William L. Marshall, and Stephen M. Hudson (New York: The Guilford Press, 1993), 235–242.

93. Ibid.

94. Rhonda Gilby, Lucille Wolf, and Benjamin Goldberg, "Mentally Retarded Adolescent Sex Offenders. A Survey and Pilot Study," *Canadian Journal of Psychiatry* 34 (1989): 543.

95. Ibid.

96. Ibid., 236.

97. Glen E. Davis and Harold Leitenberg, "Adolescent Sex Offenders," *Psychology Bulletin* 101 (1987): 417–427.

98. Lana Stermac and Frederick Matthews, "Issues and Approaches to the Treatment of Developmentally Disabled Sexual Offenders," as cited in Lana Stermac and Peter Sheridan, "The Developmentally Disabled Adolescent Sex Offender," in *The Juvenile Sex Offender*, ed. Howard E. Barbaree, William L. Marshall, and Stephen M. Hudson (New York: The Guilford Press, 1993), 235–242.

99. See generally: William Rowe et al., *Sexuality and the Developmentally Handicapped: A Guidebook for Health Care Professionals* (New York: Edwin Mellen, 1987).

100. Nancy W. Cowardin, "Preventing Sexual Exploitation of Adolescents with Exceptional Needs" as cited in Lana Stermac and Peter Sheridan, "The Developmentally Disabled Adolescent Sex Offender," in *The Juvenile Sex Offender*, ed. Howard E. Barbaree, William L. Marshall, and Stephen M. Hudson (New York: The Guilford Press, 1993), 235–242."

101. Ibid.

102. Ellen. Brantlinger, "Mildly Mentally Retarded Secondary Students' Information about and Attitudes toward Sexuality and Sexuality Education," *Education and Training of the Mentally Retarded* 20(2) (1985): 100.

REFERENCES

"5th-Graders Accused of Having Sex in Class." *Chicago Tribune*, April 5, 2007, 6.

Associated Press. "Woman, 19, Charged in Online Sex Ring." CBS News, http://www.cbsnews.com/stories/2007/07/12/national/printable3052371.shtml (June 21, 2001).

Brantlinger, Ellen. "Mildly Mentally Retarded Secondary Students' Information about and Attitudes toward Sexuality and Sexuality Education." *Education and Training of the Mentally Retarded* 20(2) (1985): 99–108.

Bumby, Kurt M., and Nancy H. Bumby. "Adolescent Females Who Sexually Perpetrate: Preliminary Findings." Paper presented at the 12th Annual Research and Treatment Conference of the Association for the Treatment of Sexual Abusers, Boston, MA, 1993.

Bumby, Nancy. H., and Kurt M. Bumby. "Adolescent Sexual Offenders." In *The Sex Offender: New Insights, Treatment, Innovations, and Legal Developments*, edited by K. B. Schwartz and R. H. Cellini, 10.1–10.16. Kingston, NJ: Civic Research Institute, Inc., 1997.

Chow, Eva W. C., and Alberto L. Choy. "Clinical Characteristics and Treatment Response to SSRI in a Female Pedophile." *Archives of Sexual Behavior* 31(2) (2002): 211–215.

CNN.com. "Letourneau Says She and Former Student Are Engaged," October 12, 2004.

Crawford, Selwyn. "Girl's 15-Year Sentence in Fw Rape Case Called Harsh." *The Dallas Morning News*, January 13, 1995, 27A.

Davis, Glen E., and Harold Leitenberg. "Adolescent Sex Offenders." *Psychology Bulletin* 101 (1987): 417–427.

Denov, Myriam S. *Perspectives on Female Sex Offending: A Culture of Denial*. Burlington, VT: Ashgate Publishing Company, 2004.

Fehrenbach, Peter A., and Caren Monastersky. "Characteristics of Female Adolescent Sexual Offenders." *American Journal of Orthopsychiatry* 58(1) (1988): 148–151.

Fehrenbach, Peter A., Wayne Smith, Caren Montastersky, and Robert W. Deisher. "Adolescent Sexual Offenders: Offenders and Offense Characteristics." *American Journal of Orthopsychiatry* 56(2) (1986): 225–231.

Fromuth, Mary Ellen, and Victoria E. Conn. "Hidden Perpetrators: Sexual Molestation in a Nonclinical Sample of College Women." *Journal of Interpersonal Violence* 12(3) (1997): 456–465.

Gilby, Rhonda, Lucille Wolf, and Benjamin Goldberg. "Mentally Retarded Adolescent Sex Offenders. A Survey and Pilot Study." *Canadian Journal of Psychiatry* 34 (1989): 542–548.

Goldston, Linda. "Children Who Molest Children: Today's Victims May Become the Aggressors of Tomorrow." *The Dallas Morning News*, June 23, 1987.

Gray, Alison, Aida Busconi, Paul Houchens, and William D. Pithers. "Children with Sexual Behavior Problems and Their Caregivers: Demographics Functioning, and Clinical Patterns." *Sexual Abuse: A Journal of Research and Treatment* 9(4) (1997): 267–290.

Groth, Nicholas A., and Jean H. Birnbaum. *Men Who Rape: The Psychology of the Offender*. New York: Plenum Press, 1979.

Hart, Timothy C., and Callie Rennison. "Reporting Crime to the Police, 1992–2000." Washington, DC: U.S. Department of Justice, Bureau of Justice Statistics (2003).

Hetherton, Jacquie. "The Idealization of Women: Its Role in the Minimization of Child Sexual Abuse by Females." *Child Abuse and Neglect* 23(2) (1999): 161–174.

Hislop, Julia. *Female Sex Offenders: What Therapists, Law Enforcement and Child Protective Services Need to Know*. Washington: Issues Press, 2001.

Hunter, John A., Jr., L. J. Lexier, D. W. Goodwin, P. A. Browne, and C. Dennis. "Psychosexual, Attitudinal, and Developmental Characteristics of Juvenile Female Sexual Perpetrators in a Residential Treatment Setting." *Journal of Child and Family Studies* 2(4) (1993): 317–326.

Johnson, Toni Cavanagh. "Female Child Perpetrators: Children Who Molest Other Children." *Child Abuse and Neglect* 13(4) (1989): 571–585.

Kubik, K. Elizabeth, E. Jeffrey Hecker, and Sue Righthand. "Adolescent Females Who Have Sexually Offended: Comparison with Delinquent Adolescent Female Offenders and Adolescent Males Who Sexually Offend." *Journal of Child Sexual Abuse* 11(3) (2002): 63–83.

Letourneau, Elizabeth J., Sonja K. Schoenwald, and Ashli J. Sheidow. "Children and Adolescents with Sexual Behavior Problems." *Child Maltreatment* 9(1) (2004): 49–61.

Mathews, Ruth, J. A. Hunter, Jr., and Jacqueline Vuz. "Juvenile Female Sexual Offenders: Clinical Characteristics and Treatment Issues." *Sexual Abuse: A Journal of Research and Treatment* 9(3) (1997): 187–199.

Mathews, Ruth, Jane Kinder Matthews, and Kathleen Speltz. *Female Sexual Offenders: An Exploratory Study*. Brandon, VT: The Safer Society Press, 1989.

Mathis, James L. *Clear Thinking about Sexual Deviations: A New Look at an Old Problem*. Chicago, IL: Nelson-Holt, 1972.

Mayer, Adele. *Women Sex Offenders*. Holmes Beach, FL: Learning Publications, Inc., 1992.

McCarty, Loretta M. "Investigation of Incest: Opportunity to Motivate Families to Seek Help." *Child Welfare* 60 (1981): 679–689.

National Center for Child Abuse and Neglect. "Study Findings: National Study of Incidence and Severity of Child Abuse and Neglect," edited by NCCAN. Washington, DC: DHEW, 1981.

Piquero, Alex R. "Assessing the Relationships between Gender, Chronicity, Seriousness, and Offense Skewness in Criminal Offending." *Journal of Criminal Justice* 28(2) (2000): 103–115.

Ray, Jo Ann, and Diana J. English. "Comparison of Female and Male Children with Sexual Behavior Problems." *Journal of Youth and Adolescence* 24(4) (1995): 439–451.

Rosencrans, Bobbie. *The Last Secret: Daughters Sexually Abused by Mothers*. Orwell, VT: Safer Society Press, 1997.

Rowe, William, Sandra Savage, Mark Ragg, and Kay Wigle. *Sexuality and the Developmentally Handicapped: A Guidebook for Health Care Professionals*. New York: Edwin Mellen, 1987.

Salter, Anna C. *Predators: Pedophiles, Rapists, and Other Sex Offenders*. New York: Basic Books, 2003.

Sarrel, Phillip M., and William H. Masters. "Sexual Molestation of Men by Women." *Archives of Sexual Behavior* 11(2) (1982): 117–131.

Stermac, Lana, and Frederick Matthews. "Issues and Approaches to the Treatment of Developmentally Disabled Sexual Offenders." In *The Juvenile Sex Offender*, edited by H. E. Barbaree, W. L. Marshall, and S. M. Hudson. New York: The Guilford Press, 1987.

Stermac, Lana, and Peter Sheridan. "The Developmentally Disabled Adolescent Sex Offender." In *The Juvenile Sex Offender*, edited by H. E. Barbaree, W. L. Marshall, and S. M. Hudson. New York: The Guilford Press, 1993.

Syed, Fariya, and Sharon Williams. "Case Studies of Female Sex Offenders." Ottawa, ON: Correctional Service of Canada, 1996.

Tardif, Monique, Nathalie Auclair, Martine Jacob, and Julie Carpentier. "Sexual Abuse Perpetrated by Adult and Juvenile Females: An Ultimate Attempt to Resolve a Conflict Associated with Maternal Identity." *Child Abuse & Neglect* 29(2) (2005): 153–167.

Terry, Karen J. *Sexual Offenses and Offenders: Theory, Practice, and Policy*. Belmont, CA: Wadsworth, 2006.

Turner, Marcia T. *Female Adolescent Sexual Abusers: An Exploratory Study of Mother-Daughter Dynamics with Implications for Treatment*. Brandon, VT: The Safer Society Press, 1994.

U.S. Department of Justice. *Uniform Crime Reports, 2005*. Washington, DC: Government Printing Office, 2006.

Vandiver, Donna M, Kelly A. Cheeseman, and Robert Worley. "A Qualitative Assessment of Registered Sex Offenders: Characteristics and Attitudes toward Registration." Paper presented at the Annual Meeting of the Southwestern Association of Criminal Justice, Fort Worth, TX, 2006.

Vandiver, Donna M. "Female Sex Offenders." In *Sex and Sexuality*, edited by Richard D. McAnulty and M. Michele Burnette, 47–80. Westport, CT: Praeger, 2006.

Vandiver, Donna M., and Jeremy Braithwaite. "Juvenile Female Sex Offenders: A Longitudinal Study of Recidivism Rates." In *American Society of Criminology*. Atlanta, GA, 2007.

Vandiver, Donna M., and Glen Kercher. "Offender and Victim Characteristics of Registered Female Sexual Offenders in Texas: A Proposed Typology of Female Sexual Offenders." *Sexual Abuse: A Journal of Research and Treatment* 16(2) (2004): 121–137.

Vandiver, Donna M., and Raymond Teske, Jr. "Juvenile Female and Male Sex Offenders: A Comparison of Offender, Victim, and Judicial Processing Characteristics." *International Journal of Offender Therapy and Comparative Criminology* 50(2) (2006): 148–165.

Vick, Jennifer, Ruth McRoy, and Bobbie Matthews. "Young Female Sex Offenders: Assessment and Treatment Issues." *Journal of Child Sexual Abuse* 11(2) (2002): 1–23.

Welldon, Estele V. *Mother, Madonna, Whore: The Idealization and Denigration of Motherhood.* London: Free Association Book, 1988.

Witt, Philip, Jackson Bosley, and Sean Hiscox. "Evaluation of Juvenile Sex Offenders." *The Journal of Psychiatry* 30(Winter) (2002): 569–592.

WSBTV.com. "3 Young Boys Arrested in Rape Case." Action News 2, WSBTV, November 19, 2007.

6

Once a Sex Offender, Always a Sex Offender?

Philip A. Ikomi

It may surprise some to know that sex offenders, adult and juvenile, have relatively low rates of recidivism. In fact, one of the most highly cited sex offender recidivism studies of adults reports approximately 19 percent of rapists and 13 percent of rapists during a four- to five-year follow-up period.[1] This is contrary to what the media tell us—media often report sex offenders who offend over and over. What is important for the consumer to know is that media often report rare or unusual cases. Juveniles have an even lower rate of recidivism when compared to adults.[2] The nature of the criterion used to gauge re-offense rate is a nagging problem. Researchers do not have a clear criterion to use. Some use sexual re-offense while others use any offense for which the perpetrator was arrested postrelease for a sexual offense. This is only one of several problems discussed in this chapter. The findings from recidivism research, however, can reveal factors that differentiate those who re-offend from those who do not, which are also discussed in this chapter.

Other related topics that are discussed in this chapter include treatment of sexual offenders and assessment tools used in the determination of the risk of re-offense. I present various treatments currently in use, especially those that were checked in the treatment provider survey that we conducted.[3] It will be noted that although there are different types of treatments, the treatments are not applied differently based on the sex of the offender or on the type of sexual offense being treated. Someone new to the field would probably think that the different sexual offenses would have different treatments but sadly, this is not the case. In this chapter the goals of treatment are identified initially, to provide a foundation for the different types of treatment identified in the subsequent section.

The assessment tools psychologists, psychiatrists, and other treatment providers use are also discussed; these provide insight into the behaviors and motivations of sexual offenses. This is a growing area as each of the tools becomes refined and each provides different information to the treatment provider. This chapter, therefore, provides the most up-to-date information regarding recidivism rates of juvenile sex offenders, along with an overview of treatment and assessment tools used in working with juvenile sex offenders.

RECIDIVISM RATES

As noted in Chapter 4, it has been found that many juvenile sex offenders do not continue to engage in sexual abuse after their initial reported offense.[4] Additionally, in Chapter 2 it was noted many youth commit sex offenses during an experimental phase of their development[5] and possibly discontinue such behavior shortly thereafter. These research findings support the notion that not all juvenile sex offenders continue to offend, but still leaves the question— how many do re-offend?

In one report summarizing several studies, researchers found that only 8 to 14 percent of the juvenile sexual offenders committed a new sex offense over an average of twenty months to eight years follow-up period.[6] Additionally, based on a committee set up to evaluate the effectiveness of treatment in 1997, the Association for the Treatment of Sexual Offenders reported that 17.7 percent of untreated sexual offenders re-offended compared to 12.3 percent of treated sexual offenders who re-offended.[7] Other more recent studies have found recidivism rates between 5 and 30 percent.[8] Some of the highest published rates of recidivism, in fact, have been 44 and 37 percent. Again this is an indication that sexual offenders do not have a high rate of re-offending generally.

"While sexual aggression may emerge early in the developmental process, there is no compelling evidence to suggest that the majority of juvenile sex offenders are likely to become adult sex offenders."

—Hunter, 2000, p. 1.

Some may want to know how many juveniles re-offend after they become adults. As noted earlier, many youth may abuse because of sexual curiosity or naivety.[9] They, therefore, do not sustain such behavior. One study conducted by one of the authors of this book assesses re-arrest rates of a cohort of 300 registered sex offenders for several years after they became adults. It was found only 13 of the 300 were re-arrested for a sexual offense during the follow-up period.[10]

Recently, in one of the more extensive recidivism studies, re-arrest rates were slightly less than 6 percent for sexual offenses. This study included a relatively large sample, 256 male juvenile sex offenders, and it followed the cohort for ten years. The boys had been incarcerated and were exposed to two different types of treatment. Again, this research shows few sex offenders are re-arrested. Some may argue (and rightfully so) that many sex offenders are not brought to the attention of law enforcement. This is one of several problems that are addressed in the following section.[11]

PROBLEMS IN DETERMINING TRUE RECIDIVISM RATES

With all of the studies discussed in the previous section, we still do not know what are the "true" rates of recidivism. Measuring sex offenses is quite difficult, given that most victims know their offender; and they may be reluctant to report. Also, most victims are younger than the offender,[12] making it difficult for them to report. It is possible that because sexual crimes are really crimes that most people would rather keep secret, crimes that would have been reported, making the recidivism rate higher, are not reported, and so we have the mistaken idea that sexual crime recidivism is low. This is only the beginning of the problem in assessing recidivism rates; several of the noted problems are outlined here.

Recidivism rates may be low because follow-up periods are too short to really determine the extent of recidivism over a longer period of time. One problem with the early studies was the length of follow-up period. It was found that when adjudicated perpetrators were followed for a shorter period, they seemed not to re-offend, when the follow-up period was longer they found that re-offense rates rose.

Recidivism rates may also be low because of the supervision under which convicted offenders who have received treatment are placed once they are released into the various communities in which they live. Clearly the offenders know that they are bound to be discovered if they did something contrary to the terms of their release from detention. They have registered as sex offenders and people in the community know or could easily find out about their history and so keep them under surveillance. These offenders presumably are also under some form of monitoring by their supervisors, which tends to reduce the opportunities for re-offense. It is thus reasonable to expect that recidivism rates will be low under these circumstances.

On the issue of recidivism, which is one measure of how effective a particular intervention has been, researchers usually want to know the length of the follow-up period. Studies have used varying periods that largely have depended on the particular study and the availability of follow-up. In studies that have used short follow-up periods, it has been found that recidivism rates have been greater than in studies that have used longer follow-up periods. One researcher suggested that follow-up periods should be as long as ten or more years after treatment.[13] The lack of uniformity in the selection of a follow-up period to determine recidivism rates is a recurrent problem in the treatment-effective literature. This lack of uniformity makes it difficult to compare recidivism rates for different treatment options or modalities. This problem also makes it impossible for one to know which modality of treatment is the most successful with recidivism rates as measures of success.

In light of all of the problems in regard to assessing recidivism rates, one may wonder what should they believe: (1) juvenile sex offenders have low rates of recidivism (as indicated by many research studies), or (2) the studies are not reliable and are fraught with too many problems; therefore, juvenile sex offenders may have higher rates of recidivism than what is reported. The answer is somewhere in between the two. The authors of this book believe that the findings of prior studies may underestimate recidivism rates, yet we do not believe all juvenile sex offenders recidivate.

RISK FACTORS

Various researchers have suggested a number of risk factors for sexual re-offending or recidivism. One of these risk factors is the expression of deviant sexual interest by juveniles. In one study, researchers found that self-reported sexual interest in children, including sexual fantasies involving child victims, child grooming behaviors, and intrusive sexual assault activities with children, was a significant risk factor for re-offending for upwards of a mean follow-up period of six years.[14]

Another risk factor for re-offending is the number of prior criminal sanctions for sexual assaults. Researchers have found that adolescents with prior convictions for sexual assault or prior criminal charges for sexual offense are at a higher risk for re-offense than those with no prior conviction. In addition, it has been found that adolescents who have committed prior sexual offenses against two or more victims are at a greater risk for re-offense than those who have not committed any sexual offenses or those who committed against only one victim. This has been shown to be the case even as long as nine years after release among youth fifteen to twenty years of age.[15] In some cases, the risk is as high as twice for adolescents with multiple victims as for those with a single victim. Other researchers have suggested that adolescents who victimize strangers are at a higher risk for re-offense. The reason for this, apparently, has to do with the greater availability of strangers relative to available potential victims known to the adolescent according to the researchers.[16]

Researchers have also found a lack of intimate peer relationships or social isolation to confer a high risk of recidivism on those adolescents who have sexually offended.[17] They suggest that lack of emotionally intimate relationships may cause lower empathy with others. In fact some researchers found that adolescents with limited social contacts were more than three times more likely to be reconvicted for a sexual crime after a follow-up period of five years.[18] It has also been found that adolescents who are yet to complete an offense-specific treatment or who refuse to be treated are at a greater risk of re-offense than those who have completed treatment.[19]

At least two factors are suggested to be promising in terms of risk factors for re-offending.[20] These are, problematic parent-adolescent relationship or parental rejection and attitudes that are supportive of sexual offending. The basis for the former is that there seems to be a moderate relationship between an adolescent's feeling of parental rejection and subsequent sexual recidivism. Some researchers have also found a relationship between poor parent-child relationship and any criminal recidivism.[21] With regard to attitudes supportive of sexual offending, it has been found that adolescents who believe that sexual assaults are welcomed by the victims are at higher risk of committing further sexual assaults.

A number of factors are considered tentative or possible risk factors because there is not enough research establishing them to be "risk factors," however, they cannot be ignored. These include high-stress family environment. Researchers found a high level of family distress was significantly correlated with violent offending. An obsessive sexual interest or sexual preoccupation is another possible factor that could trigger re-offense in the adolescent. Adolescents who offend sexually and who are preoccupied with thoughts and images of sexual activity are likely at a greater risk of sexual assault. So also are adolescents who are highly impulsive and have a history of sexual offending. Some researchers have suggested that such adolescents are at a greater risk of re-offending sexually.[22]

Researchers who have examined the victims of sexual offenses have suggested that adolescent male sexual offenders who selected male victims are at a greater risk of re-offending sexually than those who did not select male

victims.[23] However, this recommendation, based on a finding of a relationship between gender of victim and likelihood of an offense was not found in
subsequent studies, casting doubts on the earlier conclusion.[24] In other victim
research, workers have found that adolescents with a history of past sexual assault against a prepubescent child have a higher risk of re-offending sexually.[25]
Other research has found that adolescents with indiscriminate choice of victims are also at a greater risk of re-offending than those with limited choices.[26]
It appears that this is because there is a greater variety of targets or a more
diverse pattern of deviant sexual interest. However, there is no empirical evidence for this as there is not research using adolescents according to the researchers.

Researchers have also found that adolescents who have used weapons or
excessive violence during sexual offense are at a greater risk of committing
further sexual assaults.[27] This may be because the adolescents get some arousal
from violence or have attitudes supportive of sexual violence. However, some
studies do seem to support the idea. In one research, adolescents who reported
using force during their sexual offense had more instances of assault-related
sexual fantasies and more deviant sexual interest and multiple victims.[28] In
another study, adolescents who used verbal threats during their sexual assaults
were more likely to have subsequent sexual assault convictions.[29]

Adolescents who have demonstrated a pattern of interpersonal aggression
in addition to their sexual offense may also be at a higher risk of re-offending
sexually.[30] This is possibly because such adolescents may have learned to cope
with difficulties by reliance on aggressive behavior. People who are generally
aggressive and show little remorse for hurtful actions are likely to be sexually
aggressive too. Some assessment tools suggest that a history of interpersonal
aggression is a recipe for continued sexual offending.

Adolescents who exhibit antisocial interpersonal orientation may also be at
a higher risk for sexual re-offense, especially because such individuals are self-
centered and would readily do things at the expense of others.[31] However no
empirical support has been found for this assertion using some risk assessment
instruments.[32] Finally, adolescents who have sexually offended and who have
demonstrated a recent escalation in anger or negative affect may also be at a
higher risk for sexual re-offense.[33]

Adolescents who are unwilling to alter their deviant sexual interests or attitudes may also be at a higher risk for sexually re-offending.[34] This may
have to do with the strength of their deviant interests, which causes them to
not want to give the interests up. On the other hand it may also be because
they do not have hope that change can occur or just lack the motivation to
seek more appropriate sexual thoughts or fantasies. There is, however, no research support for this idea, which comes from the fact that authors of risk

assessment instruments for adolescents suggest that adolescents who are resistant to treatment are at a higher risk for re-offense sexually.

Some researchers have suggested that juvenile sexual offending has more in common with coercive behaviors such as bullying than with sexual gratification.[35] One could see a plausible reason for such a suggestion in the fact that perhaps too many juvenile sexual offenders subsequently go on to commit offenses that are violent in nature during periods when they are being monitored for re-offense. Besides, many sexual offenders also commit nonsexual offenses. In fact, recidivism rates for sexual offenders committing nonsexual offenses are higher than for sexual offenses. Thus, juvenile sexual offenders may not be all that different from other juvenile delinquents.

In 1989 some researchers, following their review of the evidence, concluded that there was no evidence that treatment effectively reduced sex offense recidivism.[36] However, eighteen years later, can we come to the same conclusion? Whereas the National Adolescent Perpetrator Network reported that there were only about twenty adolescent sexual offense treatment programs nationally in 1982, the body reported that there were more than 520 at the time of the report in 1988.[37] Presently, they are in thousands nationally. To answer the question of effectiveness of treatment it is apropos to first look at the variety of treatments offered because treatment effectiveness depends on a variety of factors, including the type of treatment and whether or not it is given in groups or individually. Group therapy has been found to be more efficacious than individual therapy.

In a study we conducted recently in a southwestern state, we were interested in answering a number of questions regarding treatment provided to juveniles who offended sexually.[38] Therefore, I would start with the different types of treatment that the surveys we made elicited. Respondents to our survey indicated that they used the following modalities in their treatment facilities, based on the fixed response format survey we dispatched to them. The modal treatment used by the treatment providers was cognitive behavioral therapy with relapse prevention. This was the approach used by seventy-five of eighty providers who responded to this question. This was closely followed by group therapy and social skills training with seventy providers giving these types of treatment. Cognitive behavioral approach came next with fifty-eight providers. The other less common approaches were covert sensitization with eleven providers, therapeutic communities with eight providers, aversion training with seven providers, and biological therapy with only two providers. It should be noted that cognitive behavioral therapy has different forms including some that were mentioned in this survey. These were cognitive behavioral therapy with family systems, cognitive behavioral therapy with psychopharmacology, and cognitive behavioral therapy with social skills training.

TREATMENT OF JUVENILE SEX OFFENDERS

Treatment of juveniles who sexually offend should not be thought of as an impossible task. In the recent decades, the number of programs for juvenile sex offenders has expanded tremendously. The expansion may reflect a general concern among society toward sexual offenses committed by juveniles. Also, a general belief that early intervention is key to disrupting a cycle of abuse is prevalent.[39]

> "...a number of encouraging clinical reports on the treatment of juvenile sex offenders have been published. While these studies are not definitive, they provide empirical support for the belief that the majority of juvenile sex offenders are amendable to treatment and achieve positive treatment outcomes."
> —Hunter, 2000, p. 3.

GOALS OF THERAPY

Several researchers and treatment providers posit that important goals of therapy include the prevention of recidivism, helping the patient gain control over their deviant sexual behavior, teaching impulse control, increasing appropriate social interaction, and correcting distorted beliefs about normal sexual behavior.[40] Other researchers say that the objectives of treatment are to prevent further victimization, halt the development of additional psychosexual problems, and help the juvenile develop age-appropriate relationships with peers.[41] Yet others have suggested that the goal of treatment is community safety.[42] To accomplish these goals various treatment approaches including those mentioned by our survey participants are used.[43]

The literature on treatment recognizes that treatment of adolescent or juvenile sex offenders has to be developmentally sensitive to the needs of juveniles because unlike adults, juvenile offenders are in a state of physical, emotional, and social development.[44] In this regard one can point to the fact that within the age group covered by juveniles, there are those undergoing pubertal changes that affect children's response to chemicals in drugs for instance. Then there are those children who have gone past puberty and are now more mature and so have a greater tolerance to the effects of certain chemicals. Socially, juveniles are still testing their environments and trying to find their niche within a complex social system and so various interventions that ordinarily adults take for granted may result in unwanted consequences for them. Emotionally, juveniles are very sensitive to novel emotional stimuli and so it may be difficult to have appropriate emotional interventions for them.

Another well-recognized issue is that treatment has to be holistic, involving a combination of resources to address all the areas sensitive to juvenile development and integration into the society.[45] This means that attention should be paid to their healthy psychosocial development, their familial needs, and their physical developmental needs. This calls for using a combination of treatment modalities that will simultaneously be effective in satisfying the various needs of the individual sex offender. Holistic treatment also implies that community needs that affect the individuals will be taken into consideration in treatment planning.

One of the goals of therapy is to make the individual better able to function in the society and not just to give the individual the ability to reduce distorted thinking and risks of sexually re-offending.[46] Accordingly, it is important to help the juvenile with the acquisition of prerequisite skills for the formation and maintenance of healthy interpersonal relationships. The skills along with therapeutic support will help pull individuals from a life of sexual offending.

However, traditional treatment approaches, according to some researchers, have tended to concentrate on reduction of the risk factors in sexual offending and the promotion of the prevention of relapse.[47] Most juveniles who have offended sexually are not motivated to enter treatment for various reasons. This lack of motivation has to be overcome if treatment is to be successful. Thus programs that are directed toward reducing risks of re-offending and reduction in sexual fantasies will be less acceptable than those that are more holistic, treating the entire individual and enhancing the integration of the individual into the society.[48]

PURPOSE OF TREATMENT

Recently, the authors of The National Task Force on *Juvenile Sexual Offending* summarized the assumptions regarding treatment. It was intended to reflect the thinking at the time regarding the provision of a comprehensive response to juveniles who have committed sexual offense.[49] These assumptions include the suggestion that after a full assessment of the juvenile's risk factors and needs have been made, individualized and developmentally sensitive interventions are required. Additionally, individualized treatment plans should be designed and from time to time, reassessed and revised. These plans should specify treatment needs, objectives, and required interventions. Treatment should be provided in the least restrictive environment necessary for community protection. The treatment methods should involve the least intrusive methods necessary to accomplish treatment objectives.

Furthermore, they specify that progress reports should be issued to the agency that mandated treatment and should be discussed with the juvenile and parents. Progress must be based on measurable objectives and observable changes as well as on the demonstrated ability to apply changes in current situations. It also acknowledged that although adequate outcome data were lacking, satisfactory treatment could require a minimum of twelve to twenty-four months. It is interesting that our survey of treatment providers in the southwestern state indicated that treatment lasted an average of twenty-four months for our sample of providers.

CONTINUUM OF CARE MODELS

A number of researchers have recommended a continuum of care models to deal with the problems of the individual juveniles who have committed sexual offenses as well as the safety needs of the community. These continua of care may include the following described in the *Oregon Report on Juvenile Sex Offenders* in 1986 as reported by Righthand and Welch:

- Short-term, specialized psychoeducational programs.
- Community-based outpatient sex offender treatment programs for juveniles remaining at home or in foster care.
- Day treatment programs.
- Residential group homes or residential facilities.
- Training schools for short-term placements providing assessments and facilitating readiness for community-based treatment.
- Secure units providing comprehensive, intensive treatment, including daily unit groups; two to three small daily groups focusing on interpersonal skill; weekly sessions on a variety of topics, such as sex offending issues, stress cycles, anger management, and social skills; parent groups; family therapy; individual treatment; substance abuse therapy, if needed; and more.

Another researcher has posited a continuum of care that is similar to the one just described. Some components of this continuum as pointed out by Righthand and Welch include:

- Locked residential treatment facilities.
- Unlocked residential treatment units made secure by staff.

- Alternative community-based living environment, such as foster care, group living homes, mentor programs, or supervised apartments.
- Outpatient groups, day programs, and special education schools.
- Diagnostic centers and services specifically designed to provide assessments tailored to sex offenders in addition to traditional diagnostic assessments.

TREATMENT APPROACHES

To accomplish the goals of treatment it is reported that intervention programs that are highly structured have been adopted, including written contracts between the treatment providers and their juvenile clients.[50] These treatment approaches include individual, group, and family interventions. Group therapies are said to be the most effective; however, empirical studies proving or establishing their effectiveness are few and for between.[51] It is also reported that co-therapy teams including male and female therapists have been recommended so that they can model equal relationships between the sexes for their clients.[52] However, there has not been an empirical demonstration that this approach is actually better than other approaches. Some researchers have suggested that although group therapy has some positive values, such as members drawing from their own experiences to facilitate the group and group exposure leading to new ways of thinking and interacting with others, there are disadvantages of group membership, which should not be lost.[53] One of these is the negative peer group pressure that could result from the process.

Once a treatment plan has been adopted, the first step is usually helping the juvenile to accept responsibility for his or her behavior.[54] But this is quite difficult and may even be complicated when legal considerations are added.[55] However, some researchers feel that progress cannot be made in treatment if the juvenile has not accepted responsibility for his or her behavior.[56] In fact, some therapists will not proceed with treatment if the juvenile does not accept responsibility for his or her behavior.[57] Some researchers have observed that once the juvenile's denials and minimizations of the effects of their behavior have been reduced, the juvenile can begin to empathize with their victims and so be motivated to make progress beyond the first steps in treatment.[58]

The National Adolescent Perpetrator Network (NAPN) and others have recommended treatment content areas that include sex education, correction of cognitive distortions (known as cognitive restructuring), empathy training, clarification of values concerning abusive versus nonabusive sexual behavior, anger management, strategies to enhance impulse control and facilitate good judgment, social skills training, reduction of deviant arousal, and relapse prevention. In addition there are other content areas such as training in vocational and basic skills, assistance with academics, resolution of personal victimization experiences, assistance with coexisting disorder or difficulties, resolution of family dysfunction and impaired sibling relationships, and development of prosocial relationship with peers, dating skills, and positive sexual identity. Similar training contents have also been used by James Worling.[59]

Cognitive Behavior Therapy. A number of treatment options have been administered in an attempt to defeat the scourge presented by juveniles with sexual behavior problems or juvenile sex offenders. These include some already mentioned in this chapter and others to be described. Among those already mentioned is the one that is touted to be the most commonly used and possibly the most effective. This is the cognitive behavioral approach. The cognitive behavioral approach comes in many forms. However, common to all forms of it is the cognitive aspect. The idea is that people are thinking beings and so could use their thinking and reasoning faculties to make changes in their lives. Cognitive approaches are designed to induce changes in thinking, behaving, or in the arousal patterns of juvenile offenders. Aspects of cognitive behavioral treatment include role-playing, modeling, homework assignments, and education regarding social skills, problem solving, and affective expression.[60] Cognitive behavioral approaches include satiation therapy, cognitive restructuring, covert sensitization, vicarious sensitization, aversion therapy, social skills training, sex education, and relapse prevention. I will now discuss these approaches in more detail.

Satiation therapy involves the use of certain stimuli to masturbate to the extent of ejaculation.[61] After ejaculation the juvenile is allowed to continue the masturbation for further ejaculation to the point where the individual becomes fed up and hopefully will give up on a life of sexual offending. It is a reprocess that is repeated until the individual is satiated. At times some sex offenders have difficulty maintaining arousal with a particular stimulus. Such individuals could be trained to change the theme of their imagined deviant fantasies to more appropriate fantasies prior to ejaculation. Some researchers have used either a masturbatory or verbal satiation. In verbal satiation, juvenile sex offenders verbally repeat some statements to themselves until they are bored.

Some researchers have described cognitive restructuring as the flagship of the cognitive behavioral group of treatment approaches.[62] In cognitive restructuring the aim is to confront the rationalizations that the juveniles use to motivate themselves into committing the offenses. Juveniles are taught to counter the thoughts that induce them to commit such offenses. For instance, if a sex offender said that the child wanted to have sex and hence he had sex with the child, then he would be told that children that young never wish to have sex with any one and hence is a wrong thing to do.

Covert sensitization involves the verbalization of feelings and experiences that led to offending followed by a variety of negative consequences that can ensue from the offense, such as being caught and detained.[63] The therapist could conduct this treatment by reading to the offender fantasies that the offender has written, and immediately following with the offender imagining serious consequences of the sexual act. In some instances the consequences of the act can be enhanced by presenting an unpleasant or noxious olfactory stimulus if the juvenile cannot create sufficient negative imagery. The negative consequences are at first presented after the fantasies and continuously moved forward until it is presented before the fantasies over a number of sessions.

Vicarious sensitization involves the juveniles listening to individualized crime scenarios depending on their crimes.[64] They are then presented with aversive video stories displaying a range of negative consequences that could result from the juvenile's sexually abusive behavior. Reports suggest that parents and juveniles think that this method is effective in reducing deviant arousal in the children. They think that it has a positive effect on the self-esteem of the children. In aversion therapy, a negative reinforcement is used in conjunction with the offender's deviant fantasies. In this case, the fantasies are followed by the aversive stimulus, such as electric shock or a malodorous agent such as valeric acid. For instance the offender could be shown the picture of an innocent nude child and immediately followed by the foul smelling valeric acid.

Studies have found that juvenile sex offenders are deficient in social skills.[65] As a result an aspect of cognitive behavioral treatment involving the learning of social skills is incorporated in the treatment of juvenile sex offenders. Social skills training involves getting juveniles to achieve competency in various interpersonal and intrapersonal skills such as understanding verbal and nonverbal cues, regulating affect, anticipating intention, listening, encouraging reciprocity, and engaging in meaningful conversation and give and take relationship with others. Competency in social skills could enable a juvenile to approach an opposite sex juvenile for friendship rather than having to engage in rape or incest. There are a number of commercially available packages for teaching social skills that have been validated empirically. Some involve the use of modeling, role-playing, participant discussion, and feedback and homework assignments.[66] Social skills training has been found to be quite effective in increasing the self-esteem of those who got the training compared to those who did not. In a similar vein, human sexuality education is also used therapeutically according to James Worling. He suggested teaching human physiology, reproduction, and sexually transmitted diseases.

Some authors have published books to teach human sexuality. One such book is *Growing through Knowing: Issues in Sexuality* by D. K. Kieren. Some topics covered in the book include coping with pubertal changes, sexual health issues, sex roles, sexual decision making, pregnancy, and the expression of love and physical intimacy. In one study it was found that child molesters were less knowledgeable than nonsex offenders about sexually transmitted diseases. Worling also mentioned anger management as another important area that is given therapeutic attention among juvenile sexual offenders. Researchers feel that many juvenile offenders offend following episodes of anger. For this reason anger management is listed as an area of focus in the treatment of sexual offending among juveniles. There are various packages used for anger management.

Relapse prevention is another therapeutic approach used with sex offenders.[67] Originally it was used with drug addicts to prevent them relapsing after a period of abstention from the use of drugs. Later a couple of researchers decided to apply it to sex offenders, treating sex offending as having characteristics similar to those that induce people to use drugs. Sex offenders are seen to be addicted to deviant sexual activity and as such need to be educated and treated with understanding as people in need of treatment rather than punishment. Relapse prevention is based on Albert Bandura's social learning theory.[68] It focuses on the denials held by the offender that are so common. They often do not accept responsibility for their offense and hold cognitive distortions that predicate their offending.

Relapse prevention also focuses on the sex abuse cycle in an attempt to identify the point where the trigger for the offense lies so as to avoid getting there before terminating the progression to an offense.[69] In relapse prevention juveniles are trained to recognize the circumstances and triggers for their abusive behavior and to prevent the recurrence or the progression beyond a certain point so that they do not re-offend. Relapse prevention is based on the reliance on offenders to manage self and prevent a recurrence of offense. Relapse prevention is actually very commonly used along with other modes of treatment.

Family therapy is another approach to treatment that is used with juvenile offenders and has been quite effective.[70] This treatment, however, has been resisted by some parents. The parents may argue that because the child is the one that has sexually misbehaved, he or she alone should be treated. The goals of family treatment include assessing family dynamics, educating parents to provide external controls on the child's behavior, and assuring the safety of any other children in the home.[71] On the other hand, other researchers have suggested that the goals of treatment are to promote positive parenting behaviors and to reintegrate the offender into the family.[72] Some have argued that adequate family support can help reduce recidivism.

Biological therapy is not very common in the treatment of juveniles. Caution is advised in the biological treatment of juveniles because of developmental concerns. In addition, not much is known about the effectiveness of drugs in the treatment of children. Nonetheless, there are indications that some adolescents have been successfully treated with some drugs. For instance, antidepressants (such as selective serotonin re-uptake inhibitors (SSRI)) have been successfully administered to juveniles.[73] Improvements have been reported in paraphilic urges and fantasies for juveniles who have been administered these drugs. Another researcher has also reported using another drug successfully to treat a sexually obsessive-compulsive seventeen-year-old boy who was referred for fetishism and lust-murder fantasies directed at ten-year-old girls.[74] Another group of researchers described how a seventeen-year-old boy who met the criteria for multiple paraphilias, e.g., pedophilia, frotteurism, sexual sadism, zoophilia, necrophilia, exhibitionism, voyeurism, bipolar type II disorder, and obsessive-compulsive disorder, did not respond to group therapy but responded to a drug over the course of one year. In his case, paraphilic urges and behaviors as well as depression and violent obsessions were reduced.[75] In a study comparing the efficacy of three SSRIs when used by persons of varying ages from seventeen years old and older, the researchers found no differences in efficacy between the three types of SSRIs.[76]

Hormonal Treatments.[77] At present not much is known about the use of antiandrogens for the treatment of juveniles with sexual behavior problems. The juveniles and their parents have to give their informed consent for such medication to be given. There are two antiandrogens that are normally used with *adult* offenders. There have been a few instances, however, of the use of both in adolescents in the last two decades. Both have been reported as being efficacious in reducing deviant sexual fantasies and the frequency of masturbation in juveniles treated with them. Both have similar adverse effects. The adverse effects of one of them include enlargement of the male breasts, depression, fatigue, weight gain, leg cramps, decreased glucose tolerance, increased prolactin levels, and damage to liver cells, which may rarely be fatal. The most frequent adverse effect is male breast enlargement, which occurs in 20 percent of cases. The adverse effects of the other antiandrogen include weight gain, hypertension, enlarged male breasts, lethargy, leg cramps, bone mineral loss, hot and cold flushes, diabetes mellitus, gallstones, adrenal suppression, and blood clot formation. Blockage of the pulmonary artery or one of its branches is the most severe adverse effect that has been reported. Researchers have suggested that in adolescents with severe mental retardation the first of these two antiandrogens may be administered especially in cases of nonsexual aggressive behavior associated with deviant sexual behavior.[78] They do not recommend the use of the second one because of its adverse effects. It has been suggested that patients should be carefully monitored when taking these drugs, especially for the effects of feminization. Biochemical monitoring of liver function is also required when taking the first one. It is recommended that hormonal treatment of adolescents be commenced after the age of sixteen years because of pubertal development.[79] Some authors feel that adolescents are more resistant to treatment than adults and as such more intensive treatment is required for adolescents.[80]

Surgical castration has been used with adults. However, there is no evidence or data to suggest that castration is a viable or ethical treatment for juvenile sex offenders.

ASSESSMENT TOOLS

A number of tools are available for assessing juvenile sex offenders. One of the goals of assessment is usually to determine the level of risk such individuals pose to community members. This is because although the individuals may have been treated, they could re-offend and as such, the community members need to be protected. Another purpose of assessment is identification of the individual's strengths and treatment requirements. The risks, strengths, and requirements for treatment will assist in decisions regarding whether or not and at what point in time the juvenile should be reunited with their family of origin. Furthermore, the level of risk and requirements for treatment would determine their access to the community and at what point in time, or the kind of further treatment to offer. In our survey of treatment providers, we found that providers used a variety of assessment tools to make the determination of the risk level and the amount of supervision necessary for each offender.

The following is a description of the assessment tools that the providers said they used. I will classify them according to the nature of what is assessed. For instance are they psychological, physiological, or personality assessment tools? This classification should be seen only as a way to lessen the burden on the reader who is trying to make some sense of the myriads of information that they have to cope with here and not as a classification system that has some esoteric empirical or theoretical underpinnings.

PHYSIOLOGICAL ASSESSMENT TOOLS

ABEL.[81] The ABEL Assessment for Sexual Interest (AASI) combines a measure of visual reaction time and responses to a detailed questionnaire. It is an objective method for evaluating sexual interest. The questionnaire includes questions involving public masturbation, fetishism, frottage (i.e., rubbing against someone in a public and usually crowded place for sexual pleasure), voyeurism, obscene phone calls, necrophilia (i.e., sexual attraction to dead people), masochism, coprophilia (i.e., sexual attraction to feces), rape, and sexual affairs outside of a committed relationship. Data are gathered regarding each of these sexual deviations, especially age of onset, age at which the deviant behaviors stopped, the number of victims, the number of times the behavior was committed, and the individual's current reported control of deviant behavior. This test is less intrusive and more ethically sound than the plethysmograph, described in the subsequent section.

Plethysmograph.[82] The plethysmograph is a device for measuring changes in the circumference of the penis. A stretchable band with mercury in it is fitted around the subject's penis. The band is connected to a machine with a video screen and data recorder. Any changes in penis size, even those not felt by the subject, are recorded while the subject views nonpornographic slides, or movies, or listens to audiotapes.

Polygraph.[83] A polygraph is an instrument that simultaneously records changes in physiological processes such as heartbeat, blood pressure, galvanic skin conductance, and respiration. The polygraph should not be used with those who are younger than fourteen. The polygraph is used to validate sex offender's self-reports. Using the polygraph with sex offenders is much like using urine analysis with drug offenders according to some authors. The polygraph is controversial because the instrument is actually a measure of physiological processes and not a measure of truth. It measures arousal and changes occur in arousal if someone lies and so some have called it a lie detector. It is accepted in court in some parts of the United States, but it is not allowed in court cases in most of the rest of the world. The Association for the Treatment of Sexual Offenders (ATSA) recommends that the standards and guidelines of recognized polygraph organizations should be followed. It has been reported that when polygraph is used with sex offenders to gather preliminary information before treatment, providers are able to get better information. It has also been reported that periodic polygraph use may have a deterrent effect on offenders to adhere to the terms of their probation. Authors have pointed out that there are no empirically based standards for use and interpretation of polygraph results.

PSYCHOLOGICAL AND BEHAVIORAL ASSESSMENT TOOLS

ERASOR.[84] Estimate of Risk of Adolescent Sexual Offense Recidivism (ERASOR) is designed to assess risk for sexual recidivism of those who are between twelve to eighteen years old and previously committed for a sexual offense. The developers, Worling and Curwen, stated that they relied on published studies of adolescent sexual offense recidivism, published checklists and guidelines regarding the clinical judgment of risk and/or protective factors for adolescents who sexually offend, and the large amount of literature on adult sexual offense recidivism to select risk factors for the ERASOR. The instrument is composed of twenty-five risk factors including sixteen dynamic and nine historical static factors. The twenty-five factors are grouped in five categories: (1) Sexual interests, attitudes, and behaviors, an example of a factor or item in this category is "attitudes supportive of sexual offending"; (2) historical sexual assaults, an example of a factor in this category is, "Ever sexually assaulted 2 or more victims"; (3) psychosocial functioning, an example of a factor in this category is, "Antisocial personality orientation"; (4) family/environment functioning, an example of a factor in this category is, "High-stress family environment"; and (5) treatment, an example of a factor in this category is, "Incomplete sexual-offense-specific treatment." Each of the twenty-five factors is rated: "Present," "Possibly or Partially Present," "Not Present," or "Unknown." Provision is also made for "other factor" for specific individual cases, for example, an adolescent who happens to be under the influence of drugs or alcohol. The dynamic factors are coded using a six-month "recency" time frame. According to the developers, the final risk estimate derived from the ERASOR is a short-term estimate for a maximum of about a year and should not actually be expected to provide for a longer period. One of the developers gives three reasons for this: (1) development in the age range for which it is used is rapidly changing in respect to several areas of functioning, including sexual, cognitive, social, and familial; (2) the recidivism data in the published literature are usually based on mean follow-up periods of under three years; and (3) sixteen of the twenty-five factors are dynamic factors and so need to be reassessed whenever there are marked changes or the passage of time. The coding manual for the instrument contains the rationale for the inclusion of each risk factor. The ERASOR is an empirically guided scale, that is, not enough is known about its efficacy to make it an entirely actuarial scale; so ultimately, a clinical judgment goes into the determination of the risk level assigned an individual that is assessed with it.

J-SOAP.[85] The Juvenile Sex Offender Assessment Protocol (J-SOAP) is an empirically based method of assessing risk of re-offense while in treatment (i.e., assessing change as a function of treatment, and at discharge). The J-SOAP is a checklist with four scales containing twenty-six items. The checklist is designed for use with twelve- to eighteen-year-old boys who have been adjudicated for sexual offenses and/or boys that have a history of inappropriate sexual behavior. Originally the J-SOAP was developed following a review of the literature covering five areas including clinical studies of juvenile sex offenders, risk assessment and outcome studies of juvenile sex offenders, risk assessment/outcome studies of adult sex offenders, risk assessment/outcome studies from the general juvenile delinquency literature, and risk assessment studies on mixed populations of adult offenders.

According to the developers, Prentky and Righthand, the scales were intended to include two major historical or static domains, that is, sexual drive/sexual preoccupation and impulsive, antisocial behavior, and two dynamic areas that could potentially reflect changes in behavior, that is, clinical treatment and community adjustment that are important for risk assessment of the juvenile sexual offender population. They felt that the latter subscales were very important because the original instrument was meant to assess risk at both discharge and change as a function of treatment. The J-SOAP was thoroughly validated using ninety-six sexual offenders ranging in age from nine years to twenty years, with an average age of fourteen, who had been referred for assessment and treatment. Inter rater agreement ranged from good to excellent for three scales but poor for one scale, which has since been revised. Three of the subscales had moderate internal consistency, while one had a high degree of internal consistency, a measure of how well items on a scale tend to measure the same construct.

J-SOAP II.[86] The Juvenile Sex Offender Assessment Protocol (J-SOAP) was revised and became J-SOAP II after validity studies that showed weaknesses in several items among the four subscales. The four subscales are "Impulsive, antisocial behavior," "Clinical intervention," "Sexual drive and preoccupation," and "Community adjustment." The J-SOAP-II is the revised J-SOAP and it now contains twenty-eight items whereas the original J-SOAP had twenty-six items and the current one replaces all previous versions of the J-SOAP. The J-SOAP II is useful in aiding with the assessment for sexual and nonsexual recidivism among juvenile offenders. The developers suggest that it should only be used as part of a comprehensive risk assessment and not as the sole risk assessment tool basically because the stakes in the decisions are too high to use just one instrument for assessment. The developers Robert Prentky and Sue Righthand also stated in the J-SOAP-II manual that attempts were made to better anchor the items in the J-SOAP in clear, behavioral terms.

In a caveat, the developers suggest that as the stakes are very high in assessing risk of juveniles re-offending, clinicians who have to bear this burden have enormous responsibility as the decisions they make would have profound impact. These clinicians should be very knowledgeable of challenges involved in the process since the youth involved are still in a state of developmental flux during which their cognitive development as well as their social and other areas are still undergoing changes,and whatever the decision that is taken on them is bound to have a lasting effect on their lives, the developers suggest. Thus users, according to the developers, should have training and experience in assessing juveniles who commit sexual offenses. They suggest that before using the J-SOAP-II users should read the manual and familiarize themselves with the contents. Furthermore, they should have several practice cases using the scales and compare their scores with others to identify and resolve any problems before using the instrument. They also suggest that users should stay abreast of developments with the literature on assessment.

Multiphasic Sex Inventory (MSI).[87] The Multiphasic Sex Inventory (MSI) is a risk assessment tool for male clients. It is a test that assesses a wide range of psychosexual characteristics of sex offenders. The MSI has an adolescent and an adult form designed for use with males. The MSI has nineteen scales, including: validity, accountability, sexual deviance, paraphilia, sexual dysfunction, sexual knowledge, and beliefs. The adolescent form has 300 items spread over the nineteen scales.

Multiphasic Sex Inventory II (MSI-II) Adolescent Male Form. The MSI-II is the adolescent male form of the risk assessment tool. It is used to access the risk of adolescents aged twelve to nineteen years. This is a research level instrument (that is, it can be used actuarially) and was designed to measure the sexual characteristics of adolescents alleged to have committed a sexual offense or misconduct. It is used to measure sexual deviance and progress during treatment. This could explain its use at the Texas Youth Commission where it is used as an intermediate measure for their sex offenders undergoing treatment. The scales are the same as the adult form, but the items have some differences because of the experience and age of the adolescents. It has an additional scale, the sex apprehension/confidence scale. The developers describe the scales as having fairly good test-retest reliability. The test is a paper and pencil test requiring true or false responses and takes about forty-five minutes. Cassette tapes are also available for those with reading difficulty although the test requires only a seventh-grade reading level. It can be scored in as little as seven minutes with the scoring templates, which are color coded for easy scoring and efficiency. The instrument requires a level one qualification for the purchase of the test. Level one qualification is based on the knowledge and training required, which is a degree in Psychology, Education, or related field and knowledge of the principles of measurement and tests. Also required is knowledge of the competent and ethical use of tests.

Risk—Sophistication-Treatment Inventory (RSTI).[88] The RSTI helps to address juvenile justice issues and provide recommendation information to juvenile court judges, child and adolescent forensic psychotherapists, and other legal authorities. The instrument has a semistructured interview scale designed to evaluate clients ages nine to eighteen years. According to the developers, the instrument is used to assess three important areas: (1) risk for dangerousness consisting of violent and aggressive tendencies, planned and extensive criminality, and psychopathic features; (2) sophistication maturity consisting of autonomy, cognitive capacities, and emotional maturity; and (3) treatment amenability, consisting of Psychopathology (Degree and Type), Responsibility and Motivation to Change, and Consideration and Tolerance of Others. Each of these areas is measured by a scale composed of fifteen items.

The client is interviewed for between fifty and sixty-five minutes and then given a form that takes between fifteen and twenty minutes to complete. The examiner requires an advanced professional degree with training to administer and interpret the instrument at a competent level of performance. In the alternative, the examiner should be licensed or certified by an agency that requires training and experience in the ethical and competent use of psychological tests. The RSTI materials include a Professional Manual detailing the instrument's instructions, reliability and validity, the semistructured Interview Booklet, and a Rating Form.

Sexual Violence Risk Assessment (SVR-20).[89] The SVR-20 is designed as a method, not a test, to assess an individual's risk of sexual offense. It is a structured clinical checklist designed to assess the risk of sexual violence in adult sex offenders. The SVR-20 consists of twenty items divided into three domains: psychosocial adjustment, sex offenses, and future plans. Apparently the providers in our survey used this instrument for juveniles as well as for adults.

Structural Assessment of Violence Risk in Youth (SAVRY).[90] The SAVRY is designed to help in the assessment of risk of violence in adolescents. The SAVRY includes ten historical risk factors, six social contextual risk factors, eight individual risk factors, and six protective factors. The SAVRY is used to make assessments of the nature of the degree of risk for adolescent violence. The instrument has twenty-four risk factors that are assessed as low, moderate, or high and six protective factors that are assessed as present or absent. The risk factors are apportioned in three domains, historical, social/contextual, and individual/clinical risk factors. The SAVRY is not a test instrument, as there are no numerical values nor cut off scores assigned, but it ensures that important items are not missed when determining the risk level of an adolescent. It is useful for assessing male or female adolescents between the ages of twelve and eighteen. The SAVRY has been translated into Dutch, German, Swedish, Norwegian, Spanish, and Catalan.

Texas Juvenile Sex Offender Risk Assessment.[91] This is an instrument used to identify predictive variables for juvenile sex offenders in order to develop community supervision strategies. This method utilizes a data collection form to compare the victims' characteristics to variables that have been associated with sexual recidivism in several research studies. The variables include current sex offense, age at first referral, prior adjudicated sex offenses, prior referrals for sex offenses, prior adjudicated felony offenses, and prior felony referrals. These variables are each scored zero, one, or two. For each juvenile, a total score is divided into two levels for the purposes of assigning a risk level whereby zero to five is rated a moderate risk and six to thirteen is rated a high risk.

Rapid Risk Assessment for Sexual Offense Recidivism (RRASOR).[92] The RRASOR was designed to screen offenders into relevant risk levels. The RRASOR is not a comprehensive method for assessing risk of sexual recidivism. The RRASOR considers prior sex offenses, age, gender of victim, and relationship to victim. The RRASOR has been integrated into the Static-99. It has been stated that the four items of the RRASOR largely account for the predictive ability of the Static 99.[93]

Static-99.[94] The Static-99 reviews the offender's age, prior convictions, and whether the offense was against an individual outside of the family. These three factors are considered "static" factors because these factors remain fixed. A score is computed based on the presence or absence of the "static" factors. The Static-99 has incorporated the factors associated with the RRASOR for determining risk of re-offense. The Static-99 is one of the most effective tools used to determine sexual recidivism.

Vermont Assessment of Sex Offender Risk (VASOR).[95] The Vermont Assessment of Sex Offender Risk is a risk assessment scale for adult male sex offenders who are at least eighteen years old. Obviously, some providers are using this instrument for juveniles, as it appeared in the responses to our survey of juvenile sexual offender providers. The VASOR is composed of two scales, a thirteen-item re-offense risk scale, and a six-item violence scale. The re-offense risk scale is designed for assessing the likelihood of sexual recidivism. The violence scale is designed for assessing the nature of an individual's violence history and offense severity.

PERSONALITY ASSESSMENT TOOLS

PCL-YV.[96] Identifying youth with psychopathic traits is critical to understanding the factors that contribute to the development of adult psychopathy. The Hare Psychopathy Checklist: Youth Version (PCL: YV) is a twenty-item rating scale for the assessment of psychopathic traits in male and female juvenile offenders aged twelve to eighteen years. To use the instrument, one has to have an advanced degree in the social sciences, medicine, or behavioral sciences. It is also necessary to be registered with a state or provincial outfit regulating the assessment and diagnosis of mental disorders and one should also have experience working with forensic populations. The PCL: YV uses a semistructured interview and emphasizes the need for using additional information from other sources to complement the information from the interview to come to a decision. The information collected includes those pertaining to the individual's interpersonal, behavioral, and affective characteristics related to traditional ideas of psychopathy. The scale yields scores for clinical use, but can also be used for classification of individuals. The scores are highly reliable and predictive.

Millon's Adolescent Clinical Inventory (MACI).[97] The MACI is designed to assess an adolescent's personality, self-reported concerns, and clinical syndromes. This test is used with thirteen- to nineteen-year-old adolescents. The MACI scores twenty-seven scales, including several personality patterns, some expressed concerns, and many clinical syndromes. It has indices to identify test-taking attitudes in addition to confused and random responding. The test can be scored in a multiplicity of ways including software, hand, optical, and mail-in scoring whereby the test is mailed to the developers for scoring. It is one of the few scales that were developed specifically for minors. It is short and easy to administer. It can help users to construct individual plans to guide youth to a healthier and better life.

CONCLUSION

In this chapter I have attempted to describe the state of affairs in the world of juvenile sex offender recidivism, treatment, and assessment. The research indicates that a high percentage of adult offenders began their sexual offending as minors. However, we also know that juvenile sex offenders are more likely to benefit from treatment than their adult counterparts. There is also evidence that juveniles benefit more from family interventions than adults partly because juveniles still live with their parents whereas many adult sex offenders live by themselves.

At this point it is not clear what the follow-up period should be when deciding on recidivism rates. Should it be one year or five years? One researcher suggested ten. There is a wealth of treatment options and a lot of them work well in terms of the objectives of the treatment, which are designed to protect the community, and help the individual offender lead a life devoid of sexual offenses. Using the assessment tools available, providers have done a decent job of protecting the communities through risk assessment and decisions based on them. However, assessment still involves a lot of clinical rather than actuarial judgment and so it is not yet as precise as it could be. Consequently, we hear of unfortunate incidents involving assessed juvenile sex offenders who were rated lower than the risk that they actually posed. This results in setback for the protective workers. However most of the time, the assessments work and juveniles are properly rated. It will be fair to conclude that at this point in time not enough is known about the nature and etiology of sexual offending for one to say whether or not "once a sex offender, always a sex offender."

NOTES

1. Karl R. Hanson and Monique T. Bussière, "Predicting Relapse: A Meta-Analysis of Sexual Offender Recidivism Studies," *Journal of Consulting and Clinical Psychology* 66(2) (1998).

2. Sue Righthand and Carlann Welch, "Juveniles Who Have Sexually Offended: A Review of the Professional Literature," Washington, DC: Office of Juvenile Justice and Delinquency Prevention, 2001, 32.

3. Philip A. Ikomi, H. Elaine Rodney, Georgetta Harris-Wyatt, and Geri Doucet, "Treatment for Juveniles Who Sexually Offend in a Southwestern State," manuscript in preparation (2008).

4. Judith V. Becker, Jerry Cunningham-Rathner, and Meg S. Kaplan, "Adolescent Sexual Offenders: Demographics, Criminal and Sexual Histories, and Recommendations for Reducing Future Offenses," *Journal of Interpersonal Violence* 1(4) (1987).

5. Michael O'Brien and Walter Bera, "Adolescent Sexual Offenders: A Descriptive Typology," *National Family Life Education Network* 1(3) (1986).

6. Ibid.

7. Karl R. Hanson, "The Effectiveness of Treatment for Sexual Offenders: Report of the ATSA Collaborative Data Research Committee." Paper presented at the 19th Annual Research and Treatment Conference of the Association for the Treatment of Sexual Abusers, San Diego, CA, November 2000.

8. Gregory A. Parks and David E. Bard, "Risk Factors for Adolescent Sex Offender Recidivism: Evaluation of Predictive Factors and Comparison of Three Groups Based upon Victim Type," *Sexual Abuse: A Journal of Research and Treatment* 18(4) (2006).

9. O'Brien and Bera, "Adolescent Sexual Offenders: A Descriptive Typology."

10. Donna M. Vandiver, "A Prospective Analysis of Juvenile Male Sex Offenders: Characteristics and Recidivism Rates as Adults," *Journal of Interpersonal Violence* 21(5) (2006).

11. Dennis Waite et al., "Juvenile Sex Offender Re-Arrest Rates for Sexual, Violent Nonsexual and Property Crimes: A 10-Year Follow-Up," *Sexual Abuse: A Journal of Research and Treatment* 17(3) (2005).

12. John A. Hunter, "Understanding Juvenile Sex Offenders: Research Findings and Guidelines for Effective Management and Treatment," in *Juvenile Justice Fact Sheet* (Charlottesville, VA: Institute of Law, Psychiatry, and Public Policy, 2000).

13. Robert Schweitzer and Jonathan Dwyer, "Sex Crime Recidivism: Evaluation of a Sex Offender Treatment Program," *Journal of Interpersonal Violence* 18(11) (2003): 1292.

14. James R. Worling and Tracy Curwen, "Adolescent Sexual Offender Recidivism: Success of Specialized Treatment and Implications for Risk Prediction," *International Journal of Child Abuse and Neglect* 24(7) (2000): 965.

15. Niklas Langstrom, "Long-Term Follow-Up of Criminal Recidivism in Young Sex Offenders: Temporal Patterns and Risk Factors," *Psychology, Crime and Law* 8(1) (2002): 41.

16. James Worling and Niklas Langstrom, "Assessment of Criminal Recidivism Risk with Adolescents Who Have Offended Sexually: A Review," *Trauma, Violence, and Abuse* 4(4)(2003): 341.

17. Ibid.

18. Niklas Langstrom and Martin Grann, "Risk for Criminal Recidivism among Young Sex Offenders," *Journal of Interpersonal Violence* 15(8) (2000): 855.

19. James Worling and Niklas Langstrom, "Assessment of Criminal Recidivism Risk with Adolescents Who Have Offended Sexually: A Review."

20. Ibid.

21. Ibid.

22. Ibid.

23. Niklas Langstrom, and Martin Grann, "Risk for Criminal Recidivism among Young Sex Offenders."

24. James R. Worling and Tracy Curwen, "Adolescent Sexual Offender Recidivism: Success of Specialized Treatment and Implications for Risk Prediction."

25. James Worling and Niklas Langstrom, "Assessment of Criminal Recidivism Risk with Adolescents Who Have Offended Sexually: A Review."

26. Ibid.

27. Ibid.

28. Ibid.

29. Timothy J. Kahn and Heather J. Chambers, "Assessing Re-offense Risk with Juvenile Sexual Offenders," *Child Welfare* 70(3) (1991): 333.

30. James Worling and Niklas Langstrom, "Assessment of Criminal Recidivism Risk with Adolescents Who Have Offended Sexually: A Review."

31. Ibid.

32. Langstrom and Grann, "Risk for Criminal Recidivism among Young Sex Offenders."

33. James Worling and Niklas Langstrom, "Assessment of Criminal Recidivism Risk with Adolescents Who Have Offended Sexually: A Review."

34. Ibid.

35. Craig T. Palmer, "Twelve Reasons Why Rape Is Not Sexually Motivated: A Skeptical Examination," *Journal of Sex Research* 25(4) (1988): 512.

36. Lita Furby, Mark R. Weinrott, and Lyn Blackshaw. "Sex Offender Recidivism: A Review" *Psychological Bulletin* 105(1) (1989), 3.

37. National Adolescent Perpetrator Network, "Preliminary Report from the National Task Force on Juvenile Sexual Offending, 1988," *Juvenile and Family Court Journal* 39(2) (1988), 5.

38. Philip A. Ikomi et al., "Treatment for Juveniles Who Sexually Offend in a Southwestern State."

39. Hunter, "Understanding Juvenile Sex Offenders: Research Findings and Guidelines for Effective Management and Treatment."

40. Priscille Gerardine and Florence Thibaut, "Epidemiology and Treatment of Juvenile Sexual Offending," *Pediatric Drugs* 6(2) (2004), 79.

41. Judith V. Becker and John A. Hunter, "Understanding and Child and Adolescent Sexual Offenders," in *Advances in Clinical Child Psychology*, vol. 19, ed. T. H. Ollendick and R. J. Prinz (New York: Plenum Press, 1997).

42. National Adolescent Perpetrator Network, "The Revised Report from the National Task Force on Juvenile Sexual Offending," *Juvenile and Family Court Journal* 44(4) (1993): 1–120.

43. Philip A. Ikomi et al., "Treatment for Juveniles Who Sexually Offend in a Southwestern State."

44. John Hunter and Robert E. Longo, "Relapse Prevention with Juvenile Sexual Abusers: A Holistic and Integrated Approach," in *The Handbook of Clinical Intervention with Young People Who Sexually Abuse*, ed. Gary O'Reilly, William L. Marshall, Alan Carr, and Richard C. Beckett (Hove: Brunner-Rutledge, 2004).

45. Ibid.

46. Ibid.

47. Tony Ward and Claire A. Stewart, "Good Lives and the Rehabilitation of Sexual Offenders," in Tony Ward, D. Richard Laws, and Stephen M. Hudson, eds. *Sexual Deviance: Issues and Controversies.* (Thousand Oaks, CA: Sage, 2003).

48. Bobbie Print and David O'Callaghan, "Essentials of an Effective Treatment Programme for Sexually Abusive Adolescents: Offense Specific Treatment Tasks," in *The Handbook of Clinical Intervention with Young People Who Sexually Abuse*, ed. Gary

O'Reilly, William L. Marshall, Alan Carr, and Richard C. Beckett (Hove: Brunner-Rutledge, 2004).

49. Sue Righthand and Carlann Welch, "Juveniles Who Have Sexually Offended: A Review of the Professional Literature."

50. Barry Morentz and Judith V. Becker, "The Treatment of Youthful Sexual Offenders," *Applied and Preventive Psychology* 4(4) (1995).

51. National Adolescent Perpetrator Network, "The Revised Report from the National Task Force on Juvenile Sexual Offending."

52. Ibid.

53. William L. Marshall and Howard E. Barbaree, "Outcome of Comprehensive Cognitive-Behavioral Treatment Programs," in *Handbook of Sexual Assault: Issues, Theories, and Treatment of the Offender*, ed. William L. Marshall, D. R. Laws, and Howard E. Barbaree (New York, Plenum Press, 1990).

54. Sue Righthand and Carlann Welch, "Juveniles Who Have Sexually Offended: A Review of the Professional Literature," Report, Washington, DC: U.S. Department of Justice, Office of Justice Programs, Office of Juvenile Justice and Delinquency Prevention, 2001.

55. Ibid.

56. Howard E. Barbaree and Franca A. Cortoni, "Treatment of the Juvenile Sex Offender within the Criminal Justice and Mental Health Systems," in *The Juvenile Sex Offender*, ed. Howard E. Barbaree, William L. Marshall, and Stephen M. Hudson (New York: Guilford Press, 1993).

57. Ibid.

58. Ibid.

59. James R. Worling, "Essentials of a Good Intervention Programme for Sexually Abusive Juveniles," in *The Handbook of Clinical Intervention with Young People Who Sexually Abuse*, ed. Gary O'Reilly, William L. Marshall, Alan Carr, and Richard C. Beckett (Hove: Brunner-Rutledge, 2004), 275–296.

60. Ibid.

61. Amanda Fanniff and Judith V. Becker, "Specialized Assessment and Treatment of Adolescent Sex Offenders," *Aggression and Violent Behavior* 11(3) (2006), 265.

62. Ibid.

63. Ibid.

64. D. Moorehead, "Efficacy of Nonpsychopharmacological Treatment for Male Sex Offenders: A Review of the Literature" (Ph.D. Dissertation, Biola University, CA, 2001), 1–65.

65. James R. Worling, "Essentials of a Good Intervention Programme for Sexually Abusive Juveniles: Offense Related Treatment Tasks," in *The Handbook of Clinical Intervention with Young People Who Sexually Abuse*, ed. Gary O'Reilly, William L. Marshall, Alan Carr, and Richard C. Beckett (Hove: Brunner-Rutledge, 2004).

66. Arnold P. Goldstein and Ellen McGinnis, *Skillstreaming the Adolescent: New Strategies and Perspectives for Teaching Prosocial Skills*, revised edition (Champaign, IL: Research Press, 1997).

67. John Hunter and Robert E. Longo, "Relapse Prevention with Juvenile Sexual Abusers," in *The Handbook of Clinical Intervention with Young People Who Sexually Abuse*, ed. Gary O'Reilly, William L. Marshall, Alan Carr, and Richard C. Beckett (Hove: Brunner-Rutledge, 2004), 275–296.

68. Albert Bandura, *Social Learning Theory* (Englewood Cliffs, NJ: Prentice-Hall, 1977).

69. John Hunter and Robert E. Longo, "Relapse Prevention with Juvenile Sexual Abusers," in *The Handbook of Clinical Intervention with Young People Who Sexually Abuse*, ed. Gary O'Reilly, William L. Marshall, Alan Carr, and Richard C. Beckett (Hove: Brunner-Rutledge, 2004).

70. Jerry Thomas, "Family Intervention with Young People with Sexually Abusive Behaviour," in *The Handbook of Clinical Intervention with Young People Who Sexually Abuse*, ed. Gary O'Reilly, William L. Marshall, Alan Carr, and Richard C. Beckett (Hove: Brunner-Rutledge, 2004), 315–342.

71. Diana M. Elliott and Kathy Smiljanich, "Sex Offending among Juveniles: Development and Response," *Journal of Pediatric Health Care* 8(3) (1994): 101.

72. Glen E. Davis and Harold Leitenberg, "Adolescent Sex Offenders," *Psychological Bulletin* 101(3) (1987).

73. Priscille Gerardine and Florence Thibaut, "Epidemiology and Treatment of Juvenile Sexual Offending," *Pediatric Drugs* 6(2) (2004).

74. John M. W. Bradford, "The Pharmacological Treatment of the Adolescent Sex Offender," in *The Juvenile Sex Offender*, ed. Howard E. Barbaree, William L. Marshall, and Stephen M. Hudson (New York: Guilford Press, 1993).

75. Priscille Gerardine and Florence Thibaut, "Epidemiology and Treatment of Juvenile Sexual Offending," *Pediatric Drugs* 6(2) (2004): 79.

76. David M. Greenberg, John M. W. Bradford, S. Curry, "A Comparison of Treatment of Paraphilias with Three Serotonin Re-Uptake Inhibitors: A Retrospective Study," *Bulletin of the American Academy of Psychiatry and Law* 24(4) (1996): 525.

77. Ibid.

78. Priscille Gerardine and Florence Thibaut, "Epidemiology and Treatment of Juvenile Sexual Offending."

79. Ibid.

80. Ibid.

81. Judith V. Becker and Cathi Harris, "The Psychophysiological Assessment of Juvenile Offenders," in *The Handbook of Clinical Intervention with Young People Who Sexually Abuse*, ed. Gary O'Reilly, William L. Marshall, Alan Carr, and Richard C. Beckett (Hove: Brunner-Rutledge, 2004), 191–202.

82. Ibid.

83. Ibid.

84. James R. Worling, "The Estimate of Risk of Adolescent Sexual Offense Recidivism (ERASOR): Preliminary Psychometric Data," *Sexual Abuse: A Journal of Research and Treatment* 16(3) (2004).

85. Robert Prentky and Sue Righthand, "*Juvenile Sex Offender Assessment Protocol-II* (SOAP-II)," http://www.csom.org/pubs/JSOAP.pdf (accessed November 2007).

86. Ibid.

87. Nichols and Molinda Assessments, Inc., Authors and Publishers of Psychosexual Test Instruments, "Original MSI and MSI-II," http://www.nicholsandmolinder.com/msi-msi_ii.html (accessed November 2007).

88. Randall T. Salekin, "Risk-Sophistication Treatment Inventory"[TM] (RSTI[TM]), https://www3.parinc.com/products/product.aspx?Productid=RSTI (accessed November 2007).

89. Douglas R. Boer, Stephen D. Hart, P. Randall Kropp, Christopher D. Webster, "Sexual Violence Risk-20 (SVR-20)," http://www3.parinc.com/products/product.aspx?Productid=SVR-20 (accessed November 2007).

90. Randy Borum, Patrick Bartel, Adelle E. Forth, "Structural Assessment of Violence Risk in Youth," in *Mental Health Screening and Assessment in Juvenile Justice*, ed. Thomas Grisso, Gina Vincent, and Daniel Seagrave (New York: Guilford Press, 2005), 311–323.

91. Texas Juvenile Probation Commission, "Texas Juvenile Sex Offender Risk Assessment Instrument: Data Collection Form, http://www.tjpc.state.tx.us/publications/forms/2004/RARCSEX0204.pdf (accessed November 2007).

92. Karl R. Hanson, "The Development of a Brief Actuarial Scale for Sexual Offense Recidivism, "Department of the Solicitor General of Canada, Ottawa, http://ww2.ps-sp.gc.ca/publications/corrections/199704_e.pdf (accessed November 2007).

93. Karl R. Hanson, "The Development Of A Brief Actuarial Scale For Sexual Offense Recidivism," Department of the Solicitor General of Canada, Ottawa.

94. Karl R. Hanson and David Thornton, "Static 99: Improving Actuarial Risk Assessment for Sex offenders," Department of the Solicitor General of Canada, Ottawa, http://ww2.ps-sp.gc.ca/publications/corrections/199902_e.pdf (accessed November 2007).

95. Robert J. McGrath and Stephen E. Hoke, "Vermont Assessment of Sex Offender Risk Manual (2001 Research edition)," http://www.csom.org/pubs/VASOR.pdf (accessed November 2007).

96. Hare's Psychopathy Checklist-Youth Version, http://www.hare.org/scales/pclyv.html (accessed December 2007).

97. Millon's Adolescent Clinical Inventory (MACI[TM]), http://www.pearsonassessments.com/tests/maci.htm (accessed November 2007).

REFERENCES

Abel Assessment for Sexual Interest. "Assessment Page 2." http://www.alphaservices.org/assessment_2.htm.

Austin, James, Johnette Peyton, and Kelly Dedel Johnson. "Reliability and Validity Study of the Static-99/RRASOR Sex Offender Risk Assessment Instruments." [Final Report submitted to the Pennsylvania Board of Probation and Parole.] Washington, DC: The Institute on Crime, Justice and Corrections, George Washington University, 2003.

Bandura, Albert. *Social Learning Theory*. Englewood Cliffs, NJ: Prentice-Hall, 1977.

Becker, Judith V., Jerry Cunningham-Rathner, and Meg S. Kaplan. "Adolescent Sexual Offenders: Demographics, Criminal and Sexual Histories, and Recommendations for Reducing Future Offenses." *Journal of Interpersonal Violence* 1(4) (1987): 431–445.

Becker, Judith V., and Cathi Harris, "The Psychophysioloical Assessment of Juvenile Offenders." In *The Handbook of Clinical Intervention with Young People Who Sexually Abuse*, edited by Gary O'Reilly, William L. Marshall, Alan Carr, and Richard C. Beckett, 191–202. New York: Psychology Press, 2004.

Becker, Judith V., and John A. Hunter, "Understanding and Treating Child and Adolescent Sexual Offenders." In *Advances in Clinical Child Psychology*, vol. 19, edited by T. H. Ollendick and R. J. Prinz, 177–197. New York: Plenum Press, 1997.

Boer, Douglass R., Steven D. Hart, P. Randall Kropp, and Christopher D. Webster. "Sexual Violence Risk Assessment-20 (SVR-20)." http://www3.parinc.com/products/product.aspx?Productid=SVR-20 (accessed November 26, 2007).

Borum, Randy, Patrick Bartel, and Adelle E. Forth. "Structural Assessment of Violence Risk in Youth." In *Mental Health Screening and Assessment in Juvenile Justice*, edited by Thomas Grisso, Gina Vincent, and Daniel Seagrave, 311–323. New York: Guilford Press, 2005.

Bourke, Michael L., and Brad Donohou. "Assessment and Treatment of Juvenile Sex Offenders: An Empirical Review." *Journal of Child Sexual Abuse* 5 (1996): 47–70.

Elliott, Diana M., and Kathy Smiljanich. "Sex Offending among Juveniles: Development and Response." *Journal of Pediatric Health Care* 8(3) (1994): 101–115.

Ertl, Melissa A., and John R. McNamara. "Treatment of Juvenile Sex Offenders: A Review of the Literature." *Child & Adolescent Social Work Journal* 14(1) (1997): 199–221.

Fanniff, Amanda M., and Judith V. Becker, "Specialized Assessment and Treatment of Adolescent Sex Offenders." *Aggression and Violent Behavior* 11(3) (2006): 265–282.

Forth, Adelle E., David S. Kosson, and Richard D. Hare. *The Hare PCL-Youth Version*. Toronto, ON: Multi-Health Systems, 2003.

Furby, Lita, Mark R. Weinrott, and Lyn Blackshaw. "Sex Offender Recidivism: A Review." *Psychological Bulletin* 105(1) (1989): 3–30.

Gerardin, Priscille, and Florence Thibaut. "Epidemiology and Treatment of Juvenile Sexual Offending." *Pediatric Drugs* 6(2) (2004): 79–91.

Goldstein, Arnold, P., and Ellen McGinnis. *Skillstreaming the Adolescent: New Strategies and Perspectives for Teaching Prosocial Skills*, revised edition. Champaign, IL: Research Press, 1997.

Greenberg, David M., John M. W. Bradford, and S. Curry, "A Comparison of Treatment of Paraphilias with Three Serotonin Re-uptake Inhibitors: A Retrospective Study." *Bulletin of the American Academy of Psychiatry and Law* 24(4) (1996): 525–532.

Gulf Hurricane Relief. "Penile Plethysmograph." http://skepdic.com/penilep.html (accessed August 2007).

Hanson, R. Karl, "Effectiveness of Treatment for Sexual Offenders: Report of the ATSA Collaborative Data Research Committee." Paper presented at the 19th Annual Research and Treatment Conference of the Association for the Treatment of Sexual Abusers, San Diego, CA (November 2000).

Hanson, R. Karl. "The Development of a Brief Actuarial Scale for Sexual Offense Recidivism" (User Report No. 1997–04.) Ottawa, ON: Solicitor General of Canada, 1997.

Hanson, R. Karl, and David Thornton, "Static 99: Improving Actuarial Risk Assessment for Sex Offenders." Department of the Solicitor General of Canada, Ottawa. http://ww2.ps-sp.gc.ca/publications/corrections/199902 e.pdf (assessed November 2007).

Hare's Psychopathy Checklist-Youth Version. http://www.hare.org/scales/pclyv.html (accessed December 2007).

Hunter, John A. "Understanding Juvenile Sex Offenders: Research Findings and Guidelines for Effective Management and Treatment." In *Juvenile Justice Fact Sheet*. Charlottesville, VA: Institute of Law, Psychiatry, and Public Policy, 2000.

Hunter, John, and Robert E. Longo. "Relapse Prevention with Juvenile Sex Abusers: A Holistic and Integrated Approach." In *The Handbook of Clinical Intervention with Young People Who Sexually Abuse*, edited by Gary O'Reilly, William L. Marshall, Alan Carr, and Richard C. Beckett, 297–314. New York: Psychology Press, 2004.

Innocent Dads. "Explaining the Abel Assessment." http://www.innocentdads.org/abel.htm (accessed August 2007).

Khan, Timothy J., and Heather J. Chambers. "Assessing Re-offense Risk with Juvenile Sexual Offenders." *Child Welfare* 70(3) (1991): 333–345.

Langstrom, Niklas. "Long-Term Follow-Up of Criminal Recidivism in Young Sex Offenders: Temporal Patterns and Risk Factors." *Psychology, Crime and Law* 8(1) (2002): 41–58.

MACI™ Inventory. "Milon's Adolescent Clinical Inventory." http://hometown.net/MACI.htm (accessed November 2007).

McGrath, Robert J., and Stephen E. Hoke. "Vermont Assessment of Sex Offender Risk Manual (2001 Research Edition)." http://www.csom.org/pubs/VASOR.pdf (accessed November 2007).

Moorehead, Douglass A. *Efficacy of Nonpsychopharmacological Treatment for Male Sex Offenders: A Review of the Literature*. Doctoral Research Paper (Dissertation), Biola University, SC, 2001.

National Adolescent Perpetrator Network. "Preliminary Report from the National Task Force on Juvenile Sexual Offending, 1988." *Juvenile and Family Court Journal* 39(2) (1988): 5–52.

National Adolescent Perpetrator Network. "The Revised Report from the National Task Force on Juvenile Sexual Offending." *Juvenile and Family Court Journal* 44(4) (1993): 1–120.

Nichols and Molinda Assessments, Inc. "Multiphasic Sex Inventory—II Adolescent Male Form." http://www.nicholsandmolinder.com/msi_ii_jm.html (accessed November 2007).

Nichols and Molinda Assessments Inc. "Authors and Publishers of Psychosexual Test Instruments." http://www.nicholsandmolinder.com/ (August 2007).

O'Brien, Michael, and Walter Bera. "Adolescent Sexual Offenders: A Descriptive Typology." *National Family Life Education Network* 1(3) (1986): 1–4

Parks, Gregory A., and David E. Bard. "Risk Factors for Adolescent Sex Offender Recidivism: Evaluation of Predictive Factors and Comparison of Three Groups Based upon Victim Type." *Sexual Abuse: A Journal of Research and Treatment* 18(4) (2006): 319–342.

Prentky, Robert, and Sue Righthand. "*Juvenile Sex Offender Assessment Protocol II (J-SOAP-II) Manual, 2003.*" http://www.csom.org/pubs/JSOAP.pdf (accessed August 2007).

Prescott, David S. "Emerging Strategies for Risk Assessment of Sexually Abusive Youth Theory, Controversy, and Practice." *Journal of Child Sexual Abuse* 13(3–4) (2004): 83–105.

Print, Bobbie, and David O'Callaghan. "Essentials of an Effective Treatment Programme for Sexually Abusive Adolescents: Offense Specific Treatment Tasks." In *The Handbook of Clinical Intervention with Young People Who Sexually Abuse*, edited by Gary O'Reilly, William L. Marshall, Alan Carr, and Richard C. Beckett, 237–274. Hove: Brunner-Rutledge, 2004.

Righthand, Sue, and Carlann Welch. "Juveniles Who Have Sexually Offended: A Review of the Professional Literature," 1–59. Washington, DC: Office of Juvenile Justice and Delinquency Prevention, 2001.

Salekin, Randall T. "Risk Sophistication Treatment Inventory." http://www3.parinc.com/products/product.aspx?Productid=RSTI (accessed November 2007).

Schweitzer, Robert, and Jonathan Dwyer. "Sex Crime Recidivism: Evaluation of a Sexual Offender Treatment Program." *Journal of Interpersonal Violence* 18(11) (2003): 1292–1310.

Texas Juvenile Probation Commission. "Texas Juvenile Sex Offender Risk Assessment Instrument Data Collection Form." http://www.tjpc.state.tx.us/publications/forms/2004/RARCSEX0204.pdf (accessed August 31, 2007).

Thomas, Jerry, "Family Intervention with Young People with Sexually Abusive Behavior." In *The Handbook of Clinical Intervention with Young People Who Sexually Abuse*, edited by Gary O'Reilly, William L. Marshall, Alan Carr, and Richard C. Beckett, 315–342. New York: Psychology Press, 2004.

Vandiver, Donna M., "A Prospective Analysis of Juvenile Male Sex Offenders: Characteristics and Recidivism Rates as Adults," *Journal of Interpersonal Violence* 21(5) (2006): 673–688.

Waite, Dennis, Adrienne Keller, Elizabeth L. McGarvey, Edward Wieckowski, Relana Pinkerton, and Gerald L. Brown. "Juvenile Sex Offender Re-Arrest Rates for Sexual, Violent Nonsexual and Property Crimes: A 10-Year Follow-Up." *Sexual Abuse: A Journal of Research and Treatment* 17(3) (2005): 313–331.

Ward, Tony, and Claire A. Stewart. "Good Lives and the Rehabilitation of Sexual Offenders." In *Sexual Deviance: Issues and Controversies*, edited by Tony Ward, D. Richard Laws, and Stephen M. Hudson, 21–44. Thousand Oaks, CA: Sage, 2003.

Worling James R. "Essentials of a Good Intervention Programme for Sexually Abusive Juveniles." In *The Handbook of Clinical Intervention with Young People Who Sexually Abuse*, edited by Gary O'Reilly, William L. Marshall, Alan Carr, and Richard C. Beckett, 275–296. Hove: Brunner-Rutledge, 2004.

Worling, James R., and Tracy Curwen. "Adolescent Sexual Offender Recidivism: Success of Specialized Treatment and Implications for Risk Prediction." *International Journal of Child Abuse and Neglect* 24(7) (2000): 965–982.

Worling, James R., and Niklas Langstrom. "Assessment of Criminal Recidivism Risk with Adolescents Who Have Offended Sexually: A Review." *Trauma, Violence & Abuse* 4(4) (2003): 341–362.

7

Our Legal Response: The Sex Offenders We Know and the Ones We Don't

Our laws regarding sex offenders reflect a lot of heart or emotion but not much from our heads—or the data. Juveniles tagged as "sex offenders" are very different from their adult counterparts. Yet, we have not given much thought to juveniles who experience the unintended consequences of what we order up for adult sex offenders. The public has the misperception that all sex offenders are predatory, with a sexual fixation and very high odds of sexual re-offending. This misperception is the result of what "the experts" told us three decades ago. Now that we know differently—it is time for a reeducation of the public.

Addressing juvenile sex offending legally boils down to a balancing act of the interests of the individual versus the interests of society. Recent legal trends suggest that the interest of the community (public safety) trumps those of the juvenile (his or her treatment). After all, juveniles don't vote, but more of the community does and public safety is what the community demands. Well, does "the community" realize that its present efforts to protect itself, especially the most vulnerable therein, might be doing far more harm than good? This harm, which includes the application of an unwarranted stigma, a denial of therapy, home, family relations, a meaningful livelihood, and in a few cases vigilante murder, are discussed here. Another whammy with many of our laws for sex offenders is that the ones who law enforcement know and monitor are not likely to be the ones to harm us but rather those not yet identified! Thus, our laws create a false sense of security.

FOR STARTERS, WE NEED TO GET OUR DEFINITIONS STRAIGHT

The sex offenders who scare us are the ones that we want to know about, register, civilly commit, monitor, maybe even ban from the earth. These are, to be precise—*the sexual predators*, especially *the violent sexual predators*. These are the ones moving about like wolves in the midst seeking that lone child or adult to snatch, rape, and often kill; the ones who make the headlines. They can strike anywhere—John Walsh's son was snatched from a mall with his mother close by; Elizabeth Smart was snatched from her bedroom; and, whatever happened to little Jon Benet Ramsey? Other sex offending that concern us include forcible rape, child molestation, immoral acts (e.g., bestiality), public indecency (visible sexual conduct generating an unwilling audience), voyeurism ("peeping Toms"), and commercial sex (prostitution, and child pornography). Most of the perpetrators of these acts are adults. Yet, the same restrictive laws that we have applied to adult offenders—we have applied to many others, for example, the college student who streaks across campus and the fourteen-year-olds who "consent" to have sex with each other. Our response to sex offenders over the past two decades has been most suitable for about 6 percent of all sex offenders—the violent, predatory types. But what of the other 94 percent—which includes juveniles?[1] By needlessly making the lives of the 94 percent of sex offenders who don't scare us exceedingly challenging we have increased our own jeopardy.

When we speak of "sex offending" let us get a bunch of stuff off of that list. For example, in Oklahoma urinating in public is a sex offense (plus it is, in at least thirteen states); prostitution between adults (in at least five states); streaking (in Pennsylvania, indeed exposing genitals in public is a sex offense in at least thirty-two states); and "consensual" sex between teens is an offense in at least twenty-nine states).[2] In Texas, if two fourteen-year-olds have sex, both could be found guilty of a felonious sex offense. In Utah, if a thirteen-year-old and a twelve-year-old agree to have sex, both would be victims and offenders in the eyes of the law. In Idaho, if two fifteen-year-olds "touch each other" (heavy petting) both could be found guilty of a felony and be required to register[3]; and, up to five years age difference between an adult and a teen who have sex is an offense in some places.[4]

The age gap between victim and offender is problematic for many states. Some states require different age gaps between a victim and a sex offender—three, four, or five years usually. These numbers seem rather arbitrary. For example if one person is fifteen, the other is seventeen—a two-year difference could make "consensual" sex between the two, statutory rape. Why? In some states the fifteen-year-old would be a minor and the seventeen-year-old a legal adult. Surely, this is not the type of sex offense that we had in mind! Our culture is saturated with images of an older male with a younger female. It is basically a norm and which youngster would not seek to follow the norms about him or her? We could say "relations" between a boy and a girl or same gender intimates should not be occurring at all—but tagging what are for many normal human expressions of sexuality with peers or near peers as criminal is kind of extreme, *n'est-ce pas?* At best, we might call the juveniles involved "mentally impaired by youth," since their brains and judgment capability will not peak until about age twenty-five. Such ill-advised "consensual" sex is for many a developmental transitory behavior, which desists with time. Recognizing this, some states have already crafted what they call a "Romeo and Juliet" fix to exclude juvenile "consensual" sex offenders from their sex offender registries.

NEXT, STOP WIDENING THE NET ON JUVENILE SEX OFFENDING

A recent effort to help protect children has the potential to contribute to this widening of the net on sex offenses—the mandatory reporting of child abuse and neglect *without* some public education. It used to be that just some people had a duty to report suspected child abuse and/or neglect—namely, physicians, counselors, and teachers. Now more and more states require everyone to report suspected abuse or face legal sanctions. Who could possibly argue with the need for everyone to share in protecting the young in our midst? Well, here's the problem—the public needs some guidance or education on what to report. Some cases are obvious, but many are not. We could all stand to pay just a bit more attention to the welfare of children. But how do you know if it's fairly innocent exploration versus a "sex offense"? In either case, we could in our ignorance brand or stigmatize a child for a long time by not responding with care.

Is the rate of sex offending increasing? Not necessarily. Numbers of any offense will go up as the population increases and the rate will go up as people feel more comfortable reporting victimizations. So, higher rates may simply mean more reporting. And, is sex offending much worse among juveniles in institutions and foster care than private homes? Since sex acts, not necessarily intercourse, are fairly common among juveniles, those in institutions or foster homes as residences are likely to have far less privacy than their counterparts in private residences and thus, the latter are less likely to be caught when engaging in such behaviors.[5]

Must we prosecute in order to treat problematic juvenile behavior? Zimring believes that policies on sex offenders coming out of Washington, DC, in recent years reflect the cynicism of correctional psychologists who actually treat the worst cases—those who have been unamenable to therapy, chronic, or predatorily violent sex offenders. Concurrently, there has been the rise of the victims' rights movement and a focus on accountability.[6] Hence, the perpetuation of the view that "all" therapy for sex offenders should include the rigid control of the offender for everyone's well-being.[7] This has been in keeping with society's overall increasing punitiveness toward all offenders regardless of age. We are now in what is called a "just desserts" era of justice where the notion of "do the crime, do the time" flourishes. Problem is, with the *Roper v. Simmons* decision in 2005, we began the process of officially accepting that mentally juveniles just don't get it. In *Roper v. Simmons* the U.S. Supreme Court put a stop to the practice of executing juveniles for acts committed before age eighteen. Why? To be in step with the rest of the world. The United States had been one of a handful of states (which until 1990 included Pakistan, Iran, Nigeria, Saudi Arabia, Yemen, and the Congo) that legally sanctioned executing juveniles. There was also new evidence from the medical community that the frontal lobe of the juvenile brain—the part largely responsible for making judgments does not fully develop until about age twenty-five. The need to exercise patience and restraint, and to utilize therapeutic interventions with juveniles, was clear. Evidently, we had already assumed as much, as evidenced by our maintenance of two different justice systems in all states—one for juveniles and another for adults.[8]

This was not always the case. Centuries ago, in the 1600s and the 1700s, we thought of juveniles as miniadults who could be subject to all of the same sanctions as adults. But somewhere along the line our thinking changed— we became reluctant to send them to a retributive fate. With no juvenile justice system, the alternative was to let juvenile offenders simply go free. The juvenile justice system (with its beginnings in the 1800s) came out of an effort to create a midpoint between the extremes of—being too harsh or doing nothing with juvenile offenders. A significant first step was the opening of the nation's first juvenile House of Refuge, where Madison Square Gardens now stands in New York City.[9] It was a residential facility for delinquent juveniles and others considered at risk for delinquency. By 1899 we had the first recognized juvenile court in Cook County, Illinois. Initially, the juvenile court operated largely under the legal principle, *parens patriae*. This is the idea that the state is the sovereign parent of all juveniles. This means that if parents or guardians are deficient in their parenting the state has the right to step in "as parent" for the child. It is this principle that allows the state to take custody of children in cases of abuse, neglect, or delinquency.

Juvenile justice has become significantly adversarial since the 1960s—but the combat between the juvenile and the state is often far from equitable. The prosecutor has substantial powers including a bounty of the state's resources to build a case. On the other hand, the juvenile is entitled to state-provided counsel if indigent, but not much else and few of "the usual suspects" are wealthy. This makes a juvenile suspect easy prey for a power-hungry prosecutor trying to make a name. Juveniles however, largely reflect the adults around them. Their beliefs about sex, the behaviors they exhibit, all come from somewhere. At times it is the media—television, movies, songs to which we expose them whether actively or by neglect. Other times it comes from us, or others to whom they are exposed. Juveniles are like sponges. Consequently, when we hear of a ten-year-old raping a four-year-old—let's not rush to burn the ten-year-old at the stake. Let's ask—why would a ten-year-old do such a thing? Might the offender have been a victim of the same?

REHABILITATE: TREAT TO THE EXTENT POSSIBLE

Zimring points out that we do not incarcerate minors for status offenses because their behaviors are such that they mature out of them.[10] Status offenses are those behaviors that are illegal for minors but not adults—examples include smoking, truancy, curfew violations, and running away. Many perceive the bulk of juvenile sexual offenses in the same light—as transitory follies of youth. The concern, however, is that these follies can have serious consequences including—innocence lost, possible pregnancy, and sexually transmitted diseases (including a few that could kill). Thus, much like for other juvenile offending—offender, victims, and their families are in need of intervention.

Zimring also notes that juvenile justice systems seem to support this line of thinking in their handling of juvenile sex offenders.[11] The first course of response for many is some sort of outpatient therapy. In utilizing outpatient therapy we release these juveniles into the community knowing that they will not be monitored at all times. Additionally, we rarely transfer these types of cases. For the most part juvenile transfers to the adult system have been reserved for juvenile homicide. A primary aim of the justice system is deterrence. Clearly, juvenile justice systems recognize the element of harm or the irrationality of punishing individuals for actions that they do not fully comprehend and are unlikely to continue. Many a therapist will note that for the juvenile sex offender there is often latent guilt and shame that inhibits the recurrence of the sex offense. If juveniles will age out of the behavior—why treat them as if they will not? Such efforts are counterproductive and expensive. Of course it is important to not be dismissive with a "boys will be boys" response as Lewis Doshay cautioned back in 1943 in his acclaimed study, *The Boy Sex Offender and His Later Career*, for *some* guilt and shame is necessary to arrest the illicit conduct.[12]

We have long accepted the idea that juveniles can be treated for they are not as fixed in their maladjustments as adults. Those we deem "untreatable" should be very few. We say "should" because politics have led to more retributive responses against certain juvenile offenses. So, what the justice system needs to do is have a proper investigation followed by a thorough assessment of the alleged juvenile sex offender. The assessment should be before instead of after a juvenile adjudication (juvenile trial).[13] Why? Hunter explains that assessments usually depend a great deal on what the juvenile has to say. If the juvenile intends to deny everything these assessments will not be very accurate. Caution: Without a parent or attorney present during these preadjudication assessments the juvenile might say things that could hurt him or her later in court.

Your sex offender treatment provider should know the pros and cons of various approaches to the juvenile's assessment. For example, which instruments are used? Problematically, many of the tests that we have used on juvenile sex offenders were normed on adults; however, there are some normed on juveniles (mentioned in Chapter 6). The juvenile's motivation is important. It will largely determine the intervention that is necessary as "sex offending" may range from naïve exploratory activity, to cause for serious concern (such as when there is a sexual compulsion or violent predatory behavior). In the worst cases of a rare uncontrollable sexual compulsion, medically supervised chemical intervention may be necessary. Nevertheless, if we force treatment when it is unnecessary we become the problem by stigmatizing a child needlessly. Research indicates that juvenile sex offenders are not different from nonsex juvenile offenders in motivations to offend, but the recidivism rate of sex offending is far less than nonsex offending recidivism.

In this it is important to identify the juvenile with pedophiliac tendencies. For such juveniles the *Diagnostic and Statistical Manual* of the American Psychiatric Association (DSM-IV-TR)[14] criteria are:

1. Over a period of at least six months, recurrent, intense, sexually arousing fantasies, sexual urges, or behaviors involving sexual activity with a prepubescent child or children (generally age thirteen or younger).

2. The fantasies, sexual urges, or behaviors cause clinically significant distress or impairment in social, occupational, or other important areas of functioning.

3. The person is at least aged sixteen years and at least five years older than the child or children in Criterion A. Note: Do not include an individual in late adolescence involved in an ongoing sexual relationship with a twelve- or thirteen-year-old.

Some suspect that the juvenile sex offenders who are most likely to recidivate sexually underreport their sex offending and as they age, a fear of social and legal reprisal leads them to act more deceptively, much like their adult counterparts.[15] Thus, an increasingly significant part of sex offender assessment is the use of the polygraph test. But, is it suitable for juveniles? Some argue that it is unnecessary because juveniles are not as deceptive as adults. On the other hand, this same point makes a case for polygraph use. Polygraph test results are not admissible as legal evidence. The concern is that it is not a foolproof technique for truth. The results are interpreted based on how it is assumed that our bodies respond when we attempt to deceive. Problem is—some savvy individuals can train their body's physiological responses to beat the test. With sex offenders, states vary on the extent to which polygraphs might be used. In some cases, legal immunity might be required before a polygraph.

What is different these days? There seems to be a larger injection of a thirst for retribution in the case of any harm regardless of the irrationality of the response. We come out much further ahead when we stick to the rehabilitation ideal. To effectively do this, the juvenile judges—who are usually not sex offender experts—must at least listen to those who are. Sex offender treatment providers (SOTP) are usually clear on their loyalty—to the client   the juvenile. Texas, for example, is doing a fairly decent job in treating its juvenile sex offenders. Most juvenile sex offenders in the state begin with some therapy in a nonstate facility, reserving state beds for violent sex offenders and those who fail in outpatient therapy. In Texas SOTP "must" be persons who are both licensed mental health counselors and licensed sex offender treatment providers. Each of these licenses requires continuing education to be maintained. Interestingly, the state's juvenile justice facilities (Texas Youth Commission) have a partial waiver from this requirement, such that treatment might be provided therein by noncredentialed persons who are at least supervised by someone with the necessary credentials. This is a serious kink in the system because Texas Youth Commission sees the toughest cases. The waiver is attributed to staffing problems. Many juvenile judges heed the therapists' recommendations most of the time, others seem less motivated to pursue juvenile rehabilitation in this "tough on crime state," and do otherwise.

Another significant hindrance to rehabilitation in juvenile justice is the transfer of significant power from judges to prosecutors. Juvenile judges have less to loose politically when they pursue juvenile rehabilitation and are thus more inclined to do so. Prosecutors, however, are from an office where the chief prosecutor is an elected person. Many prosecutors want to campaign that they are tough crime fighters. They are judged on how many convictions they get and regrettably, juveniles make easy convictions. Juveniles are usually unsophisticated in defending themselves. This is even more likely to be the case when the juvenile is from a low-income family; the juvenile is no match for the resources and wit of the prosecution. Thus, in states like Florida and Arizona where prosecutors have the option to file a case in the juvenile justice system or the adult system—with vulnerable juvenile defendants prosecutors too often opt for the adult system—seemingly, to make a name for themselves. Hence, the need to return transfer decisions to the juvenile judge.

CURTAIL THE USE OF SEX OFFENDER REGISTRIES FOR JUVENILE SEX OFFENDERS

Sex offender registration usually requires that the offender render his or her name, address, details on the conviction offense, a DNA sample, fingerprint, photographs, social security number, and date of birth. The database is usually searchable by zip code or name. The U.S. Supreme Court has concluded that sex offender registries do not violate the sex offender's constitutional rights.[16] In all, by 2001, about 386,000 sex offenders were registered, given data for forty-nine states. The state with the most sex offenders registered was California (88,000), followed by Texas with 30,000.[17] Thirty-six states have laws requiring juveniles to register—but laws vary on whether this information might be made public.[18] Some states have "Romeo and Juliet" ("consensual" sex between juveniles) exceptions to registration. At least six states have different registration laws for juveniles versus adults: Arkansas, Missouri, Montana, North Carolina, Oklahoma, and Wisconsin.[19]

All states now have a sex offender registry often named after a local child victim of an adult sexual predator, for example, in Wisconsin, its "Amy's Law." These registries can be searched anonymously by anyone online in all states except Vermont and New York, where searchers must first identify themselves.[20] More states should consider this to deter abuse by vigilantes. If we keep registries public more states need laws prohibiting the misuse of the information.

Fourteen states have such laws.[21] In short, the public sex offender registry has become our modern-day version of a scarlet letter branding.

Consider the following case:[22] As a prank, a high school senior in Oklahoma flashed a group of female gym students while on the way to the toilet. The police were notified and the student was taken into custody. Pretrial he was held for four months until pleading guilty to indecent exposure. He received a suspended sentence, community service, but also placement on the sex offender registry. Stigmatized, the juvenile dropped out of high school and moved away from his family to another town. Finding and keeping jobs became difficult. His mother claimed that "[i]t seemed like after that happened, he didn't care." Her son apparently killed himself days before he would have turned twenty in 2000. The mother believed that the sex offender registry was largely to blame and questioned its use for a nonviolent, nonchronic, nonpredatory sex prank.

Sex offender registries have been around for decades but they were limited to law enforcement use in investigating crimes. California, for example, has had a sex offender registry since 1947.[23] The idea of requiring sex offenders to register themselves, began to build after Jacob Wetterling, an eleven-year-old boy was abducted. Wetterling had gone bike riding with his brother and a friend on October 22, 1989, in St. Joseph, Minnesota, when he was abducted. Thereafter, his family led the effort to see that Minnesota had a registry of all sex offenders in the state. They then pushed for what became the federal Jacob Wetterling Crimes against Children and Sexually Violent Offender Registration Act, a provision of President William "Bill" Clinton's Violent Crime Control and Safe Streets Act passed in 1994. The law requires that all states have a sex offender registry or lose federal funding. By 2002, at least thirty-eight states included juveniles in their sex offender registration requirements.[24]

The Wetterling Act was amended in 1996 by a federal version of New Jersey's Megan's Law. In July 1994, Megan Kanka, a seven-year-old Hamilton, New Jersey, girl was lured next door by a previously convicted sex offender, thirty-three-year-old Jesse Timmendequas. He invited her over to see his new puppy and subsequently raped and murdered her. Kanka's parents argued that had they known that their neighbor was a sex offender they could have exercised more care in seeing to Megan's safety. The parents advocated successfully for a state law requiring the public availability of a sex offender registry and community notification of the presence of sex offenders. Two years later a federal version of the law was passed also called Megan's Law (1996). The premises of the law are: (a) sex offenders pose a risk of sexual re-offending; (b) protecting the public can be achieved with this effort; and (c) public safety trumps individual privacy. The law left it up to the states to work out the details of how to make the registry available to the public and how to execute the public notifications.

Megan's Law was amended further by the Pam Lyncher Sex Offender Tracking and Identification Act (1996). Pam Lyncher, a realtor, was attacked while meeting a supposed client. The Lyncher Act requires the Federal Bureau of Investigation (FBI) to maintain a national sex offender database to facilitate tracking across states. It also requires that sex offenders convicted of an aggravated sex offense or multiple registration offenses register for life. Wetterling was again amended in 1997 to include more transient persons such as military personnel and college students. The latter aspect was refined in 2000 as the Campus Sex Crimes Prevention Act, which requires a registered sex offender who works at or attends an institution of higher education to report his or her status to the campus police or other law enforcement agency with jurisdiction over the institution.

Then, July 27, 2006, President George W. Bush signed the federal Adam Walsh Child Protection and Safety Act. Six-year-old Adam Walsh, the son of John and Reve Walsh, was abducted and decapitated in July 1981. He had gone to a store with his mother about a mile from their Hollywood, Florida, residence. While his mother talked to a salesperson Adam went to another section of the store. He was out of her sight for about five to ten minutes when she realized that he was gone. Two weeks later his head was found in a Vero Beach canal. To date, there have been no prosecutions in this case. Thereafter, Adam's father, John Walsh became an ardent victims' advocate. He has served as host of the popular television series *America's Most Wanted* and he cofounded the National Center for Missing and Exploited Children. He was also instrumental in seeing to the passage of the federal Adam Walsh Law twenty-five years after his son's murder. The law eliminates statutes of limitations when children are victims of felony sex offenses. It requires that state sex offender registry information is compiled into one big federal sex offender database that is publicly available. The law includes mandatory minimum sentences for serious sex offenders and sanctions for offenders who fail to comply with their registration obligations. It also provides funds for the civil commitment of sex offenders and for law enforcement training toward reducing the sexual violation of minors facilitated by the Internet. Since the federal Megan's Law in 1996, aggravated sexual violence offenders have been required to register for life. Seventeen states already require lifetime registration for *all* sex offenders and thirty-three states require *some* offenders to register for life.[25] The Walsh law expands the registry to any "criminal offense that has an element involving a sex act or sexual contact with another." It exempts "consensual" sex "victims" who are at least thirteen and "offenders" up to four years older; but requires some juvenile sex offenders to register.

The Walsh Law has three categories of offenders that distinguish how long a person is required to register:

For category 1: Registration is required every year for fifteen years. With a clean record for ten years, persons can petition for removal from the registry. Voyeurism is an example of a category 1 offense.

For category 2: Registration is required for every six months for twenty-five years. Compelling prostitution is an example of a category 2 offense.

For category 3: Registration is required every three months for life. This applies to chronic and/or violent offenders.

The problem with the Walsh classification is that it is based on the nature of the sex offense instead of risk of sexual re-offending.[26] Although we have had a national registry since 2005,[27] the uploads have been slow; however, the Adam Walsh Law requires that this process is completed by 2009. Not adopting the Adam Walsh Law by 2009 will mean a reduction in certain federal funds that could be available to the state.

ARE REGISTRIES ANY GOOD?

For law enforcement, they aid investigations by allowing the authorities to rule out the usual suspects. But a registry need not be public for that to happen. Fact is, many regular folks, even parents of young children, don't check the registries. Have you? Most sex offenses that come to the attention of the police are not done by these usual suspects but by persons previously unsuspected.[28] Registries, then, give folks a dangerously false sense of safety. So the best defense is to see everyone as a potential sex offender. Guard yourself and the minors in your charge from ALL potentially dangerous scenarios (e.g., teenage babysitters or kin whom you do not know well, etc.). Sex offenders can be bold. It is not uncommon for "true" sex offenders to visit homes and ingratiate themselves into a victim's family (often as part of an effort to convince the victim that their "special secrets" are "okay").

Also when we widen the net on the sex offenses that will require registration, it creates a strain for law enforcement to keep up. The result is that in many states they have lost track of several sex offenders (e.g., California has lost track of 44 percent (33,000 out of 76,350) of its sex offenders and Florida cannot account for 7,000 of its group).[29] For juveniles, registries unseal what would be sealed or expunged juvenile records. The federal Children's Safety Act (2005) required juveniles to be included in registries. In so doing, we made it much harder for juveniles to follow through on sincere plans to change for the better.

The research says that over 80 percent of these offenders (adults or juveniles) will improve themselves if given the chance. Instead, many juveniles in their naiveté succumb to a guilty plea in exchange for a reduced charge, which often includes sex offender registration, not recognizing the long-standing impact of registration.[30]

Another negative of the registry is that it has created a stigmatized class—sex offenders—and made this class more difficult to monitor. As is, we have made it difficult for sex offenders to find a home, sending many into homelessness. A *USA Today* survey (2007) revealed that two-thirds of states requiring registration allow offenders to register as homeless; at least twelve states list hundreds of sex offenders without addresses and, some states report that the numbers of homeless registered sex offenders is increasing given residency restrictions and landlord discrimination. Further some states that insist on an address may accept addresses for shelters, highway markers, and post office boxes.[31] On the other hand, it is possible that some of these claims of homelessness might be false to throw off monitoring—not to facilitate sexual offending—but to facilitate normal living. We have also made it more difficult for these youngsters to pursue college, given the harassment and stigma that could happen. There is also stigma for the sex offender's family. This might further discourage families from reporting victimizations involving families and friends. Thus, some juvenile sex offenders might go without needed treatment—making what could be a relatively minor behavior problem worse.

Since the baseline predictors of both sexual and nonsexual juvenile offending are so similar,[32] it is irrational to focus almost exclusively on the circumstances of sex offenses. We should reserve these public registries for the most dangerous—the chronic and/or violent predators. All sex offenders might be required to register but limit the information on juvenile registrants to law enforcement and school safety officers. Consider periodic, say—annual assessments by a group of experts for more concerning cases. Minnesota, for example, allows sex offenders to appeal their sex offender registry status every two years and to have registry requirements adjusted as necessary; also notification is per the assessed danger of the person and on a need-to-know basis.[33]

IT IS CLEAR THAT TO FACILITATE JUVENILE REHABILITATION WE NEED TO UTILIZE PUBLIC SEX OFFENDER REGISTRIES MOST SPARINGLY FOR JUVENILE SEX OFFENDERS

For starters we could exclude "Romeo and Juliet" offenders and juvenile pranksters from public sex offender registration. Consider the following cases:

Brandon M., a high school senior, met a fourteen-year-old girl through church. Her parents allowed them to date for about a year; however, when they learnt sex was involved they had Brandon prosecuted. He was convicted of sexual assault and added to the state's registry. He expects to be on the registry for life.[34]

Leah Dubuc[35] is a twenty-two-year-old college student in Michigan. At age ten, while playing with her stepbrothers, ages eight and five, they "flashed" each other. Also, while fully clothed they all pretended to be having sex. DuBuc pled guilty to twelve charges of criminal sexual conduct. She was then required to spend eighteen months in residential treatment. She characterized her behavior as "stupid child's play," which led to her being on the public sex offender registry until she turns thirty-seven. Her name was not added to the registry until DuBuc turned eighteen. She petitioned unsuccessfully to have her name on the registry available to law enforcement only. DuBuc notes that "she leads Bible study, has taught English in Japan and volunteers at a homeless shelter. 'Look at everything I've done,' she says. 'Let me go on with my life.'" The consequences of her registration have included receiving angry messages at her home and via e-mail, denial of minimum wage jobs, and internships for her social work degree. Also, as an adult on the sex offender registry she is prohibited from entering schools. Thus, she must miss her nine-year-old brothers' hockey matches and her ten-year-old sister's dance recitals.

> The state ... fired a West Texas juvenile justice guard it didn't know until recently was a registered sex offender ... The firing revealed a blind spot in the state's system of background checks for juvenile justice employees: Private companies charged with running a handful of facilities don't always check the juvenile records of prospective employees ... The employee was identified as David Andrew Lewis, 23, who was charged with indecency with a 5-year-old girl when he was 15 years old.[36]

Troubling in this case is the rather wide (ten-year) age gap between the juvenile and his victim. If this young man had a sex-offending compulsion it would be a problem employing him with a population of vulnerable juveniles. But does he have a problem? We would need a lot more information. For example, was this the juvenile's only sex offense incident? Was he remorseful and empathetic to his victim? Was it part of youthful folly?

Okay, okay, we can hear the victims' rights advocates shouting—"what about the victims? Don't they get to move on?" In short, "two wrongs do not make a right." Both parties—victim and offender—need the appropriate opportunities to heal.

ALSO, LET US MAKE THE SEX OFFENDER REGISTRY INFORMATION AS CORRECT AS POSSIBLE AND LET US BUILD IN SAFEGUARDS AGAINST VIGILANTISM

The information on the registry could be misleading. In 2007 Human Rights Watch reported that most states fail to list the age of the offender at the time of the sex offense that got them on the registry.[37] The result is that as the juvenile sex offender gets older, someone looking on the registry, which includes the age of the victim, and the current age of the offender could get the mistaken impression that the offender is an adult sex offender. Consider the following cases of Marcus A., and Jim as described by Human Rights Watch.

At age twenty, Marcus had sex with his fifteen-year-old girlfriend. Being an adult, this was statutory rape. However, his present problem:

> [The] state's sex offender website "lists my age, which is now forty-seven, and my victim's age, who I later married, as fifteen. It makes me look like a child rapist. I live alone now. I moved to a new neighborhood . . . and I worry that everyone will just think I am some dirty old man living alone who likes to have sex with children.[38]

Similarly, when Jim was ten, he touched his six-year-old sister's vagina repeatedly. He also forced her on different occasions to touch his penis. At age fifteen, Jim was convicted (as if he were an adult) of child molestation. He served three years in an Arizona jail and since his release he has been required to register every three months and he is subject to community notification for life. In his community this involves publishing details about his vehicle. However, the registry states his present age and the age of his victim when the offense occurred—thus, suggesting Jim is an adult sex offender. Jim has curtailed his plans for much of a future and lives in dread of the public's scowls. He has even contemplated suicide. The circumstances have caused his entire family considerable pain. Alabama, Minnesota, New Jersey, and North and South Dakota have attempted to fix this problem.

HOW DO WE COMPARE WORLDWIDE?

We are one of eight nations with registries: Canada, France, Australia, United Kingdom, Ireland, Japan, and South Korea—but these countries limit their registries to law enforcement. South Korea is the only other country that does community notification and we are the only country with residency restrictions.[39] United States laws have a vindictive retributive twist.

PUBLIC OR COMMUNITY NOTIFICATION ABOUT JUVENILE SEX OFFENDERS

The premises of community notification are: (a) deterrence from sex offending and (b) that it protects the public. But does it? The first such law
was the Community Protection Act (1990) in Washington State. Thereafter,
the federal Megan's Law (1996) required sex offender registration and public
community notification in all states. Indeed, all states required some community notification—but to whom and how has been left to locals to decide.
Notification techniques tend to include providing a toll-free number with
information, postings on the Internet, letters, door-to-door flyers, and community meetings. Many law enforcement agencies discontinued community
notification because they did not believe in their utility and sometimes no one
showed up. Flyers and letters seem more effective.[40] In practice some states
attempt to notify only after gauging the offender's likelihood to re-offend. In
Wisconsin this amounts to about 39 percent of released sex offenders.[41] In
Minnesota, a panel of experts decide if the risk of an offender when released is
such that notification is necessary and for how long.[42] In New Jersey the state's
Megan's Law was amended to exclude those committing sex offenses before
age fourteen from community notification. Fortunately some states require
that juveniles register, but exempt them from public notification. Nevertheless, per the Adam Walsh Law states will lose some federal law enforcement
dollars if they do not do notifications.

DO NOTIFICATIONS WORK?

We do not have enough data to say, plus it is difficult to measure a noneffect
(i.e., what did not happen). Notifications could be a deterrent or a disincentive.
They might also drive some sex offenders away (by encouraging sex offenders in states with rigid notification practices to move to more lenient states),
unmonitored, unsupported, facing housing and job difficulties, and being the
subject of ridicule and battery. Think about it—do you really want to have sex
offenders unemployed, idle? What do you think will happen then?

The Association for the Treatment of Sexual Abusers (ATSA) recommends
limiting notifications to the most serious cases and to those in the immediate
surroundings (since juveniles are not that mobile).[43] It argues that juveniles,
unlike adults, are forced to deal with peers. This makes them more vulnerable
to stigmatization. The associated emotions can be beyond that which some
juveniles can handle. ATSA also opposes transferring juvenile sex offenders

to the adult system. They argue that in juvenile justice, juveniles are more likely to be properly assessed, to get treatment, to take responsibility, and to consider the needs of victims.

Our time notifying people would be better spent teaching children to be wary of strangers and nonstrangers. There is at least one such program based in Illinois—as part of a school safety initiative. We should also encourage juveniles to communicate concerns with us no matter what. Then of course, when they do communicate, we should not react in such a way that it will be the last time that they do. This does not mean tolerating inappropriate behaviors, but being willing to teach when these teachable moments occur.

THE CIVIL COMMITMENT OF SEXUALLY VIOLENT PREDATORS

Washington was the first state to enact a civil commitment law for sex offenders back in 1990. The effort was prompted by the case of Earl Shriner, an adult sex offender who served ten years for assaulting two adolescent girls. While incarcerated he verbalized plans to continue offending on release and he did. Sexual violent predator (SVP) laws allow the civil commitment of sex offenders who pose the most risk of harm to a secure facility after serving a prison sentence. In such cases the burden of proving dangerousness is on the state. These laws are controversial because in essence they are like an indefinite extension of a prison sentence.

States with civil commitment laws are Arizona, California, Florida, Illinois, Iowa, Kansas, Massachusetts, Minnesota, Missouri, North Dakota, New Jersey, South Carolina, Texas, Virginia, Washington, and Wisconsin. At least four of these provide for civilly committing juveniles. In Texas, a "sexually violent predator" is someone with a behavioral abnormality, such that there is a history of repeated sexual violence for which the person has at least one conviction. The other states might be slightly broader in their definition of a sexually violent predator, requiring the presence of a mental disorder that makes future violent sex offending likely. Commitment then, would be required as long as the threat of harm exists.

THE ILLS OF RESIDENCY RESTRICTIONS

The imposition of residency restrictions on sex offenders began in Alabama in 1996.[44] The law stated that no adult sex offender could live or work within 2,000 feet of a school or childcare facility. Now at least twenty-seven states (including Alabama, Arkansas, California, Florida, Georgia, Illinois, Indiana, Iowa, Kentucky, Louisiana, Ohio, Oklahoma, Oregon, and Tennessee) have these laws. Other restricted areas may be bus stops, parks, and playgrounds.

But why should we care where the sex offender sleeps? It's where the person is when awake and moving about unsupervised that matters and we do not restrict sex offenders from moving about.[45] Aren't potential victims at the grocery store? The church? The gym? Or on the local bus? While some laws ban sex offender residency—they don't ban presence in those same areas. A Minnesota study revealed that sex offenders inclined to re-offend were far more likely to travel to neighborhoods where they thought they would not be recognized rather than seek victims where they live.[46]

In addition, the residency restrictions have created a housing crisis, especially in urban areas. Some cities are so congested the restrictions pretty much exclude sex offenders from being there (e.g., Atlanta, Tulsa, and Des Moines). Significantly, federal law prohibits public housing for those subject to lifetime registration.[47] Some suspect the residency restrictions are the fruit of politically sinister motives to protect property values by keeping certain types out.[48] The result is that some sex offenders lie about their addresses or fail to register. The laws also seem to chase sex offenders into rural areas where they are more difficult to monitor, to earn a living, and to access treatment.[49] Treatment and a supportive family are crucial to the rehabilitation of many juvenile sex offenders.[50] Consequently, a lot of our tax dollars get spent tracking these persons. For example, when residency restrictions went into effect in Iowa, the state lost track of half of its sex offenders. Also, some people who marry and have children might have to leave their home. And, what if a childcare center moves to where the sex offender works or lives? The registered sex offender has to move! There are lawsuits challenging such situations with the intention of having these statutes revised. After all, we still call this nation "land of the free" with basic rights to live and to earn a living.

Like notification, residency restrictions also force offenders into rural areas where they are more difficult to monitor.[51] In July 2007, Wisconsin considered a law requiring that sex offenders return to the county in which they lived before their conviction (to avoid having the registry chase them). What would work better are residency restriction laws to control and monitor the most dangerous sex offenders (sexual predators—chronic forcible rapists, and psychiatrically diagnosed pedophiliac child molesters)—those on tier three. This might include requiring a DNA sample and prohibiting access to minors—wherever they may be. We could also make greater use of electronic monitoring. Other requirements would be personalized.[52] The bottom line is that some true sex offenders exist and registries and restrictions will not change the naiveté, ignorance, miseducation, or youthful misjudgment that makes juveniles vulnerable.

Recently, New Jersey took its efforts a step further by banning registered sex offenders from using the Internet. Makes sense—since no matter where one lives, via the World Wide Web a sex offender could travel the world and arrange to meet a potential victim in a nonrestricted zone.

JUVENILE SEX OFFENDERS AND SCHOOL

For some time just about everyone dealing with a juvenile sex offender case knew about the juvenile sex offender's status except school personnel. Laws on this issue regarding school have emerged out of concern for the safety of fellow students and staff. Sometimes when school counselors and principals were informed of a juvenile status they were bound from disclosing to other staff. In the case of a clear threat of harm, the counselors, per the *Tarasoff* decision would have a clear duty to warn potential victims. Of the fifty million[53] in our public schools in 2003, 22,540 were taken into custody for sex offenses in 2003.[54] Of course there must be care not to needlessly stigmatize students. The legal novelties include that Washington State bans juvenile sex offenders from attending the same school as their victim; Delaware requires that the principal be notified of a juvenile sex offender status; and, Arkansas requires parents of a juvenile sex offender to notify the juvenile's school of the status. Often, this did not happen; so, last year the law was changed to have a juvenile's safety plan automatically sent to his or her school.[55]

ON UTILIZING DEOXYRIBONUCLEIC ACID (DNA) BANKS

Did you know that the Federal Bureau of Investigation (the FBI) has a national Combined DNA Index System (CODIS), which law enforcement can search to help clear cases? Additionally, over thirty-two states are collecting DNA samples on adults convicted of certain crimes including sex offenses. Three states require juveniles adjudicated delinquent to submit DNA samples.[56] In Texas, for example, it recently became law that DNA samples be collected on those juvenile sex offenders for whom a stay in the state's residential facility (TYC) was required (this includes juvenile offenders who committed violence or who failed to comply with outpatient sex offender therapy). In some cases samples are collected from mostly arrested adults—but with juveniles privacy concerns necessitate limits on DNA collection and use.

There are two basic reasons for having a DNA bank: (1) to facilitate investigations, and (2) to deter offending by increasing the certainty that if one offends he or she will be caught. The latter reflects what is called in criminal justice and criminology a "deterrence" approach. Deterrence theory influenced the policy orientation of Bill Clinton and George W. Bush. The approach argues that legal sanctions deter when three basic elements are present: (1) celerity; (2) severity; and (3) certainty. On celerity—the faster we punish offenders the less likely they are to repeat their negative action. Say, for example, your three-year-old Little Susie takes a cookie from the cookie jar after you told her not to. Instead of tapping her on the wrist right after the offense, you wait until a week later, walk up to her, and tap her on the wrist saying, "naughty." Little Susie will look at you as if you are crazy. Anyone present when you do this (unaware of what happened before) will have a similar response. The same with crime: when we execute someone ten years after a homicide, after the public has forgotten the gravity of the crime—the execution has less of a deterrent effect. The time lag makes it difficult to connect the offense and its consequence.

Severity has to do with the proportionality of the response to the offense. If the punishment is not severe enough, neither the offender nor the general public is likely to be deterred. If it is too severe, then the public may begin to sympathize with the offender, as was the case in 1994 when American teenager Michael Fay was caned in Singapore for spray-painting six cars. Thus, it needs to be severe enough for most to say "no" to the act or omission.

Certainty refers to how sure it is that if a person commits an offense, he or she will be caught and sanctioned. The more certain it is that we will be caught when we do wrong, the less likely we are to do wrong. The collection of DNA for law enforcement databases is supposed to be deterrent in that such banks increase the likelihood that a known offender will be caught if he or she re-offends. The question is whether we can administer our laws to achieve these three elements of deterrence so potential sex offenders believe that we mean business?[57]

A peril here is that more and more states are adding offenses to the list for which they want DNA collected. For example, Pennsylvania added burglaries and robberies to their list in 2002![58] Imagine the fiscal strain on tax dollars! It's too much! Hence, there is a DNA backlog—such that DNA information might not get uploaded into the database for up to a year![59] We have already invested three trillion dollars in DNA technology for crime fighting.[60] So, we should limit these DNA banks to those offenders who concern us the most—namely—murderers, and violent and/or chronic sex offenders. Another question is—given the recent literature that the juvenile brain isn't fully developed until about age twenty-five—how rational are juveniles in calculating their odds of being caught? Assessing risk requires rationality. Yet, many juveniles persist in taking risks. They know speeding kills—but they do it anyway with a "that won't happen to me" attitude.

CONCLUSION

The way that we have done things lately regarding juvenile sex offenders impedes the liberty and privacy of many people who are no threat to us. This has not been what we profess to be "the American way!" We have been very harsh on sex offenders when other crooks are more likely to re-offend like robbers, burglars, and killers. The public misperceives that most sex offenders will re-offend. Thus, a need to educate the public so that they can support empirical approaches that work. For example a review of the literature reveals that predictive of juvenile sex offense recidivism are—a history of family violence, a history of other offending not necessarily sexual, having a younger victim, having two or more victims, a stranger victim, a male victim, older age of initial offending, multiple female victims, victim blaming, and rigid sexual attitudes.[61] Plus, we know that rapists are more likely to recidivate than child molesters.[62] We also know that when recidivism happens it is usually within a few years of release.[63]

Quite simply then we should let the research inform what we do with juvenile sex offenders. Before laws are passed, especially those that might severely impact the lives of the next generation of citizens, we should take care to consider all foreseeable consequences. This can be done by study groups of scholars and practitioners engaged in policy analysis efforts. Having failed to do this before, many of the recent sex offender laws were passed. Thus, corrections to these laws are now due. We have allowed a reactive response to a few high-profile cases to lead us into a mode of legal "trial and error"—such that we have been willing to sacrifice the lives of many to save a few. This cost is too high for adult sex offenders, juvenile sex offenders, and for society as a whole. What the public needs to know is that the laws that we have created in regard to sex offenders may have made us far less safer than before these laws were passed.

NOTES

1. Parker Howell, "Sex Abuse Cases Hit Record Number. Better Awareness, Enforcement Cited," *Knight Ridder Tribune Business News*, 2007, 98.

2. Human Rights Watch, "No Easy Answers," Human Rights Watch, 19, no. 4G, http://hrw.org/reports/2007/us0907/3.htm#_Toc176672559) (accessed November 15, 2007), n.p.

3. Franklin Zimring, *An American Travesty: Legal Responses to Adolescent Sexual Offending* (Chicago: University of Chicago Press, 2004), 13.

4. Human Rights Watch, "No Easy Answers," Human Rights Watch, 19, no. 4G, http://hrw.org/reports/2007/us0907/3.htm#_Toc176672559 (accessed November 15, 2007), n.p.

5. Zimring, *An American Travesty: Legal Responses to Adolescent Sexual Offending*, 54.

6. Ibid., 97.

7. Ibid., 98.

8. Ibid., 105.

9. Thomas J. Benard, *The Cycle of Juvenile Justice* (New York: Oxford University Press, 1992), 62.

10. Zimring, *An American Travesty: Legal Responses to Adolescent Sexual Offending*, 108–109.

11. Ibid., 109.

12. Lewis J. Doshay, *The Boy Sex Offender and His Later Career* (New York: Grune and Stratton, 1943), 168.

13. John A. Hunter, "Understanding Juvenile Sex Offenders: Research Findings and Guidelines for Effective Management and Treatment," in *Juvenile Justice Fact Sheet* (Charlottesville, VA: Institute of Law, Psychiatry, and Public Policy, 2000).

14. American Psychiatric Association, *Diagnostic and Statistical Manual of Mental Disorder, Fourth Edition, Text Revision* (Washington, DC: American Psychiatric Association, 2000), 572.

15. J. Hindman and J. M. Peters, "Polygraph Testing Leads to Better Understanding Adult and Juvenile Sex Offenders," *Federal Probation* 3 (2001): 14.

16. *Connecticut Department of Safety v. Doe* (2003) 538 US 1(2003); *Smith v. Doe* (2003). 538 US 84 (2003).

17. FindLaw: Community Notification Laws, http://criminal.findlaw.com/crimes/more-criminal-topics/sex-offenders/community-notification-laws.html (accessed November 15, 2007), n.p.

18. Angela Rozas, "Do Young Sex Offenders Belong on Adult Register," *Chicago Tribune*, January 16, 2007, 1.

19. National Center of Sexual Behavior of Youth, "Frequently Asked Questions about Children with Sexual Behavior Problems," http://www.ncsby.org/pages/registry.htm (accessed November 15, 2007).

20. Human Rights Watch, "No Easy Answers," Human Rights Watch, 19, no. 4G, http://hrw.org/reports/2007/us0907/6.htm#_Toc176672576) (accessed November 15, 2007), n.p.

21. Human Rights Watch, "No Easy Answers," Human Rights Watch, 19, no. 4G, http://hrw.org/reports/2007/us0907/8.htm#_Toc176672592 (accessed November 15, 2007), n.p.

22. Human Rights Watch, "No Easy Answers," Human Rights Watch, 19, no 4G, http://hrw.org/reports/2007/us0907/5.htm#_Toc176672570) (accessed November 15, 2007), n.p.

23. California Apartment Association, "Jacob and Megan's Law Registered Sex Offenders and the Impact on the Rental Industry" (2006).

24. Michael Caldwell, "What We Do Not Know about Juvenile Sexual Reoffense Risk," *Child Maltreatment* 7(4) (2002): 291.

25. Human Rights Watch, "No Easy Answers," Human Rights Watch, 19, no. 4G, http://hrw.org/reports/2007/us0907/5.htm#_Toc176672570 (accessed November 15, 2007), n.p.

26. Margo Pierce, "Sex in the Time of Hysteria," *The Cleveland Free Times*, November 21, 2007, n.p.

27. Human Rights Watch, "No Easy Answers," Human Rights Watch, 19, no. 4G, http://hrw.org/reports/2007/us0907/5.htm#_Toc176672570 (accessed November 15, 2007), n.p.

28. Anthony Petrosino and Carolyn Petrosino, "The Public Safety Potential of Megan's Law in Massachusetts: An Assessment from a Sample of Criminal Sexual Psychopaths," *Crime and Delinquency* 45(1) (1999): 148.

29. Human Rights Watch, "No Easy Answers," Human Rights Watch, 19, no. 4G, http://hrw.org/reports/2007/us0907/5.htm#_Toc176672570 (accessed November 15, 2007). n.p.

30. Mary Reinhart, "Legislators Try to Ease Laws for Sex Crimes by Youths: Family Appeals Sway Conservative Lawmakers to Back Bills to Alter Statutes," *Knight Ridder Tribune Business News*, February 11, 2007, 1.

31. Wendy Koch, "More Sex Offender Transient, Elusive; Homeless Life May Increase Crime Risk," *USA Today*, November 19, 2007, 1.

32. Scott Ronis and Charles Borduin, "Individual, Family, Peer and Academic Characteristics of Male Juvenile Sexual Offenders," *Journal of Abnormal Child Psychology* 35(2) (2007): 153.

33. Human Rights Watch, "No Easy Answers," Human Rights Watch, 19, no. 4G, http://hrw.org/reports/2007/us0907/3.htm#_Toc176672559) (accessed November 15, 2007), n.p.

34. Human Rights Watch, "No Easy Answers." Human Rights Watch, 19, no. 4G, http://hrw.org/reports/2007/us0907/1.htm#_Toc176672549 (accessed November, 15, 2007.)

35. Martha T. Moore, "Sex Crimes Break the Lock on Juvenile Records; Some States List Minors in Their Registries; Federal Law May Follow Suit," *USA Today*, July 10, 2006, 5A.

36. Emily Ramshaw, "Sex Offender Fired as TYC Guard: Firms That Run Youth Centers Don't Always Check Juvenile Records," *Knight Ridder Tribune Business News*, March 8, 2007, 1.

37. Human Rights Watch, "No Easy Answers," Human Rights Watch, 19, no. 4G, http://hrw.org/reports/2007/us0907/6.htm#_Toc176672576) (accessed November 15, 2007), n.p.

38. Ibid.

39. Human Rights Watch, "No Easy Answers," Human Rights Watch, 19, no. 4G, http://hrw.org/reports/2007/us0907/6.htm#_Toc176672576 (accessed November 15, 2007), n.p.

40. Koch, "More Sex Offender Transient, Elusive; Homeless Life May Increase Crime Risk," 1.

41. Karen Rivedal, "Sex Offender Notification Policies All over the Board," *Knight Ridder Tribune Business News*, March 5, 2007.

42. Human Rights Watch, "No Easy Answers," Human Rights Watch, 19, no. 4G, http://hrw.org/reports/2007/us0907/3.htm#_Toc176672559) (accessed November 15, 2007), n.p.

43. ATSA, 2000, n.p., http://www.atsa.com/ppjuvenile.html.

44. Jeffrey T. Walker, "Eliminate Residency Restrictions for Sex Offenders," *Criminology and Public Policy* 6(4) (2007): 864.

45. Rivedal, "Sex Offender Notification Policies All over the Board," 1.

46. Minnesota Department of Corrections, 2003, as cited in Jill S. Levenson and Leo Cotter, "The Effect of Megan's Law on Sex Offenders Reintegration," *Journal of Contemporary Criminal Justice* 21(1) (2005).

47. 42 USC § 13663 (2004).

48. Kay Nolan, "Waukesha Passes Sex Offender Regulation: Residences near Schools, Other Facilities Prohibited," *McClatchy Tribune Business News*, November 6, 2007, 1.

49. Koch, "More Sex Offender Transient, Elusive; Homeless Life May Increase Crime Risk," 1.

50. Jill S. Levenson and Leo P. Cotter, "The Impact of Megan's Law on Sex Offender Reintegration," *Journal of Contemporary Criminal Justice* 21(1) (2005): 173.

51. Koch, "More Sex Offender Transient, Elusive; Homeless Life May Increase Crime Risk," 1.

52. Rivedal, "Sex Offender Notification Policies All over the Board," 1.

53. Michele McNeil, "Concerned about Juvenile Sex Offenders, States Move to Tighten Their Regulations," *Education Week* 26(36) (2007): 18.

54. Howard N. Snyder, "Sexual Assault of Young Children as Reported to Law Enforcement: Victim, Incident and Offender Characteristics" (Washington, DC: Bureau of Justice Statistics: National Center for Juvenile Justice, NCJ 182990, 2000), 18.

55. McNeil, "Concerned about Juvenile Sex Offenders, States Move to Tighten Their Regulations," 18.

56. Ralph B. Taylor et al., "Revise Policies Mandating Offender DNA Collection," *Criminology and Public Policy* 6(4) (2007): 855.

57. Ibid., 854.

58. Ibid., 855.

59. Ibid., 856.

60. Ibid., 857.

61. Gregory A. Parks and David E. Bard, "Risk Factors for Adolescent Sex Offender Recidivism: Evaluation of Predictive Factors and Comparison of Three Groups Based

upon Victim Type," *Sexual Abuse: A Journal of Research and Treatment* 18(4) (2006): 322.

62. Andrew Harris and Karl Hanson, Public Safety and Emergency Preparedness Canada, "Sex Offender Recidivism: A Simple Question," 2004, http://Ww2. Psepc-Sppcc.Gc.Ca/Publications/Corrections/Pdf/200403-2_E.Pdf (accessed August 24, 2007), 7.

63. State Of Ohio Department of Rehabilitation and Correction, "Ten Year Recidivism Follow-Up of 1989 Sex Offender Releases" (2001), i.

REFERENCES

American Psychiatric Association. *Diagnostic and Statistical Manual of Mental Disorder, Fourth Edition, Text Revision*. Washington, DC: American Psychiatric Association, 2000.

Benard, Thomas J. *The Cycle of Juvenile Justice*. New York: Oxford University Press, 1992.

Caldwell, Michael. "What We Do Not Know about Juvenile Sexual Reoffense Risk." *Child Maltreatment* 7(4) (2002): 291–302.

California Apartment Association, 2006. "Jacob and Megan's Law Registered Sex Offenders and the Impact on the Rental Housing Industry," April 28, 2006. Paper no. 24. http://www.caanet.org/AM/Template.cfm?Section=Web_Site& TEMPLATE=/CM/ContentDisplay.cfm&CONTENTID=14337. (Accessed November 1, 2007).

Doshay, Lewis J. *The Boy Sex Offender and His Later Career*. New York: Grune and Stratton, 1943.

Harris, Andrew, and Karl Hanson. Public Safety and Emergency Preparedness Canada, "Sex Offender Recidivism: A Simple Question," 2004. http://Ww2.Psepc-Sppcc.Gc.Ca/Publications/Corrections/Pdf/200403-2_E.Pdf (accessed August 24, 2007).

Hindman, J., and J. M. Peters. "Polygraph Testing Leads to Better Understanding Adult and Juvenile Sex Offenders." *Federal Probation* 3 (2001): 8–15.

Howell, Parker. "Sex Abuse Cases Hit Record Number. Better Awareness, Enforcement Cited." *Knight Ridder Tribune Business News*, February 4, 2007, 1.

Human Rights Watch. "No Easy Answers." Human Rights Watch, 19, no. 4G. http:// hrw.org/reports/2007/us0907/3.htm#_Toc176672559) (accessed November 15, 2007).

Human Rights Watch. "No Easy Answers." Human Rights Watch, 19, no. 4G. http:// hrw.org/reports/2007/us0907/6.htm#_Toc176672576). (accessed November 15, 2007).

Human Rights Watch, "No Easy Answers." Human Rights Watch, 19, no. 4G. http:// hrw.org/reports/2007/us0907/5.htm#_Toc176672570) (accessed November 15, 2007).

Human Rights Watch. "No Easy Answers." Human Rights Watch, 19, no. 4G. http://
hrw.org/reports/2007/us0907/1.htm#_Toc176672549 (accessed November,
15, 2007.)

Human Rights Watch, "No Easy Answers." Human Rights Watch, 19, no. 4G. http://
hrw.org/reports/2007/us0907/5.htm#_Toc176672570) (accessed November
15, 2007).

Human Rights Watch, "No Easy Answers." Human Rights Watch, 19, no. 4G. http://
hrw.org/reports/2007/us0907/5.htm#_Toc176672570) (accessed November
15, 2007).

Hunter, John A. "Understanding Juvenile Sex Offenders: Research Findings and
Guidelines for Effective Management and Treatment." In *Juvenile Justice Fact
Sheet*. Charlottesville, VA: Institute of Law, Psychiatry, and Public Policy,
2000.

Koch, Wendy. "More Sex Offender Transient, Elusive; Homeless Life May Increase
Crime Risk." *USA Today*, November 19, 2007, 1.

Levenson, Jill S., and Leo P. Cotter. "The Impact of Megan's Law on Sex Offender
Reintegration." *Journal of Contemporary Criminal Justice* 21(1) (2005): 49–66.

———. "The Effect of Megan's Law on Sex Offenders Reintegration." *Journal of
Contemporary Criminal Justice* 21(1) (2005): 49–66.

McNeil, Michele. "Concerned about Juvenile Sex Offenders, States Move to Tighten
Their Regulations." *Education Week* 26(36) (2007): 28–31.

Moore, Martha T. "Sex Crimes Break the Lock on Juvenile Records; Some States List
Minors in Their Registries; Federal Law May Follow Suit." *USA Today*, July
10, 2006, 5A.

National Center of Sexual Behavior of Youth. "Frequently Asked Questions about Children with Sexual Behavior Problems." http://www.ncsby.org/pages/registry.
htm (accessed November 15, 2007).

Nolan, Kay. "Waukesha Passes Sex Offender Regulation: Residences near Schools,
Other Facilities Prohibited." *McClatchy Tribune Business News*, November 7,
2007, 1.

Parks, Gregory A., and David E. Bard. "Risk Factors for Adolescent Sex Offender
Recidivism: Evaluation of Predictive Factors and Comparison of Three Groups
Based upon Victim Type." *Sexual Abuse: A Journal of Research and Treatment*
18(4) (2006): 319–342.

Petrosino, Anthony, and Carolyn Petrosino. "The Public Safety Potential of Megan's
Law in Massachusetts: An Assessment from a Sample of Criminal Sexual Psychopaths." *Crime and Delinquency* 45(1) (1999): 140–158.

Pierce, Margo. "Sex in the Time of Hysteria." *The Cleveland Free Times*, November 21, 2007, http://www.freetimes.com/stories/15/29/sex-in-the-time-of-
hysteria (accessed November 28, 2007).

Ramshaw, Emily. "Sex Offender Fired as TYC Guard: Firms That Run Youth Centers
Don't Always Check Juvenile Records." *Knight Ridder Tribune Business News*,
March 8, 2007, 1.

Reinhart, Mary. "Legislators Try to Ease Laws for Sex Crimes by Youths: Family Appeals Sway Conservative Lawmakers to Back Bills to Alter Statutes." *Knight Ridder Tribune Business News*, February 11, 2007, 1.

Rivedal, Karen. "Sex Offender Notification Policies All Over the Board." *Knight Ridder Tribune Business News*, March 5, 2007, 1.

Ronis, Scott, and Charles Borduin. "Individual, Family, Peer and Academic Characteristics of Male Juvenile Sexual Offenders." *Journal of Abnormal Child Psychology* 35(2) (2007): 153–163.

Rozas, Angela. "Do Young Sex Offenders Belong on Adult Register." *Chicago Tribune*, January 16, 2007, 1.

Snyder, Howard N. "Sexual Assault of Young Children as Reported to Law Enforcement: Victim, Incident and Offender Characteristics." Washington, DC: Bureau of Justice Statistics: National Center for Juvenile Justice. NCJ 182990, 2000.

State Of Ohio Department of Rehabilitation and Correction. "Ten Year Recidivism Follow-Up of 1989 Sex Offender Releases." 2001.

Taylor, Ralph B., John Goldkamp, Doris Weiland, Clarissa Breen, R. Maria Garcia, Lawrence Presley, and Brian R. Wyant. "Revise Policies Mandating Offender DNA Collection." *Criminology and Public Policy* 6(4) (2007): 851–862.

Walker, Jeffrey T. "Eliminate Residency Restrictions for Sex Offenders." *Criminology and Public Policy* 6(4) (2007): 863–870.

Zimring, Franklin. *An American Travesty: Legal Responses to Adolescent Sexual Offending.* Chicago: University of Chicago Press, 2004.

LEGAL CASES

Connecticut Department of Safety v. Doe (2003) 538 US 1(2003).

Smith v. Doe (2003). 538 US 84 (2003).

8

Putting All the Pieces Together: Separating Fact from Fiction

It is not uncommon for people to draw inaccurate conclusions when little is known about some phenomenon; juvenile sex offenders are no exception. A comparable situation of what we know about juvenile sex offenders today is the state of knowledge regarding HIV and AIDS during the 1980s. One of my first recollections of hearing about HIV and AIDS was when the news broke of Rock Hudson contracting the disease. Given that little was known about the disease, many of us heard the following pieces of information: the disease was contracted if you were gay or had many sexual partners. This led many of us to believe we were immune. Later, however, I heard it could be contracted by donating blood; it was a lethal disease; it could be contracted through kissing; and the myths continued. Two problems fueled the phenomenon: (1) research was lacking on the topic; and (2) people were fearful of it so they often jumped to conclusions. The combination of the two problems leads to panic and misconceptions. Similar to juvenile sex offending, not enough research has been conducted to be fully informed and people are fearful of it. There is cause for hope, however. As noted throughout this book, more and more research is being conducted on this population of offenders.

HAVE WE GONE TOO FAR IN DEFINING WHO IS A JUVENILE SEX OFFENDER?

A salient problem exists for juvenile sex offenders as compared to adult sex offenders: the definition of what is sexual abuse becomes even murkier. As noted in Chapter 1, sexual experimentation is a normal part of one's development.

With so much public and media attention on sex offenders in the last decade, the pendulum has swung in the direction of conservatism: anyone and everyone who deviates in an overt or even latent way should be labeled as a sexual deviant, regardless of their age or the context under which it occurred. This has led to the following cases: a seventeen-year-old boy in Georgia was incarcerated for having consensual oral sex with a fifteen-year-old girl; a thirteen-year-old boy in Illinois pleaded guilty to sexual abuse after he rang the doorbell of a thirteen-year-old girl and grabbed her breast;[1] an eight-year-old was removed from school for sexually harassing a female classmate after he grabbed the girl's buttocks in gym class.[2] While these cases are by no means the "norm" of those who have been labeled as juvenile sex offenders, they do pique our interests and call into question exactly what constitutes a sexual offense. Creating blanket laws where all offenders are treated the same may in fact create additional injustices. Being able to assess situations in their context may be key to distinguishing sexual deviant behavior from normal experimentation and typical horseplay (which should be admonished, but not severely punished).

WHAT ARE COMMON CHARACTERISTICS OF JUVENILE SEX OFFENDERS?

We have noted several times throughout this book that not all juvenile sex offenders are the same, yet we have also found many of those who sexually offend share some commonalities.

- The majority are male.
- Most do not use violence to commit sexual abuse; most use simple coercion.
- Most have victims slightly younger than themselves.
- The younger the victim is, the more likely it is a relative.
- Rarely do they victimize strangers.
- Most choose female victims (yet males can be victims).
- Current research shows few are re-arrested for another sex offense after the initial sex offense is reported.
- Many have a history of being sexually abused (yet this does not explain why they commit abuse; a substantial portion of those who are sexually abused do not go on to abuse others).

While these are the "common" characteristics, it should also be recognized that some juveniles (a very small percentage) do not fit this prototype; they may be female or they may be young (younger than thirteen); they may choose an adult as a victim. These unusual groups make up a very small portion of sex offenders.

CAN JUVENILE SEX OFFENDERS BE CURED?

At the beginning of this book we noted one of the purposes of the book was for reflection toward this problem. The reader should know that while this book covers the most up-to-date findings, it is possible and likely that many of the facts will be revised as the research efforts continue. Just as it was once true that AIDS was quickly followed by death (currently many people are living much longer than anticipated), the treatment for juvenile sex offenders should not be thought of as "impossible."

Throughout this book the Association for the Treatment of Sexual Abusers (ATSA) has been mentioned and often relied on as a source for information. This is one of the largest organizations for sexual abusers and one of the most reliable. Unfortunately many organizations for sexual abusers actually advocate sexual interactions between adults and children. To become a member of ATSA one must submit documentation verifying their credentials and submit other references. Just a few years ago when I applied, I found the process cumbersome and lengthy, yet for a good reason. The Association is made up of some of the best researchers and clinicians in the country. Their current statement regarding "curing" sex offenders is that they currently cannot be cured; yet they can be managed. What does this mean? A common example many practitioners and researchers of sexual abuse give is a comparison to alcoholics. Many alcoholics have ceased drinking alcohol for years and sometimes decades. However, we would not tell a recovering alcoholic who has not drank for several decades, "You're cured now; go celebrate by having a beer." For sex offenders, the same is true: their behavior can be curtailed, but we would never tell them, "You're cured; go celebrate and have all the neighborhood kids over for a sleepover."

The issue for juveniles is slightly more complex than this, however. For example while we can *treat* (not cure) someone who has pedophilia tendencies, not all juvenile sex offenders have true pedophilia. Also, as noted in several of the chapters, many juveniles outgrow the behavior on their own or with minimal guidance from a professional. Do we know how to distinguish between those who will outgrow such tendencies on their own and those who need treatment? Well, sort of. We know there are several key factors that distinguish the two groups. As noted in Chapter 1 (Weinrott's), research has shown the juveniles who blame the victim, have cognitive distortions (they didn't fight back—it must be OK, etc.), have deviant arousal (become sexually aroused to deviant behavior—i.e., violence), and use force or threat of force to gain sexual consent.[3] These factors, however, are probabilistic in nature; meaning if they are present it is *probable* they will persist (as opposed to committing crimes only during their adolescence, adolescence-limited). Thus, we are not 100 percent sure they will persist. This is true for most social science phenomena; there is no bulls-eye or "proven" factor that can predict such behavior.

So to answer the question can we cure juvenile sex offenders: the answer is no. However, there is a "but" and a big one—but we have a host of assessment tools that can determine the severity of the problem and there are several treatment techniques (as outlined in Chapter 7) that have been successful for those who stick with the treatment and have the support. One should be hopeful, however, as with HIV/AIDS, many people are living well beyond their initial expectancies and treatment has vastly improved; we predict the future for treatment of juvenile sex offenders will continue to improve.

ARE SEX OFFENDER REGISTRATION LAWS THE PROBLEM OR THE ANSWER?

Some have described sex offender registration laws as "feel good legislation."[4] The facts are that each of the different sex offender registration laws (Jacob Wetterling Act, Megan's Law, Adam Walsh Law, etc.) were created after someone lost a loved one to a violent sexual offender who also committed murder. While this is not a bad thing, the laws were based on reactions to hearing heartrending stories of each victim's family's experience. They were reactionary laws, not based on sound research derived by the experts, but from a mere knee-jerk reaction to a sequence of horrible events. No disrespect is intended to such families, but who would support a law if we knew it did not help reduce future victims? Here are the facts regarding sex offender registration laws and juveniles:

- Violent sexual predators make up only a small portion of registered sex offenders.[5]
- Instances of vigilantism have occurred where the offenders become targets of others' harassment and violence.[6]

- Many registered offenders find it difficult to maintain ties to the community and relationships with significant people who were part of their support system.[7]

- Research has not been published to assess the effects of juveniles who have had to register.

- Sex offender registries may give a false sense of "knowing where all the sex offenders are."

- Many juveniles who commit sex offenses desist after their adolescence (yet may be required to register through their adulthood in some states).

So one may ask, what good do such laws do? Crime control advocates contend such laws assist in the investigation of ongoing sex crimes.[8] We would like to point out, however, that having a nonpublic sex offender registration (i.e., only open to law enforcement officials) would still allow law enforcement officials to investigate sex crimes. A compromise, however, as suggested by ATSA, may be to include only the most serious sex offenders included in the public registry.

Can Juvenile Sexual Offenses be Prevented?

While it may not be possible to fully eradicate all sexual offenses, many can be prevented. As noted in Chapter 2, there are many different causes for sexual offenses and not all offenses are for the same reason. In order to reduce sexual offending, the sources need to be addressed. The following explanations were cited as sources of potential offending: sexual deviancy escalating into sexual abuse, cognitive distortions, deviant fantasies paired with masturbation, exposure to violence/abuse, peer influence (i.e., showing off for or with friends), lack of attachment, and coming from a dysfunctional family. Again, many of the factors occur in combination with other elements. For example, we all know someone who came from a dysfunctional family, yet they are not a sex offender. In order to prevent sexual abuse, one prevailing thought surfaces: problem behavior must be dealt with immediately and not escalate. For example, excessive use of pornography or holding cognitive distortions (girls just like to play hard to get; they really want to be seduced/have sex with me), needs to be addressed immediately. Parents, caretakers, and teachers need to remain in consistent communication about problem behaviors.

Children need to be taught socially appropriate sexual behavior beginning at a very young age. Parenting classes also should include such curricula. Students who have been known or suspected of being exposed to violence also need intervention. While this is not an easy problem to solve (as many children who are abused are done so by a family member, usually a parent), factors that may insulate the child engaging in deviancy need to be in place. For example, establishing additional resources for the child may reduce later problems. In addition to an education component regarding appropriate sexual behaviors, at-risk children (i.e., those who do not form bonds easily with others) should also be identified and provided with additional resources. Resources can include one-on-one sessions with a counselor to monitor progress or establishing a mentor for the child. Providing additional support for a child at risk may be beneficial in the long run.

THERE IS NO "TYPICAL" SEX OFFENDER, BUT THEY CAN BE CATEGORIZED

A common theme throughout this book is that juveniles who sexually offend vary a great deal in their characteristics. However, among the diversity, several groups of sex offenders have been identified; they include: (1) those with slight boundary issues (i.e., may explore sexuality with someone the individual is babysitting or has access to); (2) youth with social deficits (usually isolated youth who do not or have not bonded with others); (3) those who commit hands-off offenses (e.g., voyeurism or exhibitionism); (4) youth with psychological problems (e.g., learning problems, mental illness); (5) antisocial youth (those who have a history of criminal offenses); (6) psychologically normal youth (those who do not show any mental abnormalities); and (7) youth who have experienced sexual abuse. Again, while these are very broad classifications, it should be noted many youth who sexually offend might fit into more than one category.

ADVICE FOR PARENTS TOWARD KEEPING ALL CHILDREN SAFE[9]

KNOW YOUR CHILD

As noted in Chapter 1, there are many warning signs someone is being abused (fear of being alone with an adult, suddenly performing poorly in school, depression, rage, etc.), but now the question may be what to do. Sex abusers tend to choose their victims carefully. They choose victims that they believe they can overcome, control, or seduce. As parents we need to see when our children are emotionally needy and reassure them or address those points that would make them vulnerable to manipulation and exploitation. Parents also need to take the time to talk to their children, even preschool age children, in a manner appropriate for their level about what is correct behavior in terms of respecting physical boundaries—theirs and others. Children should be clear that others ought not to touch them in certain ways and on certain parts of their bodies, nor talk to them about certain kinds of touching.

As the child grows older, update the information, teaching them to use correct physiological terms along with the appropriate values that go along with certain behaviors. Note that children are often misinformed about sexual matters by their peers—but if you are a source of correct information—you lessen their vulnerability to sexual myths.

TRUST NO ONE QUICKLY

Because most children who are the victims of a sexual offense are victimized by someone they know—assume that the sex offender could be anyone at all. How well do you really know Grandpa So-and-So or Auntie So-and-So, the neighbor, or that sixteen-year-old volunteering to babysit? Be vigilant. Why is Coach So-and-So or Father So-and-So really interested in helping little Bobby after hours? Do not be quick to leave your child with anyone—even when in a crunch.

CHECK WHAT YOU DO AND WHAT YOU HAVE AROUND THE HOUSE

Children can develop inappropriate sexual behaviors if there is exposure to adult sex acts or child pornography repeatedly—seemingly normalizing such behaviors. Those dirty videos that you think they don't know about—you'd be amazed how many times that child has seen them! Also, caution about the World Wide Web where access to such images is all too easy and now with streaming videos—one need not go looking for it—type in an innocent word for a science project and it's right there. Such materials are also more available on prime-time television and video games. Children tend to learn from media and peers ideas that may become internalized via fantasies and masturbation.

PARENTS NEED TO STAY ALERT!

Pay attention to how the child gets along with others. Does he or she respect the word "no" when others use it? Does the child respect the boundaries of others? Pay attention to the special vulnerability of children with disabilities—physical and/or mental, those with mental retardation, or autism.

GUARD BOTH YOUR BOYS AND YOUR GIRLS

Do not assume that boys are safe because they are boys. Research indicates that when juveniles victimize males sexually it is more a matter of having had the opportunity to do so, than a preference for males for sex. One phallometric study of juvenile sex offender arousal revealed that when exposed to both male and female sexual stimuli, arousal was usually greater with female sexual stimuli than male stimuli even for those juveniles who had male victims. This suggests that the offending was more about opportunity and far less about the sexual contact itself.[10] There is no shortcut for vigilance!

KEEP LINES OF COMMUNICATION OPEN

Encourage or foster a relationship with your child where he or she feels comfortable communicating with you. This doesn't mean that you have to be your child's buddy—you can clearly be a trusted parent by making time to talk to your child and listening carefully to him or her. Having meals with your child or driving somewhere seems to facilitate conversation. Also, talk about the possibility of a sexual victimization—not just by the stranger hiding in the bushes, but by people they know—friends, relatives, and peers. Yes—it is an uncomfortable topic and some parents would rather not—but the fact is, the risk of sexual victimization exists. Often, it is mothers who have these conversations with their children if they occur at all.[11] What would certainly be helpful is advocating that such discussions be a part of sex education curricula in schools at age-appropriate levels from preschool and throughout the rest of their education experience. Presently what we have been doing is teaching children from their preschool years that anything dealing with genitalia is taboo. So, especially in African American and Hispanic cultures, certain conversations even about normal sexuality do not occur.[12]

BREAK THROUGH YOUR OWN DENIAL

If you learn that your child has behaved sexually inappropriately whether alone (e.g., masturbating in public) or with someone else—fight the urge to deny that such a thing could possibly be. Objectively seek the facts and get the help necessary from someone with experience working in this area (not all therapists/counselors will know what to do). If you do not know a sex offender treatment provider in your state, contact a pediatrician or any physician available to you for assistance or referral to the appropriate party. Stay calm and nonjudgmental so that you do not make the child—whether child offender or child victim—feel particularly stigmatized over the event. If the victim lives in the same house, then resist the urge to focus on the needs of one child to the neglect of the other(s).

Know what is legally required in your state in such matters—for example in Texas, if the victim of sexual harm is a minor the law states that anyone who knows or suspects it has a duty to report it to Child Protective Services or law enforcement. So if you solicit the input of another, anyone at all, but especially a sex offender treatment provider, depending on the gravity of the situation, making a report to the authorities may be a must. In assessing the offender three basic points are considered: (a) the risk the person poses; (b) what's necessary given the situation; and (c) how responsive the juvenile is likely to be to intervention.

REASSURE THE CHILD THAT YOU LOVE HIM OR HER

Whether your child is the victim or the offender, that child needs to be reassured that you love him or her. Often the abuser will threaten the child with a loss of love if the abuse becomes known. The victim will need to know that it was not his or her fault. Choose your words carefully to communicate this point. Let them know that telling was the right thing to do. Unless, it is absolutely necessary, avoid sending one of the children out of the home. Of course, be smart about it. Have clear rules to avoid further victimization and carefully monitor the children.

AVOID INTERROGATING THE CHILD

In the case that a criminal investigation becomes necessary, if you ask the child about the specifics of the incident too much, you risk confusing the child and desensitizing the child, which could impede a prosecution should such become necessary. Let the child know what you plan to do about the situation and respect his or her wishes as much as possible.

A comprehensive assessment will involve the use of multiple methods to gain information about the juvenile's:

- developmental history
- intellectual and cognitive functioning
- educational achievement, academic performance
- employment, recreation, leisure
- physical health
- psychological adjustment, mental health, personality
- substance use and abuse
- sexual development, attitudes, behaviors, interests, preferences
- family structure and dynamics
- interpersonal relationships, peers/associates, intimate relationships
- prior legal involvement, history of delinquent and criminal behavior
- response to prior interventions, motivation to change.[13]

Common juvenile sex offender assessment instruments include:

- *Estimate of Risk of Adolescent Sexual Offense Recidivism (ERASOR)* by Worling and Curwen, 2001.
- *Juvenile Sex Offender Assessment Protocol-II (J-SOAP-II)* by Prentky and Righthand, 2003.
- *Juvenile Sexual Offense Recidivism Risk Assessment Tool-II (JSORRAT-II)* by Epperson, Ralston, Fowers, DeWitt, and Gore, 2006.

In addition, a polygraph examination might be necessary. Polygraph evidence is not admissible in court proceedings because they depend on physiological responses in heart rate, blood pressure, and respiration to indicate attempts at deception. It is not an infallible way of assessing truth as one can train oneself to control these responses. It is unlikely, however, that a juvenile would have invested the effort necessary for mastering such deception.

Another assessment approach is the use of phallometric measures such as a penile plethysmograph. For this a juvenile is exposed to images, videos, and audio stimuli to see which stimuli leads to an arousal response as indicated by both physiological response and time spent looking at each image. This technique, though assumed fairly valid, is not infallible as arousal responses can be manipulated. (See Chapter 7 for more information about assessment tools.)

WHAT HAPPENS AT SCHOOL?

School is where we develop much of our skills at getting along. Teachers are a very big part of that. School might contribute to juvenile sex offending when the attitudes and values modeled by the staff—in how they dress, talk, and behave—might suggest to students with deviant sexual notions that those notions are acceptable.[14] Additionally, school security could be problematic. Incidents at school often happen in those out-of-sight places, corridors, corners, and restrooms.

The other concern for many school personnel is how to distinguish fairly normal sexual explorations from cases requiring professional and perhaps legal intervention. Some behaviors that warrant concern include an encounter between persons with a clear power differential and an encounter between persons who tend to not normally associate with each other.

When incidents happen school officials should take them seriously to assure both the offender and the victim's families. Keep confidences to the extent possible. If the offending child is still a risk, moving him/her off campus will likely be necessary. Otherwise, it is important to keep the juvenile in a normal setting so that he or she might improve in functioning. But what about the victim? In many cases the victim might *not* perceive him or herself to be victimized (as in consensual cases)—but if the victim is uncomfortable, then it is the offender who should be transferred out.

WHO REALLY NEEDS TO KNOW ABOUT A JUVENILE SEX OFFENDER IN THE SCHOOL?

Many school personnel and some parents of victims have been pushing for notification when a juvenile sex offender is in their midst. A prickly matter, for such wide disclosure can mean the increase of a heavy negative stigma for the offender and in some cases specific victims. Some would argue—tell the principal, vice principal, teachers, and custodians. Well—people talk—may as well tell everyone. Here's the catch though—in school, on the school bus, et cetera, your child could be sexually victimized by anyone. So we do not need to point out Johnny. The child sitting next to Johnny could be a sex offender too—we just have not caught her yet. So why not have policies in place to protect all the children—no matter what? For example, at one mega church that we know, children in the Sunday school are not allowed to go to the restroom alone. Schools could develop a similar safety plan.

How Might the Justice System Respond?

Avoid the politics. Let sound research guide it toward affecting that old juvenile justice goal of rehabilitation. Get prosecutors out of the mix in terms of their having the power to transfer juveniles to the adult system. Prosecutors just get too political and downright irrational, pandering to public fear. Properly investigate the allegations. To reconstruct the incident, get the: victim's story, offender's version, what relevant others (family, peers) have to say, offender's past, and a thorough mental health assessment. In many cases the judge could try something like deferred adjudication. In such cases, the juvenile gets sent to treatment—saving residential placement for the most dangerous (violent, compulsive, or noncooperative).

Because juvenile justice is about rehabilitation it must include families. Often delinquency is a mere symptom of problems in the family. For starters consider: Whether the offender was a victim of sexual abuse? The competence of the parents? The presence of sexual boundary problems in the family?[15] What does the offender need, and if the victim or other children are in the home, what do they need? Does the offender, and/or the family blame the victim? Blame could be delivered nonverbally. Plus, if the victim and nonsupportive others are not in the same residence, consider having contact with the victim monitored. Note the following case involving a thirteen-year-old victim in a children's home who said that her teenage brothers molested her for years:

> During telephone calls her mother made constant demands that she should be allowed to return home, accused her of causing illness in the family due to the allegations, and insisted that she should "pull herself together and get over the abuse." The mother also colluded with the brothers in helping them to make telephone calls to the victim, where they would continue to verbally abuse and threaten her.[16]

The Bottom Line

In regard to juvenile-perpetrated sexual offenses, the problem is at least twofold in that it involves juveniles, who are not yet set in their ways, and the behavior, sexual abuse, is in fact a serious one that evokes strong emotion from most. While research exists, it is not enough to answer all of our questions. The quality and quantity of the research in this area has increased over the past decade and we suspect it will continue; thus, it is always the key to be informed of newly developed research in this area.

Given that little information was available on juvenile sex offenders, many policymakers jumped the gun to develop policy—unfortunately such policy may not be the most effective. We, therefore, need to remain flexible and willing to examine the policy that currently exists. We must be able to admit the policy created may not be advantageous to the victim, the offender, or to society. The current policy is not set in stone; we must be willing to fix the problems we have created.

Parents who are our most valuable resources, our frontline workers so to speak, must be attentive, informed, and willing to become involved. Parents who have experienced juvenile sexual offense (whether their children have been victimized or sexually offended) can share a great deal of experience and information with the public. As noted throughout these chapters, communication is a key element. Parents must be in communication with their children and with those who have access to their children, such as teachers and care providers.

In the future, it is highly likely we will know a great deal more about juvenile sex offenders, including how to detect them and, most importantly, how they should be treated. As research continues to be conducted and more is known about sex offenders, it is also likely rational approaches will be developed to treat both victims of juvenile sex offenders and the offenders themselves.

NOTES

1. Angela Rozas, "Do Young Sex Offenders Belong on Adult Register," *Chicago Tribune*, January 16, 2007, 1.

2. Beth Stallings, "Boy, 8 Accused of Sexual Harassment," *Morning Journal*, March 25, 2006.

3. Sue Righthand and Carlann Welch, "Juveniles Who Have Sexually Offended: A Review of the Professional Literature" (Washington, DC: Office of Juvenile Justice and Delinquency Prevention, 2001).

4. Robert Freeman-Longo, "Revisiting Megan's Law and Sex Offender Registration: Prevention or Problem," American Probation and Parole Association (2005).

5. Parker Howell, "Sex Abuse Cases Hit Record Number. Better Awareness, Enforcement Cited," *Chicago Tribune*, January 16, 2007, 1.

6. Jill S. Levenson and Leo Cotter, "The Effect of Megan's Law on Sex Offenders Reintegration," *Journal of Contemporary Criminal Justice* 21(1) (2005); Richard Tewksbury, "Experiences and Attitudes of Registered Female Sex Offenders," *Federal Probation* 68(3) (2004); Donna M Vandiver, Kelly A. Cheeseman, and Robert Worley, "A Qualitative Assessment of Registered Sex Offenders: Characteristics and Attitudes toward Registration." Paper presented at the Annual Meeting of the

Southwestern Association of Criminal Justice, Fort Worth, TX, 2006). October 2006.

7. Levenson and Cotter, "The Effect of Megan's Law on Sex Offenders Reintegration"; Tewksbury, "Experiences and Attitudes of Registered Female Sex Offenders"; Vandiver, Cheeseman, and Worley, "A Qualitative Assessment of Registered Sex Offenders: Characteristics and Attitudes toward Registration."

8. Winter Denning, "Sex Offender Laws: Some Legislative Responses," in *Sexual Assault: The Victims, the Perpetrators, and the Criminal Justice System*, ed. F. P. Reddington and B. W. Kreisel (Durham, NC: Carolina Academic Press, 2005).

9. Some of the suggestions are adapted from: Stop It Now, *Do Children Sexually Abuse Other Children? Preventing Sexual Abuse among Children and Youth* (Brandon, VT: The Safer Society Press, 2007), 15.

10. M. R. Weinrott, M. Riggan, and S. Frothingham, "Reducing Deviant Arousal in Juvenile Sex Offenders Using Vicarious Sensitization," *Journal of Interpersonal Violence* 12(5) (1997): 711.

11. David Finkelhor, "Prevention: A Review of Programs and Research," in *A Sourcebook on Child Sexual Abuse*, ed. David Finkelhor et al. (Newbury Park, CA: Sage, 1986), 233.

12. John Bancroft, "Normal Sexual Development," in *The Juvenile Sex Offender*, ed. Howard Barbaree and William Marshall (New York: Guilford Press, 2006), 22, 27.

13. Center for Sex Offender Management, "The Importance of Assessment in Sex Offender Management: An Overview of Key Principles and Practices" (Silver Spring, MD: CSOM, 2007), 3.

14. Carol Carson, "Looking After Young Sexual Abusers: Child Protection, Risk Management and Risk Reduction," in *Children and Young People Who Sexually Abuse Others: Current Development and Practice Responses*, ed. Marcus Erooga and Helen Masson (London: Routledge, 2006), 60.

15. Tony Morrison and Julie Henniker, "Building a Comprehensive Inter-Agency Assessment and Intervention System for Young People Who Sexually Harm: The Aim Project," in *Children and Young People Who Sexually Abuse Others: Current Development and Practice Responses*, ed. Marcus Erooga and Helen Masson (London: Routledge, 2006), 38–39.

16. Kevin Epps, "Looking After Young Sexual Abusers: Child Protection, Risk Management and Risk Reduction," in *Children and Young People Who Sexually Abuse Others: Current Development and Practice Responses*, ed. Marcus Erooga and Helen Masson (London: Routledge, 2006), 70.

REFERENCES

Bancroft, John. "Normal Sexual Development." In *The Juvenile Sex Offender*, edited by Howard Barbaree and William Marshall. New York: Guilford Press, 2006.

Carson, Carol. "Looking After Young Sexual Abusers: Child Protection, Risk Management and Risk Reduction." In *Children and Young People Who Sexually Abuse Others: Current Development and Practice Responses*, edited by Marcus Erooga and Helen Masson. London: Routledge, 2006.

Center for Sex Offender Management. "The Importance of Assessment in Sex Offender Management: An Overview of Key Principles and Practices." Silver Spring, MD: CSOM, 2007.

Denning, Winter. "Sex Offender Laws: Some Legislative Responses " In *Sexual Assault: The Victims, the Perpetrators, and the Criminal Justice System*, edited by F. P. Reddington and B. W. Kreisel, 321–333. Durham, NC: Carolina Academic Press, 2005.

Epps, Kevin. "Looking After Young Sexual Abusers: Child Protection, Risk Management and Risk Reduction." In *Children and Young People Who Sexually Abuse Others: Current Development and Practice Responses*, edited by Marcus Erooga and Helen Masson. London: Routledge, 2006.

Finkelhor, David. "Prevention: A Review of Programs and Research." In *A Sourcebook on Child Sexual Abuse*, edited by David Finkelhor, Sharon Araji, Larry Baron, Angela Browne, Stefanie Doyle Peters, and Gail Elizabeth Wyatt, 224–254. Newbury Park, CA: Sage, 1986.

Freeman-Longo, Robert. "Revisiting Megan's Law and Sex Offender Registration: Prevention or Problem." *American Probation and Parole Association* (2005): 1–20.

Howell, Parker. "Sex Abuse Cases Hit Record Number. Better Awareness, Enforcement Cited." *Knight Ridder Tribune Business News*, 2007, 1.

Levenson, Jill S., and Leo Cotter. "The Effect of Megan's Law on Sex Offenders Reintegration." *Journal of Contemporary Criminal Justice* 21(1) (2005): 49–66.

Morrison, Tony, and Julie Henniker. "Building a Comprehensive Inter-Agency Assessment and Intervention System for Young People Who Sexually Harm: The Aim Project." In *Children and Young People Who Sexually Abuse Others: Current Development and Practice Responses*, edited by Marcus Erooga and Helen Masson, 31–50. London: Routledge, 2006.

Righthand, Sue, and Carlann Welch. "Juveniles Who Have Sexually Offended: A Review of the Professional Literature," 1–59. Washington, DC: Office of Juvenile Justice and Delinquency Prevention, 2001.

Rozas, Angela. "Do Young Sex Offenders Belong on Adult Register." *Chicago Tribune*, January 16, 2007, 1.

Stallings, Beth. "Boy, 8 Accused of Sexual Harassment." *Morning Journal*, March 25, 2006, 1.

Stop It Now. *Do Children Sexually Abuse Other Children? Preventing Sexual Abuse among Children and Youth*. Brandon, VT: The Safer Society Press, 2007.

Tewksbury, Richard. "Experiences and Attitudes of Registered Female Sex Offenders." *Federal Probation* 68(3) (2004): 30–33.

Vandiver, Donna M., Kelly A. Cheeseman, and Robert Worley. "A Qualitative Assessment of Registered Sex Offenders: Characteristics and Attitudes toward

Registration." Paper presented at the Annual Meeting of the Southwestern Association of Criminal Justice, Fort Worth, TX, 2006.

Weinrott, M. R., M. Riggan, and S. Frothingham. "Reducing Deviant Arousal in Juvenile Sex Offenders Using Vicarious Sensitization." *Journal of Interpersonal Violence* 12(5) (1997): 704–728.

Bibliography

13WHAM.com. "These Sex Offenders Are Protected." (Assessed November 28, 2007).

"5th-Graders Accused of Having Sex in Class." *Chicago Tribune*, April 5, 2007, 6.

Abel Assessment for Sexual Interest. "Assessment Page 2," http://www.alphaservices. org/assessment_2.htm. (Accessed November 15, 2007).

Abel, Gene G., Candice A. Osborn, and Deborah A. Twigg. "Sexual Assault through the Life Span: Adult Offenders with Juvenile Histories." In *The Juvenile Sex Offender*, edited by Howard E. Barbaree, William S. Marshall, and Stephen M. Hudson, 104–116. New York: The Guilford Press, 1993.

American Psychiatric Association. *Diagnostic and Statistical Manual of Mental Disorders, Fourth Edition*. Washington, DC: American Psychiatric Association, 1994.

American Psychiatric Association. *Diagnostic and Statistical Manual of Mental Disorder, Fourth Edition, Text Revision*. Washington, DC: American Psychiatric Association, 2000.

Araji, Sharon. *Sexually Aggressive Children: Coming to Understand Them*. Thousand Oaks, CA: Sage Publications, 1997.

Associated Press. "Woman, 19, Charged in Online Sex Ring." CBS News, http:// www.cbsnews.com/stories/2007/07/12/national/printable3052371.shtml. (Accessed November 15, 2007).

Association for the Treatment of Sexual Abusers. "The Effective Legal Management of Juvenile Sex Offenders." ATSA, http://www.atsa.com/ppjuvenile.html. (Accessed November 24, 2007).

Austin, James, Johnette Peyton, and Kelly Dedel Johnson. *Reliability and Validity Study of the Static-99/RRASOR Sex Offender Risk Assessment Instruments*. [Final Report submitted to the Pennsylvania Board of Probation and Parole.] Washington, DC: The Institute on Crime, Justice, and Corrections, George Washington University, 2003.

Bancroft, John. "Normal Sexual Development." In *The Juvenile Sex Offender*, edited by Howard Barbaree and William Marshall. New York: Guilford Press, 2006.

Bandura, Albert. *Social Learning Theory*. Englewood Cliffs, NJ: Prentice-Hall, 1977.

Barbaree, Howard, and William Marshall. *The Juvenile Sex Offender*, edited by Howard Barbaree and William Marshall. New York: Guilford Press, 2006.

Bartholomew, Kim. "Avoidance of Intimacy: An Attachment Perspective." *Journal of Social and Personal Relationships* 7(2) (1990): 147–178.

Becker, Judith V. "Treating Adolescent Sexual Offenders." *Professional Psychology: Research and Practice* 21(5) (1990): 362–365.

Becker, Judith V., and Cathi Harris, "The Psychophysioloical Assessment of Juvenile Offenders." In *The Handbook of Clinical Intervention with Young People Who Sexually Abuse*, edited by Gary O'Reilly, William L. Marshall, Alan Carr, and Richard C. Beckett, 191–202. New York: Psychology Press, 2004.

Becker, Judith V., and John A. Hunter, "Understanding and Treating Child and Adolescent Sexual Offenders." In *Advances in Clinical Child Psychology*, vol. 19, edited by T. H. Ollendick and R. J. Prinz, 177–197. New York: Plenum Press, 1997.

Becker, Judith V., Jerry Cunningham-Rathner, and Meg S. Kaplan. "Adolescent Sexual Offenders: Demographics, Criminal and Sexual Histories, and Recommendations for Reducing Future Offenses." *Journal of Interpersonal Violence* 1(4) (1987): 431–445.

Benard, Thomas J. *The Cycle of Juvenile Justice*. New York: Oxford University Press, 1992.

Boer, Douglass R., Steven D. Hart, P. Randall Kropp, and Christopher D. Webster. "Sexual Violence Risk Assessment-20 (SVR-20)." http://www3.parinc.com/products/product.aspx?Productid=SVR-20 (accessed November 26, 2007).

Borum, Randy, Patrick Bartel, and Adelle E. Forth. "Structural Assessment of Violence Risk in Youth." In *Mental Health Screening and Assessment in Juvenile Justice*, edited by Thomas Grisso, Gina Vincent, and Daniel Seagrave, 311–323. New York: Guilford Press, 2005.

Bourke, Michael L., and Brad Donohou. "Assessment and Treatment of Juvenile Sex Offenders: An Empirical Review." *Journal of Child Sexual Abuse* 5 (1996): 47–70.

Brantlinger, Ellen. "Mildly Mentally Retarded Secondary Students' Information about and Attitudes toward Sexuality and Sexuality Education." *Education and Training of the Mentally Retarded* 20(2) (1985): 99–108.

Bremer, Janis F. "Serious Juvenile Sex Offenders: Treatment and Long-Term Follow-Up." *Psychiatric Annals* 22(6) (1992): 326–332.

Brownmiller, Susan. *Against Our Will: Men, Women, and Rape*. New York: Ballantine Books, 1975.

Bumby, Kurt M., and Nancy. H. Bumby. "Adolescent Females Who Sexually Perpetrate: Preliminary Findings." Paper presented at the 12th Annual Research and Treatment Conference of the Association for the Treatment of Sexual Abusers, Boston, MA, 1993.

Bumby, Nancy. H., and Kurt. M. Bumby. "Adolescent Sexual Offenders." In *The Sex Offender: New Insights, Treatment, Innovations, and Legal Developments*, edited by K. B. Schwartz and R. H. Cellini, 10.1–10.16. Kingston, NJ: Civic Research Institute, Inc., 1997.

Burt, Martha R., and Rochelle Semmel Albin. "Rape Myths, Rape Definitions, and Probability of Conviction." *Journal of Applied Social Psychology* 11(3) (1981): 212–230.

Burton, David L., and William Meezan. "A Preliminary Examination of Racial Differences in Trauma and Sexual Aggression among Adolescent Sexual Abusers." *Smith College Studies in Social Work* 77(1) (2007): 101–121.

Butler, Stephen, and Michael C. Seto. "Distinguishing Two Types of Adolescent Sex Offenders." *Journal of American Child Adolescent Psychiatry* 41(1) (2002): 83–90.

Caldwell, Michael. "What We Do Not Know about Juvenile Sexual Reoffense Risk." *Child Maltreatment* 7(4) (2002): 291–302.

California Apartment Association. "Jacob and Megan's Law Registered Sex Offenders and the Impact on the Rental Housing Industry," April 28, 2006. Paper no. 24, http://www.caanet.org/AM/Template.cfm?Section=Web_Site&TEMPLATE=/CM/ContentDisplay.cfm&CONTENTID=14337. (Accessed November 1, 2007).

Calley, Nancy. "Integrating Theory and Research: The Development of a Research-Based Treatment Program for Juvenile Male Sex Offenders." *Journal of Counseling and Development* 85(2) (2007): 131–142.

Carpentier, Melissa, Jane F. Silovsky, and Mark Chaffin. "Randomized Trial of Treatment for Children with Sexual Behavior Problems: Ten-Year Follow-Up." *Journal of Consulting and Clinical Psychology* 74(3) (2006): 482–488.

Carson, Carol. "Looking After Young Sexual Abusers: Child Protection, Risk Management and Risk Reduction." In *Children and Young People Who Sexually Abuse Others: Current Development and Practice Responses*, edited by Marcus Erooga and Helen Masson. London: Routledge, 2006.

Center, David, Derek Hughes, and Stuart Kirby. "Paedophilia: Pathology, Criminality, or Both? The Development of a Multivariate Model of Offense Behaviour in Child Sexual Abuse." *Journal of Forensic Psychiatry* 9 (1998): 532–555.

Center for Sex Offender Management. "The Importance of Assessment in Sex Offender Management: An Overview of Key Principles and Practices." Silver Spring, MD: CSOM, 2007.

Chaiken, Jan, and Marcia R. Chaiken. *Varieties of Criminal Behavior*. Santa Monica, CA: Rand, 1982.

"Characteristics and Recidivism Rates as Adults." *Journal of Interpersonal Violence* 21(5) (2006): 673–688.

Chow, Eva W. C., and Alberto L. Choy. "Clinical Characteristics and Treatment Response to SSRI in a Female Pedophile." *Archives of Sexual Behavior* 31(2) (2002): 211–215.

CNN.com. "Letourneau Says She and Former Student Are Engaged." October 12, 2004. Accessed January 15, 2005, http://www.cnn.com/2004/US/10/12/letourneau.king/.

Connecticut Department of Safety v. Doe (2003) 538 US 1(2003).

Crawford, Selwyn. "Girl's 15-Year Sentence in Fw Rape Case Called Harsh." *The Dallas Morning News*, January 13, 1995, 27A.

Davis, Glen. E., and Harold Leitenberg. "Adolescent Sex Offenders." *Psychology Bulletin* 101 (1987): 417–427.

Denning, Winter. "Sex Offender Laws: Some Legislative Responses " In *Sexual Assault: The Victims, the Perpetrators, and the Criminal Justice System*, edited by F. P. Reddington and B. W. Kreisel, 321–333. Durham, NC: Carolina Academic Press, 2005.

Denno, Deborah. "Considering Lead Poisoning as a Criminal Defense." *Fordham Urban Law Journal* 20(3) (1993): 377–400.

Denov, Myriam S. *Perspectives on Female Sex Offending: A Culture of Denial.* Burlington, VT: Ashgate Publishing Company, 2004.

Dodge, Kenneth, Gregory Pettit, John Bates, and Ernest Valente. "Social Information-Processing Patterns Partially Mediate the Effect on Early Physical Abuse on Later Conduct Problems." *Journal of Abnormal Psychology* 104(4) (1995): 632–643.

Doshay, Lewis J. *The Boy Sex Offender and His Later Career.* New York: Grune and Stratton, 1943.

Edwards, Carla, and Rebecca Hendrix. "Traumagenic Dynamics in Adult Women Survivors of Childhood Sexual Abuse vs. Adolescent Male Sex Offenders with Similar Histories." *Journal of Offender Rehabilitation* 33(2) (2001): 33–45.

Elliott, Diana M., and Kathy Smiljanich. "Sex Offending among Juveniles: Development and Response." *Journal of Pediatric Health Care* 8(3) (1994): 101–105.

Epps, Kevin. "Looking After Young Sexual Abusers: Child Protection, Risk Management and Risk Reduction." In *Children and Young People Who Sexually Abuse Others: Current Development and Practice Responses*, edited by Marcus Erooga and Helen Masson. London: Routledge, 2006.

Erooga, Marcus, and Helen Masson. "Children and Young People with Sexually Harmful or Abusive Behaviors: Underpinning Knowledge, Principles, Approaches and Service Provision." In *Children and Young People Who Sexually Abuse Others: Current Development and Practice Responses*, edited by Marcus Erooga and Helen Masson, 3–17. London: Routledge, 2006.

Ertl, Melissa A., and John R. McNamara. "Treatment of Juvenile Sex Offenders: A Review of the Literature." *Child & Adolescent Social Work Journal* 14(1) (1997): 199–221.

Fanniff, Amanda M., and Judith V. Becker, "Specialized Assessment and Treatment of Adolescent Sex Offenders." *Aggression and Violent Behavior* 11(3) (2006): 265–282.

Fehrenbach, Peter A., and Caren Monastersky. "Characteristics of Female Adolescent Sexual Offenders." *American Journal of Orthopsychiatry* 58(1) (1988): 148–151.

Fehrenbach, Peter A., Wayne Smith, Caren Montastersky, and Robert W. Deisher. "Adolescent Sexual Offenders: Offenders and Offense Characteristics." *American Journal of Orthopsychiatry* 56(2) (1986): 225–231.

Fergusson, David, and Michael Lynskey. "Physical Punishment/Maltreatment during Childhood and Adjustment in Young Adulthood." *Child Abuse and Neglect* 21(7) (1997): 617–630.

Finkelhor, David. "Abusers: Special Topics." In *A Sourcebook on Child Sexual Abuse*, edited by David Finkelhor, Sharon Araji, Larry Baron, Angela Browne, Stefanie Doyle Peters, and Gail Elizabeth Wyatt, 119–142. Newbury Park, CA: Sage, 1986.

———. "Prevention: A Review of Programs and Research." In *A Sourcebook on Child Sexual Abuse*, edited by David Finkelhor, Sharon Araji, Larry Baron, Angela Browne, Stefanie Doyle Peters, and Gail Elizabeth Wyatt, 224–254. Newbury Park, CA: Sage, 1986.

Finkelhor, David, and Angela Browne. "Initial and Long Term Effects: A Conceptual Framework." In *A Sourcebook on Child Sexual Abuse*, edited by David Finkelhor, Sharon Araji, Larry Baron, Angela Browne, Stefanie Doyle Peters, and Gail Elizabeth Wyatt. Newbury Park, CA: Sage, 1986.

Forth, Adelle E., David S. Kosson, and Richard D. Hare. *The Hare PCL-Youth Version*. Toronto, ON: Multi-Health Systems, 2003.

Freeman-Longo, Robert. "Revisiting Megan's Law and Sex Offender Registration: Prevention or Problem." *American Probation and Parole Association* (2005): 1–20.

Fromuth, Mary Ellen, and Victoria E. Conn. "Hidden Perpetrators: Sexual Molestation in a Nonclinical Sample of College Women." *Journal of Interpersonal Violence* 12(3) (1997): 456–465.

Furby, Lita, Mark R. Weinrott, and Lyn Blackshaw. "Sex Offender Recidivism: A Review" *Psychological Bulletin* 105(1) (1989): 3–30.

Gerardin, Priscille, and Florence Thibaut. "Epidemiology and Treatment of Juvenile Sexual Offending." *Pediatric Drugs* 6(2) (2004): 79–91.

Gibson, Camille. "Juvenile Sex Offenders." In *Youth Delinquency and Violence*, edited by Marilyn McShane and Frank P. Williams III. Westport, CT: Greenwood Praeger Publishing, 2007.

Gilby, Rhonda, Lucille Wolf, and Benjamin Goldberg. "Mentally Retarded Adolescent Sex Offenders. A Survey and Pilot Study." *Canadian Journal of Psychiatry* 34 (1989): 542–548.

Goldstein, Arnold. *The Psychology of Group Aggression*. Chichester, UK: John Wiley & Sons, 2002.

Goldstein, Arnold, P., and Ellen McGinnis. *Skillstreaming the Adolescent: New Strategies and Perspectives for Teaching Prosocial Skills*, revised edition. Champaign, IL: Research Press, 1997.

Goldston, Linda. "Children Who Molest Children: Today's Victims May Become the Aggressors of Tomorrow." *The Dallas Morning News,* June 23, 1987.

Goleman, Daniel. "Early Violence Leaves Its Mark on the Brain." *New York Times,* October 3, 1995, p. C1.1.

Graves, Roger, Kim Openshaw, Frank Ascoine, and Susan Ericksen. "Demographic and Parental Characteristics of Youthful Sexual Offenders." *International Journal of Offender Therapy and Comparative Criminology* 40(4) (1996): 300–317.

Gray, Alison, Aida Busconi, Paul Houchens, and William D. Pithers. "Children with Sexual Behavior Problems and Their Caregivers: Demographics Functioning, and Clinical Patterns." *Sexual Abuse: A Journal of Research and Treatment* 9(4) (1997): 267–290.

Greenberg, David M., John M. W. Bradford, and Susan Curry, "A Comparison of Treatment of Paraphilias with Three Serotonin Re-Uptake Inhibitors: A Retrospective Study. *Bulletin of the American Academy of Psychiatry and Law* 24(4) (1996): 525–532.

Groth, Nicholas A., and Jean H. Birnbaum. *Men Who Rape: The Psychology of the Offender.* New York: Plenum Press, 1979.

Gulf Hurricane Relief. "Penile Plethysmograph." http://skepdic.com/penilep.html (accessed August, 2007).

Haney, Craig, Burtis Banks, and Philip Zimbardo. "Interpersonal Dynamics in a Simulated Prison." *International Journal of Criminology and Penology* 1(1) (1973): 74–150.

Hanna, Janan. "Teen Rape Suspect Could Face Adult Trial." *Chicago Tribune,* 1998, 1.

Hanson, R. Karl. The Development of a Brief Actuarial Scale for Sexual Offense Recidivism. User Report No. 1997–04. Ottawa, ON: Solicitor General of Canada, 1997.

———. "Effectiveness of Treatment for Sexual Offenders: Report of the ATSA Collaborative Data Research Committee." Paper presented at the 19th Annual Research and Treatment Conference of the Association for the Treatment of Sexual Abusers, San Diego, CA (November 2000).

———. "Introduction to the Special Section on Dynamic Risk Assessment with Sex Offenders." *Sexual Abuse: A Journal of Research and Treatment* 14(2) (2002): 99–101.

Hanson, R. Karl, and Monique T. Bussière. "Predicting Relapse: A Meta-Analysis of Sexual Offender Recidivism Studies." *Journal of Consulting and Clinical Psychology* 66(2) (1998): 348–362.

Hanson, R. Karl, and David Thornton, "Static 99: Improving Actuarial Risk Assessment for Sex Offenders." Department of the Solicitor General of Canada, Ottawa. http://ww2.ps-sp.gc.ca/publications/corrections/199902 e.pdf. (Assessed November 2007).

Hare's Psychopathy Checklist—Youth Version. http://www.hare.org/scales/pclyv.html (assessed December 2007).

Harris, Andrew, and Karl Hanson. Public Safety and Emergency Preparedness Canada, "Sex Offender Recidivism: A Simple Question," 2004. http://Ww2.Psepc-Sppcc.Gc.Ca/Publications/Corrections/Pdf/200403-2_E.Pdf (accessed August 24, 2007).

Hart, Timothy. C., and Callie. Rennison. "Reporting Crime to the Police, 1992–2000." Washington, DC: U.S. Department of Justice, Bureau of Justice Statistics (2003).

Hawley, Clyde, and Robert Buckley. "Food Dyes and Hyperkinetic Children." *Academy Therapy* 10(1) (1974): 27–32.

Hetherton, Jacquie. "The Idealization of Women: Its Role in the Minimization of Child Sexual Abuse by Females." *Child Abuse and Neglect* 23(2) (1999): 161–174.

Hindman, J., and J. M. Peters. "Polygraph Testing Leads to Better Understanding Adult and Juvenile Sex Offenders." *Federal Probation* 3 (2001): 8–15.

Hislop, Julia. *Female Sex Offenders: What Therapists, Law Enforcement and Child Protective Services Need to Know*. Washington: Issues Press, 2001.

Howell, Parker. "Sex Abuse Cases Hit Record Number. Better Awareness, Enforcement Cited." *Knight Ridder Tribune Business News*, February 4, 2007, 1.

Human Rights Watch, "No Easy Answers." Human Rights Watch, 19, no. 4G. http://hrw.org/reports/2007/us0907/5.htm#_Toc176672570) (accessed November 15, 2007).

Human Rights Watch. "No Easy Answers." Human Rights Watch, 19, no. 4G. http://hrw.org/reports/2007/us0907/3.htm#_Toc176672559) (accessed November 15, 2007).

Hummel, Peter, Volker Thomke, and Hartmut Oldenburger. "Male Adolescent Sex Offenders against Children: Similarities and Differences between Those Offenders with and Those without a History of Sexual Abuse." *Journal of Adolescence* 23(3) (2000): 305–317.

Hunter, John A. "Understanding Juvenile Sex Offenders: Research Findings and Guidelines for Effective Management and Treatment." In *Juvenile Justice Fact Sheet*. Charlottesville, VA: Institute of Law, Psychiatry, and Public Policy, 2000.

Hunter, John A., Judith V. Becker, Meg S. Kaplan, and D. W. Goodwin. "The Reliability and Discriminative Utility of the Adolescent Cognition Scale for Juvenile Sexual Offenses." *Annals of Sex Research* 4(3–4) (1991): 281–286.

Hunter, John A., Robert Hazelwood, and David Sleslinger. "Juvenile Perpetrated Sex Crimes: Patterns of Offending and Predictors of Violence." *The FBI Law Enforcement Bulletin* 69(3) (2000): 1–7.

Hunter, John A., Jr., L. J. Lexier, D. W. Goodwin, P. A. Browne, and C. Dennis. "Psychosexual, Attitudinal, and Developmental Characteristics of Juvenile Female Sexual Perpetrators in a Residential Treatment Setting." *Journal of Child and Family Studies* 2(4) (1993): 317–326.

Hunter, John, and Robert E. Longo. "Relapse Prevention with Juvenile Sex Abusers: A Holistic and Integrated Approach." In *The Handbook of Clinical Intervention with Young People who Sexually Abuse*, edited by Gary O'Reilly, William L. Marshall,

Alan Carr, and Richard C. Beckett, 297–314. New York: Psychology Press, 2004.

Innocent Dads. "Explaining the Abel Assessment." http://www.innocentdads.org/abel. htm (accessed August, 2007).

Jackson, Miles. "Teen Sentenced to 10 Years for Sex Assault." *The Daily Journal*, September 22, 2007, p.1.

Johnson, Cori. "Student Acceptance of Rape Myths." Paper presented at the annual meeting of the *Academy of Criminal Justice Sciences*. Cincinnati, OH: March 2008.

Johnson, Toni Cavanagh. "Female Child Perpetrators: Children Who Molest Other Children." *Child Abuse and Neglect* 13(4) (1989): 571–585.

Khan, Timothy, J., and Heather J. Chambers. "Assessing Reoffense Risk with Juvenile Sexual Offenders." *Child Welfare* 70(3) (1991): 333–345.

Knight, Raymond A., and Robert A. Prentky. "Exploring Characteristics for Classifying Juvenile Sex Offenders." In *The Juvenile Sex Offender*, edited by Howard E. Barbaree, William L. Marshall, and Stephen M. Hudson, 45–83. New York: Guilford Press, 1993.

Koch, Wendy. "More Sex Offender Transient, Elusive; Homeless Life May Increase Crime Risk." *USA Today*, November 19, 2007, 1.

Kubik, Elizabeth K., Jeffrey E. Hecker, and Sue Righthand. "Adolescent Females Who Have Sexually Offended: Comparison with Delinquent Adolescent Female Offenders and Adolescent Males Who Sexually Offend." *Journal of Child Sexual Abuse* 11(3) (2002): 63–83.

Lacasse, Anne, and Morton J. Mendelson. "Sexual Coercion among Adolescents: Victims and Perpetrators." *Journal of Interpersonal Violence* 22(4) (2007): 424–437.

Lane, Sandy. "The Sexual Abuse Cycle." In *Juvenile Sexual Offending*, edited by Sandy Lane and Gail Ryan. San Francisco, CA: Jossey-Bass Inc., 1997.

Langstrom, Niklas. "Long-Term Follow-Up of Criminal Recidivism in Young Sex Offenders: Temporal Patterns and Risk Factors." *Psychology, Crime and Law* 8(1) (2002): 41–58.

Letourneau, Elizabeth. J., Sonja K. Schoenwald, and Ashli J. Sheidow. "Children and Adolescents with Sexual Behavior Problems." *Child Maltreatment* 9(1) (2004): 49–61.

Levenson, Jill S., and Leo P. Cotter. "The Impact of Megan's Law on Sex Offender Reintegration." *Journal of Contemporary Criminal Justice* 21(1) (2005): 49–66.

Lightfoot, Lynn O., and Howard E. Barbaree. "The Relationship between Substance Use and Abuse and Sexual Offending in Adolescents." In *The Juvenile Sex Offender*, edited by Howard E. Barbaree, William L. Marshall, and Stephen M. Hudson. New York: The Guilford Press, 1993.

Londono, Ernesto. "Case of Juvenile Molester Sends Victim's Parents on Legislative Mission." *Washington Post* August 7, 2006, 4.

MACI™ Inventory. "Milon's Adolescent Clinical Inventory," http://hometown.net/ MACI.htm. (Accessed November 2007).

Marshall, William L., and A. Eccless. "Issues in Clinical Practice with Sex Offenders." *Journal of Interpersonal Violence* 6(1) (1991): 68–93.

Marshall, William L., Stephen M. Hudson, and Sharon Hodkinson. "The Importance of Attachment Bonds in the Development of Juvenile Sex Offending." In *The Juvenile Sex Offender*, edited by Howard E. Barbaree, William L. Marshall, and Stephen M. Hudson. New York: The Guilford Press, 1993.

Masson, Helen, and Marcus Erooga. In *Children and Young People Who Sexually Abuse Others: Current Development and Practice Responses*, edited by Marcus Erooga and Helen Masson, 3–17. London: Routledge, 2006.

Mathews, Ruth, J. A. Hunter, Jr., and Jacqueline Vuz. "Juvenile Female Sexual Offenders: Clinical Characteristics and Treatment Issues." *Sexual Abuse: A Journal of Research and Treatment* 9(3) (1997): 187–199.

Mathews, Ruth, Jane Kinder Matthews, and Kathleen Speltz. *Female Sexual Offenders: An Exploratory Study*. VT: The Safer Society Press, 1989.

Mathis, James L. *Clear Thinking about Sexual Deviations: A New Look at an Old Problem*. Chicago, IL: Nelson-Holt, 1972.

Mayer, Adele. *Women Sex Offenders*. Holmes Beach, FL: Learning Publications, Inc., 1992.

McCall, Nathan. *Makes Me Wanna Holler: A Young Black Man in America*. New York: Random House, 1994.

McCarty, Loretta M. "Investigation of Incest: Opportunity to Motivate Families to Seek Help." *Child Welfare* 60 (1981): 679–689.

McGrath, Robert J., and Stephen E. Hoke. "Vermont Assessment of Sex Offender Risk Manual (2001 Research edition)." http://www.csom.org/pubs/VASOR.pdf (accessed November 2007).

McGuire, R., J. Carlisle, and B. Young. "Sexual Deviations as Conditioned Behavior: A Hypothesis." *Behavior Research and Therapy* 2 (1965): 185–190.

McNeil, Michele. "Concerned about Juvenile Sex Offenders, States Move to Tighten Their Regulations." *Education Week* 26, (36)(2007): 28–31.

Metzner, Jeffrey, and Gail Ryan. "Sexual Abuse Perpetration." In *Conduct Disorder in Children and Adolescents*, edited by Pirooz Sholevar. Washington, DC: America Psychiatric Publisher, 1995.

Moffitt, Terrie E. "Adolescence-Limited and Life-Course-Persistent Antisocial Behavior: A Developmental Taxonomy." *Psychology Review* 100(4) (1993): 674–701.

Moore, Martha T. "Sex Crimes Break the Lock on Juvenile Records; Some States List Minors in Their Registries; Federal Law May Follow Suit." *USA Today*, July 10, 2006, 5A.

Moorehead, Douglass A. *Efficacy of Nonpsychopharmacological Treatment for Male Sex Offenders: A Review of the Literature*. Doctoral Research Paper (Dissertation), Biola University, NC, 2001.

Morrison, Tony, and Julie Henniker. "Building a Comprehensive Inter-Agency Assessment and Intervention System for Young People Who Sexually Harm: The

Aim Project." In *Children and Young People Who Sexually Abuse Others: Current Development and Practice Responses*, edited by Marcus Erooga and Helen Masson, 31–50. London: Routledge, 2006.

Muir, Grant, Kimberly Lonsway, and Diana Payne. "Rape Myth Acceptance among Scottish and American Students." *The Journal of Social Psychology* 136(2) (1996): 261–262.

Myers, Wade C. *Juvenile Sexual Homicide*. London: Academic Press, 2002.

National Adolescent Perpetrator Network. "Preliminary Report from the National Task Force on Juvenile Sexual Offending, 1988." *Juvenile and Family Court Journal* 39(2) (1988): 5–52.

National Adolescent Perpetrator Network. "The Revised Report from the National Task Force on Juvenile Sexual Offending." *Juvenile and Family Court Journal* 44(4) (1993): 1–120.

National Center for Child Abuse and Neglect. "Study Findings: National Study of Incidence and Severity of Child Abuse and Neglect," edited by NCCAN. Washington, DC: DHEW, 1981.

National Center of Sexual Behavior of Youth. "Frequently Asked Questions about Children with Sexual Behavior Problems," http://www.ncsby.org/pages/registry.htm. (Accessed November 1, 2007).

National Task Force on Juvenile Sexual Offending. *Juvenile and Family Court Journal*, 1993.

Nichols and Molinda Assessments, Inc. "Authors and Publishers of Psychosexual Test Instruments." http://www.nicholsandmolinder.com/ (August 2007).

Nichols and Molinda Assessments, Inc. "Multiphasic Sex Inventory—II Adolescent Male Form." http://www.nicholsandmolinder.com/msi_ii_jm.html (accessed November 2007).

Nolan, Kay. "Waukesha Passes Sex Offender Regulation: Residences near Schools, Other Facilities Prohibited." *McClatchy Tribune Business News*, November 7, 2007.1.

O'Brien, Michael, and Walter Bera. "Adolescent Sexual Offenders: A Descriptive Typology." *National Family Life Education Network* 1(3) (1986): 1–4.

O'Reilly, Gary, William L. Marshall, Alan Carr, and Richard C. Beckett, Eds. *The Handbook of Clinical Intervention with Young People Who Sexually Abuse*, 237–274. Hove: Brunner-Rutledge, 2004.

Oxnam, Paul, and James Vess. "A Personality- Based Typology of Adolescent Sexual Offenders Using the Million Adolescent Clinical Inventory." *New Zealand Journal of Psychology* 35(1) (2006): 36–44.

Parks, Gregory A., and David E. Bard. "Risk Factors for Adolescent Sex Offender Recidivism: Evaluation of Predictive Factors and Comparison of Three Groups Based upon Victim Type." *Sexual Abuse: A Journal of Research and Treatment* 18(4) (2006): 319–342.

Pavlov, Ivan. *Conditioned Reflexes*. Oxford: Clarendon Press, 1927.

Peters, Doyle, Gail Elizabeth Wyatt, and David Finkelhor. "Ch 1: Prevalence." In *A Sourcebook on Child Sexual Abuse*, edited by David Finkelhor, Sharon Araji,

Larry Baron, Angela Browne, Stefanie Doyle Peters, and Gail Elizabeth Wyatt, 15–59. Newbury Park: CA: Sage, 1986.

Peterson, Zoe, and Charlene Muehlenhard. "Was It Rape? The Function of Women's Rape Myth Acceptance and Definitions of Sex in Labeling Their Own Experiences." *Sex Roles* 51(3–4 (2004): 129–144.

Petrosino, Anthony, and Carolyn Petrosino. "The Public Safety Potential of Megan's Law in Massachusetts: An Assessment from a Sample of Criminal Sexual Psychopaths." *Crime and Delinquency* 45(1) (1999): 140–158.

Pierce, Margo. "Sex in the Time of Hysteria." *The Cleveland Free Times*, November 21, 2007, http://www.freetimes.com/stories/15/29/sex-in-the-time-of-hysteria. (Accessed November, 28, 2007).

Piquero, Alex R. "Assessing the Relationships between Gender, Chronicity, Seriousness, and Offense Skewness in Criminal Offending." *Journal of Criminal Justice* 28(2) (2000): 103–115.

Pittman, Travis. "13-Year-Old Sex Offender Voluntarily Returns to Custody," 2007, August 31. http//:www.king5.com (accessed November 15, 2007).

Poole, D., D. Leidecke, and M. Marbibi. "Risk Assessment and Recidivism in Juvenile Sex Offenders: A Validation Study of the Static-99." Austin: Texas Youth Commission, 2000.

Prentky, Robert, and Sue Righthand. *"Juvenile Sex Offender Assessment Protocol II (J-SOAP-II) Manual, 2003."* http://www.csom.org/pubs/JSOAP.pdf (accessed August, 2007).

Prentky, Robert, Bert Harris, Kate Frizzell, and Sue Righthand. "An Actuarial Procedure for Assessing Risk with Juvenile Sex Offenders." *Sexual Abuse: A Journal of Research and Treatment* 12(2) (2000): 71–93.

Prescott, David S. "Emerging Strategies for Risk Assessment of Sexually Abusive Youth Theory, Controversy, and Practice." *Journal of Child Sexual Abuse* 13(3–4) (2004): 83–105.

Print, Bobbie, and David O'Callaghan. "Essentials of an Effective Treatment Programme for sexually abusive adolescents" In *The Handbook of Clinical Intervention with Young People who Sexually Abuse*, edited by Gary O'Reily, William L. Marshall, Alan Carr, and Richard C. Beckett, Vol. 1, 237–274, Routledge, 2004.

Rachmen, S. "Sexual Fetishisms: An Experimental Analogue." *Psychological Record* 16(3) (1966): 293–296.

Ramshaw, Emily. "Sex Offender Fired as TYC Guard: Firms That Run Youth Centers Don't Always Check Juvenile Records." *Knight Ridder Tribune Business News*, March 8, 2007, 1.

Ramsland, Katherine. "Albert H. Fish." Tru TV Crime Library (February 15, 2007). Retrieved November 1, 2007, from http://www.crimelibrary.com/serial_killers/notorious/fish/11.html.

———. "The Paper Boy." Tru TV Crime Library (February 15, 2007). Retrieved November 1, 2007, from http://www.crimelibrary.com/serial_killers/notorious/fish/11.html.

Ray, Jo Ann, and Diana J. English. "Comparison of Female and Male Children with Sexual Behavior Problems." *Journal of Youth and Adolescence* 24(4) (1995): 439–451.

Reinhart, Mary. "Legislators Try to Ease Laws for Sex Crimes by Youths: Family Appeals Sway Conservative Lawmakers to Back Bills to Alter Statutes." *Knight Ridder Tribune Business News*, February 11, 2007, 1.

Righthand, Sue, and Carlann Welch. "Juveniles Who Have Sexually Offended: A Review of the Professional Literature," 1–59. Washington, DC: Office of Juvenile Justice and Delinquency Prevention, 2001.

Rivedal, Karen. "Sex Offender Notification Policies All over the Board." *Knight Ridder Tribune Business News*, March 5, 2007, 1.

Robertiello, Gina, and Karen Terry. "Can We Profile Sex Offenders? A Review of Sex Offenders Typologies." *Aggression and Violent Behavior* 12(5) (2007): 508–518.

Ronis, Scott, and Charles Borduin. "Individual, Family, Peer and Academic Characteristics of Male Juvenile Sexual Offenders." *Journal of Abnormal Child Psychology* 35(2) (2007): 153–163.

Rosencrans, Bobbie. *The Last Secret: Daughters Sexually Abused by Mothers.* Orwell, VT: Safer Society Press, 1997.

Rowe, William, Sandra Savage, Mark Ragg, and Kay Wigle. *Sexuality and the Developmentally Handicapped: A Guidebook for Health Care Professionals.* New York: Edwin Mellen, 1987.

Rozas, Angela. "Do Young Sex Offenders Belong on Adult Register." *Chicago Tribune,* January 16, 2007, 1.

Ryan, Gail. "Sexually Abusive Youth: Defining the Population." In *Juvenile Sexual Offending: Causes, Consequences and Corrections*, edited by Gail Ryan and Sandy Lane, 3–9. San Francisco, CA: Jossey-Bass, 1997.

Ryan, Gail. "The Families of Sexually Abusive Youth." In *Juvenile Sexual Offending*, edited by Ryan Gail and Sandy Lane, 136–154. San Francisco, CA: Jossey-Bass, 1997.

Ryan, Gail. "Theories of Etiology." In *Juvenile Sexual Offending*, edited by Gail Ryan and Sandy Lane, 19–58. San Francisco, CA: Jossey-Bass, 1997.

Ryan, Gail, Thomas J. Miyoshi, Jeffrey L. Metzner, Richard D. Krugman, and George E. Fryer. "Trends in a National Sample of Sexually Abusive Youths." *Journal of the American Academy of Child and Adolescent Psychiatry* 35(1) (1996): 17–25.

Salekin, Randall T. "Risk Sophistication Treatment Inventory." http://www3.parinc.com/products/product.aspx?Productid=RSTI (accessed November, 2007).

Salter, Anna. *Treating Child Sex Offenders and Victims: A Practical Guide.* Newbury Park, CA: Sage, 1988.

———. *Predators: Pedophiles, Rapists, and Other Sex Offenders.* New York: Basic Books, 2003.

Sarrel, Phillip M., and William H. Masters. "Sexual Molestation of Men by Women." *Archives of Sexual Behavior* 11(2) (1982): 117–131.

Scavo, Rebecca, and Bruce D. Buchanan. "Group Therapy for Male Adolescent Sex Offenders: A Model for Residential Treatment." *Residential Treatment for Children and Youth* 7(2) (1989): 59–74.

Schoenthaler, Stephen, and Walter Doraz. "Types of Offenses Which Can Be Reduced in an Institutional Setting Using Nutritional Intervention." *International Journal of Biosocial Research* 4(2) (1983): 74–84.

Schultz, Pamela. *Not Monsters: Analyzing the Stories of Child Molesters.* Oxford: Rowman & Littlefield Publishers, Inc., 2005.

Schweitzer, Robert, and Jonathan Dwyer. "Sex Crime Recidivism: Evaluation of a Sexual Offender Treatment Program." *Journal of Interpersonal Violence* 18(11) (2003): 1292–1310.

Shaw, Julie. "Rape Suspect 14, to Be Tried as a Juvenile." *The Philadelphia Inquirer,* July 20, 2006.

Shi, Lin, and Jason Nichol. "Into the Mind of a Juvenile Sex Offender: A Clinical Analysis and Recommendation from an Attachment Perspective." *The American Journal of Family Therapy* 35(5) (2007): 395–402.

Smallbone, Stephen W., and Lynley Milne. "Associations between Trait Anger and Aggression Used in the Commission of Sexual Offenses." *International Journal of Offender Therapy and Comparative Criminology* 44(5) (2000): 606–617.

Smith v. Doe (2003). 538 US 84 (2003).

Smith, Wayne R., and Caren Monastersky. "Assessing Juvenile Sexual Offenders' Risk for Reoffending." *Criminal Justice and Behavior* 13(2) (1986): 115–140.

Snyder, Howard N. "Sexual Assault of Young Children as Reported to Law Enforcement: Victim, Incident and Offender Characteristics." Washington, DC: Bureau of Justice Statistics: National Center for Juvenile Justice. NCJ 182990, 2000.

Stallings, Beth. "Boy, 8 Accused of Sexual Harassment." *Morning Journal,* March 25, 2006, 1.

Stanley, Melinda A., and Samuel M. Turner. "Current Status of Pharmacological and Behavioral Treatment of Obsessive-Compulsive Disorder." *Behavior Therapy* 26(1) (1995): 163–186.

State Of Ohio Department of Rehabilitation and Correction. "Ten Year Recidivism Follow-up of 1989 Sex Offender Releases." 2001.

Steele, Brandt, and Gail Ryan. "Deviancy: Development Gone Wrong." In *Juvenile Sexual Offending,* edited by Gail Ryan and Sandy Lane, 59–76. San Francisco, CA: Jossey-Bass, 1997.

Stermac, Lana, and Frederick Matthews. "Issues and Approaches to the Treatment of Developmentally Disabled Sexual Offenders." In *The Juvenile Sex Offender,* edited by Howard E. Barbaree, William L. Marshall, and Stephen M. Hudson. New York: The Guilford Press, 1987.

Stop It Now. *Do Children Sexually Abuse Other Children? Preventing Sexual Abuse among Children and Youth.* Brandon, VT: The Safer Society Press, 2007.

Syed, Fariya, and Sharon Williams. "Case Studies of Female Sex Offenders." Ottawa, ON: Correctional Service of Canada, 1996.

Sykes, Gresham, and David Matza. "Techniques of Neutralization: A Theory of Delinquency." *American Sociological Review* 22(6) (1957): 664–670.

Tardif, Monique, Nathalie Auclair, Martine Jacob, and Julie Carpentier. "Sexual Abuse Perpetrated by Adult and Juvenile Females: An Ultimate Attempt to Resolve a Conflict Associated with Maternal Identity." *Child Abuse & Neglect* 29(2) (2005): 153–167.

Taylor, Ralph B., John Goldkamp, Doris Weiland, Clarissa Breen, R. Maria Garcia, Lawrence Presley, and Brian R. Wyant. "Revise Policies Mandating Offender DNA Collection." *Criminology and Public Policy* 6(4) (2007): 851–862.

Terry, Karen J. *Sexual Offenses and Offenders: Theory, Practice, and Policy.* Belmont, CA: Wadsworth, 2006.

Tewksbury, Richard. "Experiences and Attitudes of Registered Female Sex Offenders." *Federal Probation* 68(3) (2004): 30–33.

Texas Juvenile Probation Commission. "Texas Juvenile Sex Offender Risk Assessment Instrument Data Collection Form." http://www.tjpc.state.tx.us/publications/forms/2004/RARCSEX0204.pdf (accessed August 31, 2007).

Thomas, Jerry. "Family Intervention with Young People with Sexually Abusive Behavior." In *The Handbook of Clinical Intervention with Young People who Sexually Abuse*, edited by Gary O'Reilly, William L. Marshall, Alan Carr, and Richard C. Beckett, 315–342. New York: Psychology Press, 2004.

Thornhill, Randy, and Craig T. Palmer. *A Natural History of Rape: Biological Bases of Sexual Coercion.* Cambridge, MA: The MIT Press, 2000.

Trivers, Robert. "Parental Investment and Sexual Selection." In *Sexual Selection and the Descent Man, 1881–1971*, edited by B. Campbell. Chicago: Aldine, 1972.

Turner, Marcia T. *Female Adolescent Sexual Abusers: An Exploratory Study of Mother-Daughter Dynamics with Implications for Treatment.* Brandon, VT: The Safer Society Press, 1994.

U.S. Department of Justice. Uniform Crime Reports, 2005. Washington, DC: Government Printing Office, 2006.

Vandiver, Donna M. "Characteristics and Recidivism Rates as Adults." *Journal of Interpersonal Violence* 21(5) (2006): 673–688.

———. "A Prospective Analysis of Juvenile Male Sex Offenders: Characteristics and Recidivism Rates as Adults." *Journal of Interpersonal Violence* 21(5) (2006): 673–688.

———. "Female Sex Offenders." In *Sex and Sexuality*, edited by Richard D. McAnulty and M. Michele Burnette, 47–80. Westport, CT: Praeger, 2006.

Vandiver, Donna M, Kelly A. Cheeseman, and Robert Worley. "A Qualitative Assessment of Registered Sex Offenders: Characteristics and Attitudes toward Registration." Paper presented at the Annual Meeting of the Southwestern Association of Criminal Justice, Fort Worth, TX, November 2006.

Vandiver, Donna M., and Glen Kercher. "Offender and Victim Characteristics of Registered Female Sexual Offenders in Texas: A Proposed Typology of Female Sexual Offenders." *Sexual Abuse: A Journal of Research and Treatment* 16(2) (2004): 121–137.

Vandiver, Donna M., and Jeremy Braithwaite. "Juvenile Female Sex Offenders: A Longitudinal Study of Recidivism Rates." Paper Presented at the Annual Meeting of the American Society of Criminology, Atlanta, GA, November 2007.

Vandiver, Donna M., and Raymond Teske, Jr. "Juvenile Female and Male Sex Offenders: A Comparison of Offender, Victim, and Judicial Processing Characteristics." *International Journal of Offender Therapy and Comparative Criminology* 50(2) (2006): 148–165.

Vick, Jennifer, Ruth McRoy, and Bobbie Matthews. "Young Female Sex Offenders: Assessment and Treatment Issues." *Journal of Child Sexual Abuse* 11(2) (2002): 1–23.

Waite, Dennis, Adrienne Keller, Elizabeth L. McGarvey, Edward Wieckowski, Relana Pinkerton, and Gerald L. Brown. "Juvenile Sex Offender Re-Arrest Rates for Sexual, Violent Nonsexual and Property Crimes: A 10-Year Follow-Up." *Sexual Abuse: A Journal of Research and Treatment* 17(3) (2005): 313–331.

Walker, Jeffrey T. "Eliminate Residency Restrictions for Sex Offenders." *Criminology and Public Policy* 6(4) (2007): 863–870.

Ward, Tony and Claire A. Stewart. "Good Lives and the Rehabilitation of Sexual Offenders." In *Sexual Deviance: Issues and Controversies*, edited by Tony Ward, D. Richard Laws, and Stephen M. Hudson, 21–44. Thousand Oaks, CA: Sage, 2003.

Weinrott, Mark. "Juvenile Sexual Aggression: A Critical Review." 91–103. Portland, OR: Center for the Study and Prevention of Violence, 1996.

Weinrott, M. R., M. Riggan, and S. Frothingham. "Reducing Deviant Arousal in Juvenile Sex Offenders Using Vicarious Sensitization." *Journal of Interpersonal Violence* 12(5) (1997): 704–728.

Welldon, Estele V. *Mother, Madonna, Whore: The Idealization and Denigration of Motherhood.* London: Free Association Book, 1988.

Williams, George. *Adaptation and Natural Selection.* Princeton: Princeton University Press, 1966.

Williams, Joan. Juvenile Sex Offenders: Predictors of recidivism. Auburn University, http://graduate.auburn.edu/auetd/search.aspx. Dissertation. (Accessed November 15, 2007).

Witt, Philip H., Jackson T. Bosley, and Sean P Hiscox. "Evaluation of Juvenile Sex Offenders." *The Journal of Psychiatry & Law* 30 (2002): 569–592.

Woodhams, Jessica. "Characteristics of Juvenile Sex Offending against Strangers: Findings from a Non-Clinical Study." *Aggression Behavior* 30(3) (2004): 243–253.

Woodhams, Jessica, Raphael Gilley, and Tim Grant. "Understanding the Factors That Affect the Severity of Juvenile Stranger Sex Offenses: The Effect of Victim Characteristics and Number of Suspects." *Journal of Interpersonal Violence* 22(2) (2007): 218–237.

Worling, James R. "Personality-Based Typology of Adolescent Male Sexual Offenders: Differences in Recidivism Rates, Victim-Selection Characteristics, and Personal

Victimization Histories." *Sexual Abuse: A Journal of Research and Treatment* 13(3) (2001): 149–166.

———. "Essentials of a Good Intervention Programme for Sexually Abusive Juveniles." In *The Handbook of Clinical Intervention with Young People who Sexually Abuse*, edited by Gary O'Reilly, William L. Marshall, Alan Carr, and Richard C. Beckett, 275–296. Hove: Brunner-Rutledge, 2004.

Worling, James R., and Tracy Curwen. "Adolescent Sexual Offender Recidivism: Success of Specialized Treatment and Implications for Risk Prediction." *International Journal of Child Abuse and Neglect* 24(7) (2000): 965–982.

Worling, James R., and Niklas Langstrom. "Assessment of Criminal Recidivism Risk with Adolescents Who Have Offended Sexually: A Review." *Trauma, Violence & Abuse* 4(4) (2003): 341–362.

Wright Thompson. Outrageous Injustice: Genarlow Wilson. (2007). http://sports.espn.go.com/espn/eticket/story?page=Wilson (accessed December 1, 2007)

WSBTV.com. "3 Young Boys Arrested in Rape Case." *Action News 2*, WSBTV.

WTOL11—News 11 WTOL—11 NEWS. http://www.wtol.com/global/story.asp?s=7415081&ClientType=Printable (accessed November 28, 2007).

Zgourides, George, Martin Monto, and Richard Harris. "Correlates of Adolescent Male Sexual Offense: Prior Adult Sexual Contact, Sexual Attitudes, and Use of Sexually Explicit Materials." *International Journal of Offender Therapy and Comparative Criminology* 41(3) (1997): 272–283.

Zimring, Franklin. *An American Travesty: Legal Responses to Adolescent Sexual Offending*. Chicago: University of Chicago Press, 2004.

Zimring, Franklin E., Alex R. Piquero, and Wesley G. Jennings. "Sexual Delinquency in Racine: Does Early Sex Offending Predict Later Sex Offending in Youth and Young Adulthood." *Criminology and Public Policy* 6(3) (2007): 507–534.

Zolondek, Stacey O., Gene G. Abel, William F. Northey, and Alan D. Jordan. "The Self-Reported Behaviors of Juvenile Sex Offenders." In *Sexual Deviance*, edited by Christopher Hensley and Richard Tewksbury. Boulder, CO: Lynne Rienner Publishers, Inc, 2003.

Index

About the Authors

CAMILLE GIBSON is a faculty member in the College of Juvenile Justice and Psychology at Prairie View A & M University in Prairie View, Texas, where she teaches in the Justice Studies Department. She is also a certified rehabilitation counselor, having worked previously as a family therapist with an emphasis on juvenile issues. In addition to juvenile sex offenders she has published on schools and delinquency, juvenile gangs, and policing.

DONNA M. VANDIVER is an Associate Professor at Texas State University, San Marcos. She received her Ph.D. in Criminal Justice from Sam Houston State University in 2002. She teaches undergraduate and graduate courses in research methods, corrections, and sex offenders. She has a number of publications on adult and juvenile sex offenders. She has developed a typology on female sex offenders and has conducted interviews with such offenders. She continues to do research on juvenile and adult sex offenders.

GUEST CONTRIBUTOR—PHILIP A. IKOMI is a Research Scientist in the Texas Juvenile Crime Prevention Center at the College of Juvenile Justice and Psychology, Prairie View A & M University in Prairie View, Texas. He has a Doctor of Philosophy degree in Psychology from Bowling Green State University, Bowling Green, Ohio. His current research focuses on juveniles who have committed sexual offenses. He has taught at both the graduate and undergraduate levels in Psychology.